TAKE-DOWN

TAKE-DOWN

THE PURSUIT AND CAPTURE OF KEVIN MITNICK, AMERICA'S MOST WANTED COMPUTER OUTLAW—BY THE MAN WHO DID IT

TSUTOMU SHIMOMURA
WITH JOHN MARKOFF

HYPERION
NEW YORK

Excerpts from "Dutch Computer Rogues Infiltrate . . . ," by John Markoff (April 21, 1991), copyright © 1991 by The New York Times Company. Reprinted by permission.

Excerpts from "Data Network Is Found Open . . . ," by John Markoff (January 23, 1995), copyright © 1995 by The New York Times Company. Reprinted by permission.

Library of Congress Cataloging-in-Publication Data

ISBN 0-7868-6210-6

Book Design by Jill Gogal

FIRST EDITION

10 9 8 7 6 5 4 3 2 1

This book is dedicated to our parents
and to the memory of John's father, Mortimer Markoff

CONTENTS

ACKNOWLEDGMENTS

This book was made possible by the efforts of a number of people. Andrew Gross, Robert Hood, Julia Menapace, and Mark Seiden gave Tsutomu technical support during many sleepless nights while he worked to unravel the December 24 break-in into his computers. Mike Bowen, John Bowler, Liudvikas Bukys, Levord Burns, Soeren Christensen, Dan Farmer, Rick Francis, Brosl Hasslacher, John Hoffman, Bruce Koball, Tom Longstaff, Mark Lottor, Jim Murphy, Joe Orsak, Martha Stansell-Gamm, and Kent Walker also provided technical and legal expertise. Carl Baldini and Paul Swere, both of RDI Computer Corporation, helped with hardware. Thanks to Sid Karin and his staff at the San Diego Supercomputer Center for their support. Our editor at Hyperion, Rick Kot, helped us translate a myriad of arcane details into an accessible story, and Tim Race, John Markoff's editor at the *New York Times,* offered his expertise. We also wish to thank our agents, John Brockman and Katinka Matson. When we began writing, Nat Goldhaber was kind enough to offer us his hospitality. Special thanks to Jimmy McClary and Leslie Terzian. Finally, Roger Dashen was a longtime friend and mentor of Tsutomu's.

take•down (tāk/ doun/) *adj. Sports.* A move or maneuver in wrestling or the martial arts in which a standing opponent is forced to the floor.

The American Heritage Dictionary of the English Language,
Third Edition

PROLOGUE

If you find three men sitting alone in a van in a shopping mall parking lot at two in the morning and one of them is holding an odd looking antenna, there's usually only one conclusion you draw.

They're cops.

I wasn't, and despite all the media frenzy that would erupt three days later, referring to me as a "cybercop" and a "cybersleuth," I had never intended to be one. In the winter of 1995 the only thing I was aspiring to be was a ski bum, and so far I wasn't doing a very good job of it. During the best ski season in memory in California, here I was stuck on a chilly morning in a parking lot in a suburb of Raleigh, North Carolina, a long way from anything resembling a ski trail.

I was holding an antenna that looked a little like a ray gun in one hand, and in my lap I was cradling a device that resembled an oversized electronic daytimer. It was emitting a soft whistling tone, much like that a modem makes when it establishes a connection.

The sound from the device had become persistent—proof I'd cornered my quarry, an elusive computer outlaw who'd managed to stay one step ahead of the FBI and at least three other law enforcement agencies for more than two years through a combination of con-artistry and sheer luck.

Along the way I'd been one of the victims. In December he

and possibly some of his cronies had electronically broken into my computers and stolen software I'd written, which if abused, could wreak havoc on the Internet community.

Now I was in a position to even the score. But none of us in the family van were police. The driver was a beefy engineer for a cellular telephone company and in the back sat a *New York Times* reporter who had tagged along following my odyssey. Ten minutes earlier our van had slowly circled a nondescript apartment complex as I swept my antenna back and forth, intently watching a digital signal-strength display for signs I was getting closer to the source of the cellular telephone call. I was determined to end my pursuit, but now, through a fog of fatigue brought on by an almost sleepless week of pursuing a vaporous trail of digital footprints through the web of computers that make up the Internet, I could feel the paranoia that can well up inside you when you push yourself too hard and too far.

Outside it was dead quiet. There were no cars or people on the street, and I felt conspicuous as our vehicle slid quietly by the apartment complex under the yellow glare of sodium vapor lights. Where was he? Was he watching us? Was he about to flee? As I watched the meter readout it suddenly fell off. He was behind us. Was he on the other side of the building? The driver turned the corner, and we saw empty fields stretching away into the darkened countryside. Our maps which we had spread out before us in the van showed a state park.

"A perfect escape route," the reporter murmured from the back seat.

We turned another corner, and the van swung back toward the front of the complex. The antenna swept back and forth and inside the darkened cab I watched as numbers on the display flickered upward again. Toward the front of the building our van slowed, and we crept through a parking lot full of empty cars. As we neared the corner of the apartments we stopped briefly. Using radio detection finding gear is a little like playing "pin the tail on the donkey." You get little cues, but still you feel like you're flying blind, floundering around in the dark. Now, however, from the way the meter jumped, I could tell we were almost on top of our target. Somewhere, within thirty meters of us, someone was crouching over a computer with an open connection to the Internet. It was impossible to decipher the meaning of the monotonous hiss that was proof he was still at his keyboard. Where was he right now?

The three of us craned our necks and peered into a cul-de-sac. From inside the complex came a light from a second-story window. How would a fugitive react if he peeked outside in the middle of the night and saw a van with an antenna inside idling in his driveway? It was obvious he'd flee, or maybe worse. I had no idea what his state of mind was. Was he alone? There was no reason to think our cyber-criminal was armed, but it was late, and a cold feeling of doubt was growing in the pit of my stomach.

"If I was him I'd be facing the window," the reporter suggested.

He was right—we might have blown everything. Weeks of painstaking, cross-country detective work would vanish, leaving us empty-handed and chagrined. We decided caution was in order. The van started moving again and rolled around the corner of the building.

PART ONE BREAK-IN

CHAPTER I

JULIA'S
RETURN

Is it possible to drive the 310 kilometers west from Echo Summit on the crest of the Sierra Nevada range to San Francisco International Airport in under two hours?

On the day before Christmas 1994 I tried it—in a snowstorm.

I thought I had a good reason. I was eager to see a friend whom I hadn't seen for more than two months and I had been feeling unsettled about where our relationship would be when she returned from her travels. We had been close friends for three years and during the last six months it had become clear that we were more than friends; we were in love. We had both agreed that during our time apart we would think about where we wanted to go with our relationship. Now I was in a hurry, because I was full of anticipation, but at the same time, I was also nervous and uncertain. What I didn't realize was that my headlong race from one side of California to the other was the opening act in an unusual adventure that was about to change my life forever.

The previous afternoon, Julia Menapace had left a message on my home answering machine in San Diego: she was at the airport in Bangkok and would be arriving in San Francisco at 1:40 the following afternoon after a fourteen-hour flight. Would I meet her?

Of course I would. I had been thinking a lot about Julia; the message suggested she'd been thinking about me too.

A tall, graceful woman who is strong and wiry, and who often wears her hair drawn back in a braid, Julia had been a programmer at Apple Computer and other high-tech companies in Silicon Valley for the better part of a decade. With an intense gaze and blue-gray eyes, Julia was often introspective but also quick to laugh. She was a talented yoga teacher and had an ethereal quality that I found completely captivating. Recently she'd been working as an independent programmer, brought in by high technology companies to work on specific software development projects.

Although she knew the inner workings of the Macintosh computer well, she never become as obsessed with computing as many of the men she worked with. She had never been completely sucked into Silicon Valley's round-the-clock hacker culture—she liked to do too many other things in life, away from the computer world where time is divided into nanoseconds. During the years we'd known each other, we'd gone on countless trips, exploring the backcountry: mountains, hot springs, beaches. We both shared a love of the wilderness, whatever the season.

Julia had a particular passion for the mountain world above six thousand meters and in the fall of 1994 she took off for the Himalaya, but before she left to climb and trek in Nepal we had a great adventure exploring the Southwest together. We hiked Bryce Canyon and Zion National Parks and wandered among the Anasazi ruins in Chaco Canyon. It was during trips like that one that I'd come to see Julia as the wonderful person she is, and we'd fallen in love. I knew she wanted to be in a committed relationship, but I had told her I needed to think about whether I was ready for a serious partnership. We hadn't spoken since right after she arrived in Katmandu, but after a couple months of contemplation I'd decided that I wanted to be with her and I thought I was able to uphold my end of a partnership.

However, I had no idea if her thoughts were tracking mine, and our relationship wasn't simple. Things remained ambiguous because she was also trying to end a seven-year-old relationship that had been drawing to a painful close for a long time. The man she had lived with had once been a friend of mine—a Silicon Valley hacker and a privacy activist who was well known for his commitment to making sure personal privacy wasn't lost in the emerging digital age. It had been a painful time before Julia left the country, but it was clear to me that their relationship hadn't been working and it was a question of when, and not if, it would end.

But I didn't know what was going to happen next. I'd missed Julia and was eager to see her. It was important for me to arrive at the airport on time—getting there, however, meant coming from the eastern side of the Sierra Nevada close to the Nevada border. Just a day earlier, I'd moved in to an A-frame cabin outside Truckee, California, a couple hundred meters from the Tahoe-Donner Ski Resort, in the midst of a cross-country skiing mecca, with Emily Sklar, a ski instructor who had been a good friend for several years.

In San Diego, where I work most of the year, I in-line skate for exercise, but as much as I like to skate, I like cross-country skiing even better. During the last three years I'd learned a cross-country skiing technique called skating that looks much like in-line skating and offers more speed than the traditional striding technique you see most skiers using. Instead of skiing in two narrow tracks, skaters glide forward, placing each ski diagonally to the trail. I also like to race and the previous winter I'd begun to take racing seriously again, and had raced in several biathlons, a combination of skiing and riflery that combines strength, speed, and control.

Of course snow isn't one of San Diego's strong points. The previous winter, the ticket agents and flight attendants on Reno Air got to know me well. Once I even packed an ice ax in my carry-on luggage and sent it through the X-ray machine. No one blinked. In that single ski season I logged more than thirty thousand kilometers between Southern and Northern California. My plan this year had been to spend the winter skiing, volunteering for the Nordic ski patrol, serving as a parttime ski instructor and, when time permitted, taking on intriguing research problems.

The kind of work I often do, computational science and computer security research, can be done from just about anywhere. And because the previous winter I'd found myself flying up from San Diego nearly every weekend, this year I'd decided simply to set up headquarters in the mountains for four months. I planned on bringing along a couple of Unix workstations and connecting my own computer network to the outside world with a high-speed digital telephone line.

Usually I spend most of each year wearing several hats. Until the winter of 1995 I was both a senior fellow at the federally funded San Diego Supercomputer Center—a facility on the University of California at San Diego campus—and a research scientist in the university's physics department. The Center provides me with an office and access to some of the world's fastest supercomputers. My work has always involved doing research in an area that has fundamentally transformed science in the last two decades—the physics of computing. Computation has emerged as a third way of conducting science, taking its place alongside traditional theoretical and experimental methods.

Where it was once necessary to prove scientific theories by doing real-world experiments, computers have become fast enough that it's now possible to create accurate simulations of real-world events. Computational physicists attempt to solve scientific problems through simulation. Ever more powerful computers make it possible to realistically simulate everything from the flow of air across the top of an airplane wing to the basic structure of matter in the hunt for the top quark.

Computational physics is also about the physics of computing itself, discovering how electrons can be marshaled to manipulate ever vaster stores of information in ever faster ways, and about designing specialized machines that surpass the performance of today's best supercomputers. Like many people in my field who were trained first as physicists, I have begun spending more and more of my time in recent years on real-world computing problems like computer security. In one sense it's a grand tradition among both physicists and computer hackers. Nobel Laureate Richard Feynman was notorious for his safecracking escapades at Los Alamos during the Manhattan project days. And Robert Morris, one of the inventors of the Unix operating system and later the chief scientist of the National Security Agency was a pioneer in understanding how to break in to computers as well as protect them.

I've always found it a compelling intellectual challenge—finding the chinks in the armor of a computer or computer network that, unprotected, might enable a digital thief to loot a bank's electronic funds or permit foreign spies to slip into the Pentagon's computers. It's a world that you can't approach just on an academic or a theoretical level. You have to get your hands dirty. The only way you can know for sure the digital locks are strong enough is if you know how to take them apart and completely understand them. My research into different paradigms for computation has provided new tools to evaluate strengths and weaknesses in computer networks.

Until I decided to move my base of operations to the mountains for the winter I had been doing more and more research on computer security at the San Diego Supercomputer Center, or SDSC, where the tone was set by the director, Sid Karin, a tall, thin, bearded, and unflappable former nuclear power engineer in his mid-fifties. Like many people who have taken circuitous routes into computing, Sid was working at General Atomics, a Southern California–based nuclear power plant contractor, when he decided he could do a better job developing the complex simulations necessary for power-plant design than the programmers who were assigned to the project. One move led to another, and today he is running the Center, a four-story building, housing a Cray C90 and Intel Paragon supercomputer, with the mission of pushing the frontiers of high-powered computing and pure science.

The Center itself, an antiseptic white four-story building set on a hillside on the university campus, is no model of architectural splendor, and we refer to it as "the box the building came in." But it's a reasonable place to do research, and it attracts a lot of people who don't like regular hours or bureaucratic routines. Sid barely blinked on the evening I skated into his office.

Which is not to say I haven't managed to rub some people at the Center the wrong way. I had an early run-in, for example, with the deputy director of operations, Dan D. Drobnis, whom I and others refer to behind his back as "D3."

One day in 1992, D3 discovered me skating in the machine room, the sprawling glass-enclosed space where the Center's main hardware is housed. He went totally nonlinear, insisting I would crash into one of his multimillion-dollar computers and swearing I would never set foot in the Center again if I came anywhere near the building in my skates.

It seemed like an extreme and unreasonable attitude. Since I was constantly crossing the room, moving between the front door and a specialized graphics workstation some thirty meters away, I thought skating made perfect sense. But I can be a pragmatist in some matters, and since that incident, I haven't exactly avoided D³, but I haven't skated into his office, either.

The worst excesses of the bureaucracy aside, life at the Supercomputer Center has for the most part been a reasonable compromise. But in December 1994, I had vowed that things would be different. Truckee, where my ski cabin is located, is twenty kilometers from Lake Tahoe, and the country around it has the advantage of being both high enough to catch the most snow and reasonably close to Silicon Valley, where many of my computer-security sponsors are located. But to get there from the lake region you typically have to cross the notorious Donner Pass, where the wagon train of the Donner Party became snowed-in in October of 1846. It was completely illogical for them to attempt a crossing that late in the season. Trapped by heavy snows and facing starvation, some of the pioneers resorted to cannibalism, and only about half of the original eighty-seven members survived.

It's a story that every California schoolchild is taught to illustrate the hardships endured by their gritty forebears. These days, though, most of the skiers who flock to the area each winter tend to pay little heed to the elements. I know a Silicon Valley software engineer whose favorite T-shirt reads "Donner Pass, Calif. Who's for Lunch?" But on that day before Christmas 1994, I developed a new respect for the Donner Pass.

I probably should have set out the night before, and had in fact briefly considered leaving then and spending the night in the city. But the weather looked like it was about to become snowy and miserable, and I was tired from a day of skiing, so I drove back to the cabin and went to sleep.

It was about 8:30 on the morning of December 24 when I swung my rented Ford Probe out of the slushy driveway of my ski cabin. A light snow was still falling, but I didn't plan to get out of the car until I was down out of the mountains, so I was dressed for California winter: T-shirt and Patagonia shorts, Oakley sunglasses, and Teva sandals. I was giving myself plenty of time for a leisurely trip through Donner Pass on Interstate 80, down the foothills, across the Central Valley, south on the freeway through Berkeley, over the Bay Bridge, and then south through San

Francisco to the airport on the west rim of the Bay. I figured I would be there by 11:30—noon, if I stopped for a strawberry milkshake at Ikeda's in Auburn.

Soon after I left I dialed Caltrans for the recorded highway report on my cell phone and got the bad news: there was "chain control" on Interstate 80 through the mountains. That meant that it was snowing much more heavily up ahead and that the California Highway Patrol would be stopping cars to see if they had chains, and if they didn't, be turning them back. My rent-a-Probe, of course, was chainless.

The report did say that Highway 50, the road that stretches from Sacramento to the south end of Lake Tahoe, was still open. I turned around and headed in the other direction, past the Squaw Valley ski resort and along the California side of the lake. But any hopes that I might skirt the storm, and scoot past chain control on Highway 50 evaporated when I reached South Lake Tahoe 90 minutes later. Ahead of me stretched a long line of cars stuck at the CHP chain control station.

I was beginning to understand how ill-equipped the Donners must have felt when they realized spring wouldn't come nearly soon enough. I whipped the Probe around and raced into town. Fifty dollars and an hour later I was in the chain-control inspection line with everyone else waiting to creep over Echo Summit on Highway 50.

It was almost 11:30 before I really got moving. Ford Motor engineers take note: your basic Probe will do 130 kilometers per hour with chains on, although it doesn't sound pretty.

I have a radar detector, which is great when you're flying along open stretches in Nevada. But in California a detector isn't very useful, for the CHP has found an effective low-tech way to beat speeders with these gadgets. Instead of using radar, they simply race down a highway entry ramp in their black-and-white interceptors, pace the unwary speeder long enough to clock him, and then smugly pull their quarry over.

On that day, I was either extremely lucky, or all the CHP cars were too busy enforcing chain control to worry about speeders.

I called on the way down to check on the arrival time of Julia's United shuttle flight from Los Angeles. It looked like I might be there late and so I asked the airline to deliver a message to her.

The message missed her in Los Angeles and so I called again and asked United to deliver a message to her on her flight, and they said they would take care of it.

The trip was more than 300 kilometers of California freeway driving, and I figure I averaged 155 kilometers per hour—a bit slower with the chains on—for the first 130 kilometers of Highway 50, certainly much faster after I stopped and took the chains off.

By 1:30, I had managed to arrive, park, and position myself just inside the airport security checkpoint just as Julia, in her lanky stride, came down the escalator in the United Airlines terminal. By her expression I could tell she was surprised to see me.

"I take it you didn't get my message," I said.

"What message?" she replied. But it didn't matter. We hugged. Later she said I had looked a little harried.

CHAPTER 2

Of all the questions raised by the first attack, one still puzzles me: was it simply an extraordinary coincidence that the initial raid was launched from Toad Hall?

Toad Hall, an exquisitely renovated two-story Queen Anne just north of San Francisco's Haight-Ashbury district and Golden Gate Park, is owned by John Gilmore, a Unix hacker, libertarian, and electronic privacy activist. John had also been the fifth employee of Sun Microsystems in 1982, years before it became a publicly held company and one of the world's leading makers of workstations and networking systems. He left Sun four years later but the millions he made from being one of the first employees at one of America's most successful companies let him purchase a beautiful home.

The name he chose for the place originally comes, of course, from the home of Mr. Toad in the Kenneth Grahame children's book classic *The Wind in the Willows.* "Toad" also happened to be the nickname of a woman John was living with when he bought the house. Either way, the name was a suitable title, because the fictional Mr. Toad was a wealthy free spirit, and so was Mr. John Gilmore.

With John and friends in residence, Toad Hall became a prototype: one of the first digitally networked homes in San Francisco, the city where new social trends always seem to be accepted first. In the fifties it was the beat generation, in the sixties the hippies, in the seventies alternative sexuality, in the eighties it was south of market skateboard punks. Now in the nineties, cyber-communes seemed to be sprouting up all over the city.

In this scheme a group of starving artists, or bicycle messengers, or even financial-district hackers will get together and rent a house or a flat or an apartment in order to pool their money to share a fifty-six-kilobit-per-second line, leased from the phone company for several hundred dollars a month, to connect to the Internet. Or if the group is more solvent, they might scrape up several thousand for specialized hardware and perhaps a thousand dollars a month for an even faster T-1 connection.

A T-1 line can give you a garden hose of computer data from the Net, compared to the strawlike modems that most people use to connect to on-line services like Compuserve, Prodigy, and American Online. A T-1 data line will transmit 1.5 million bits of information a second. That's enough to download the complete text of *Moby-Dick* in twelve seconds, or to watch a full-screen movie in real time. (Before things get really interesting, however, digital network speeds will need to increase by roughly two orders of magnitude—the equivalent of a fire hydrant—something unlikely to happen until after the turn of the century.)

I take the Net for granted as part of my work, but I can understand why people who must pay their own way might want to co-op. Still, the commune idea seems an odd one to me. If the Internet is about building "virtual communities"—electronic collections of people with no face-to-face contact—doesn't it seem strange that they feel a need to live together, too? In any case, John Gilmore was starting a trend, not following one, when he moved into the Queen Anne in 1987. It had two flats, one for himself and his girlfriend, the other initially for use by a friend he eventually bought out. From the beginning, this was to be no mere residential building; it was a place to live on-line. A coaxial Ethernet networking cable soon snaked its way through the entire house. There were also computer workstations occupying various places, from bedroom desks to basement tables, for use by the various residents, house guests, and drop-in visitors who lived in and hung out in Toad Hall. Where other people might put a coat rack, in the entrance hallway to his second-floor flat, John had placed a Sun SPARCstation ELC.

In keeping with Internet nomenclature, Toad Hall acquired the Internet domain name toad.com, whose gateway to the rest of the world was a Sun SPARCstation computer in the building's basement. This digital domain was run by John and an eclectic band of programmers and hardware gurus, who together had a diverse political outlook, and while privacy was a priority, computer security at Toad was often pretty loose.

John's Toad Hall experiment eventually spawned an early Internet cooperative called The Little Garden, named after a Chinese restaurant in Palo Alto where the first organizing meeting took place. Started by a well-known San Francisco computer hacker named Tom Jennings, The Little Garden was one of the first low-cost ways of getting directly hooked up to the Internet. Unlike today's live-in cyber communes, though, The Little Garden didn't require being physically located in Toad Hall to enjoy its electronic benefits. A member bought two modems and put one at his home and one in the basement of Toad Hall. This second modem was connected through a router to Toad Hall's network link to the Internet and as a result members were permanently on the Net.

The setup was economical, because Pacific Bell offered unmetered residential phone service. So it was possible from a business telephone to leave your data line connected around the clock for a single monthly fee that members chipped in to The Little Garden. If the line was dropped, your modem at the Little Garden would call you back at no charge. Toad Hall eventually had more than a dozen phone lines running into it, and the Pac Bell installers probably wondered what kind of boiler-room racket John and his gang were running in there.

For the past five years, Toad Hall had been Julia's home—for John Gilmore was the "other man," with whom her relationship had been souring even before she and I had met. During the Christmas holidays John was away visiting his relatives in Florida, and so Julia and I had Toad Hall to ourselves when we arrived around 4 P.M. on the afternoon of her flight from Nepal.

John, now forty, was someone I'd known from hacker circles, and even as a friend, for a number of years. Several years earlier he had helped found a second company based on some of the principles of an organization called the Free Software Foundation. The idea behind the company, known as Cygnus Support, was not to sell software directly but, instead, to give it away and then sell the support and maintenance that corporations would require to make full use of the programs such as computer languages and security tools that Cygnus developed. It's a powerful idea, and the company was thriving, even in a world dominated by Microsoft.

A thin man with shoulder-length blond hair and a beard, who sometimes wore the flowing flower-child clothes that had been in fashion in the Haight-Ashbury during the sixties, John had thrown himself into the new start-up with a passion that consumed most of his waking hours. Initially he hadn't minded that Julia and I spent time backpacking together while he worked long hours on his new start-up, because hiking didn't interest him. But once Julia and I had become more intimately involved, things grew chilly between him and me.

Julia and I sent out for dinner from an Italian place called Bambino's. When it came, we undressed and sank into the indoor hot tub, eating while we soaked.

The upstairs bathroom in Toad Hall is an unusual room. It is faced with a white and pink marble floor and wainscoting surrounding a dark green jacuzzi tub and other fixtures. A large asparagus fern sits on the window ledge, centered above the cascading waterfall of the tub's larger faucet. The fronds of the fern tumble down toward the water. Julia had put on a cassette tape of Karma Moffet playing Himalayan intruments, and then lit candles; the only other light came from four overhead spotlights that dimly illuminated each corner of the tub.

"This is just amazing," Julia murmured through the steamy air. She said she had fantasized continually about a long soak in hot water while trekking in the frigid Himalayas, where water is carried by hand from its source and becomes hot only when heated over flames, and where there is never enough to sit in. And at high altitude in the Solu Khumbu region of Nepal, the only heat had come from the sun, the small cooking fire, and the occasional woodstove fueled by wood scraps or dung.

While we ate Julia told me stories of her adventures. In the kitchen of a lodge where she stayed she met and befriended a

Sherpa guide named Tshering and a mountain guide from Seattle named Rachel DeSilva, who had led a group of 12 women to climb a 6,000-meter trekking peak in the region named Mara. Afterward they had invited her to climb another mountain named Lobuche, which lay to the north toward Everest. She had made it to just below the summit.

I sat entranced. "I wish I had been there too," was all I could find to say.

Julia had spent her birthday at the Tengboche monastery to celebrate the Mani Rimdu festival. She showed me a red string necklace that she had received when a Tibetan Lama had blessed her on her thirty-fifth birthday.

"Near noon that same day, I heard the sound of long horns, cymbals, and drums," she recalled. "Then an avalanche poured in slow motion down the south face of Ama Dablam."

Later in the trip she had stopped at one point to watch a sunset over Everest through the gathering mist, and she said it was so stark and beautiful that she cried. "I thought of you," she told me, "and wished you were there to share it with me."

As we soaked, I told her about what had happened to me while she was gone. When Julia left I had been waiting for a $500,000 per year research grant from the National Security Agency, the nation's electronic intelligence-gathering organization. The NSA has two missions: one, its foreign spying mission and the other its responsibility for the security of all the government's computers and communications. In the fall an information security division in the agency had told me they would fund a project permitting me to assemble a team of experts to do research in new areas of computer security. I was ready to go and I had commitments from people to start work, but the agency had dragged its feet for months. Finally I had gotten tired of being jerked around, and two of my researchers had been forced to take other jobs.

"I thought everything would be ironed out and I'd come back to find you happily at work with your team," she said.

"No it wasn't," I answered. "They're amazingly inept, just like any government bureaucracy."

We talked for a while about the NSA and how so many people in the civil liberties community fear them as Big Brother as well

as anyone associated with them, arguing that they become corrupted by association. But that had never seemed accurate to me.
Everything I'd seen indicated they were a largely incompetent
organization tied up in endless regulations that could do little
good or evil. And people are quite capable of making up their
own minds.

"I don't want to deal with them," I said

"I'm sorry it didn't work out, Tsutomu," she said quietly.

We soaked for a while, both of us lost in thought. Finally I
changed the subject.

"I want to tell you something I've been thinking about," I
said. "I've thought about a lot of things while you were away. I'd
really like to try having a committed relationship with you, if
you're willing to."

Julia smiled. She didn't say anything, but she reached over and
held me closely.

It seemed like we would now be able to share a lot of time
together. I told her I'd taken a leave of absence from the university and now I was looking forward to skiing and getting away. I
was finally pursuing my long-held plan to spend a winter in the
mountains, spending the mornings and late afternoons skiing
and the mid-days and evenings thinking and working on my
research projects.

"Why don't you come with me and live in the mountains?" I
suggested. "You can come ski and it will be good to be outside."

We woke at about 1 P.M. the next day and Julia—who grew up
on the East Coast and is still learning to deal with mild California
winters—told me that she had seen the first morning light before
she fell asleep and thought to herself, *It's Christmas and there is no
sign of it here.* She was still jet-lagged and also feeling what she
feared was flu coming on. We decided to spend the day inside,
catching up on talk and sleep. It was chilly out, so Julia turned up
Toad Hall's central heat, still eager to soak up the warmth of civ-
ilization after two months in the Himalaya.

A bit later, while she rested, I was walking around the house,
and several times went past the Sun SPARCstation in the hallway.
It was a reminder that I probably had new electronic mail, but I
didn't feel like checking it.

At just about that moment, however, ominous bits of data were flowing through the Ethernet cable that wound through Toad's rooms and hallways. From somewhere, perhaps thousands of kilometers away, an electronic intruder had taken control of toad.com by remotely commandeering the SPARCstation in the basement. And while the two of us spent the day together two floors above, the electronic hijacker was using toad.com as a staging base to launch an attack on the computers in my own beach house some 800 kilometers south.

I didn't realize it that afternoon, but the intruder had made himself "root" of toad.com. The root account is an all-powerful computer system administrator, an entity who can control every operation of a Unix machine. It is usually reserved for a computer's caretaker or administrator. On a Unix computer like the SPARCstation in the basement of Toad Hall, being root is like being God. Once he has become root, a computer user can create and delete accounts and files, read any other user's mail or documents, monitor someone else's every keystroke, or tamper with a computer's software to leave behind programs that create secret backdoors for easier entry next time.

Whoever it was that invaded the system had a reasonable degree of computer network sophistication—or at least an awareness of the lax security of toad.com. Whoever it was also had obviously picked out my computers in San Diego as a specific target, whether out of a personal vendetta or because they assumed I had valuable files.

As one of a small group of high-level computer security researchers in the country, I have machines that store sensitive information, like reports on little-known bugs, loopholes, and system vulnerabilities that have been discovered on various types of widely used hardware and software, and I also have a range of computer security tools. However, I had taken many security precautions, and material that I considered extremely valuable wasn't accessible. Still, some of the information and tools were within reach of the determined intruder, and in the wrong hands they could be used for breaking into other civilian or government computer systems, or sold on the corporate espionage market.

That evening we ordered dinner out again—Indian food this time. While we waited for the food to arrive, Julia began to

unpack from her trip and I spent some time setting up a new
portable computer I had picked up from a friend's house the day
before after leaving the airport. Made by RDI, a San Diego–area
company I consult for, it was a compact Unix workstation and I
had volunteered to test the new model for them. I briefly thought
about connecting it to the Toad Hall network, but I didn't. I had
no idea someone was spending Christmas Day committing a
felony over the Internet.

Julia woke the next morning still feeling sick, so instead of going
for a day hike in the Headlands across the Bay in Marin County,
as we had planned, we spent another quiet day at Toad Hall. It
was cold and gray out, and the only time we left the house was
briefly at midday, when we wandered over to Haight Street to
have lunch at Cha Cha Cha, a tapas place that attracts an eclectic crowd, ranging from those who live in the Haight to white
collar financial district types and people of various ethnicities and
hues from all over the city. John was arriving home that evening,
and there were clearly matters that he and Julia needed to talk
about. I had things to do in the South Bay area and if everything
worked out well, in a few days Julia would come skiing with me.
    "I'll see you soon, I love you," she said as I went to the door.
    "Take care of yourself," I said, and we embraced.
    Shortly after 8 P.M., I climbed into the rented Probe and began
the 50-kilometer drive south to Silicon Valley, where I had
arranged to visit a friend named Mark Lottor. A young hardware
hacker and Internet whiz, Mark, who was thirty-one years old,
was a friend with whom I'd spent a lot of time exploring cellular
telephone technology. Mark is on the short side with brown hair
falling carelessly across his forehead, but he has an adventurous
hobby: hopping freight trains for an occasional hobo's sojourn
around the West. Most of the time, though, he is attending to
Network Wizards, the small company that he runs from his
home in Menlo Park, which makes and sells a variety of useful
computing tools ranging from computer temperature sensors to
cellular telephone network diagnostic and surveillance tools that
are popular with cellular companies and law enforcement officials. Together we had taken apart the software that sits at the

heart of Oki's cellular telephone. Mark had originally spotted it as a well-designed piece of technology, and I'd read his review of the Oki 900 and bought one as well. Once we knew how the software worked we figured out how to control it with a personal computer. For just a little more than one hundred dollars his hardware and software allows an Oki and an inexpensive personal computer to rival bulky commercial diagnostic products that cost many thousands of dollars.

Most people know Mark for his biannual survey of computers directly connected to the Internet, the electronic equivalent of a Commerce Department census. He has written software that systematically "walks" through the Internet, querying each major computer domain. As with the human census, many computers choose not to answer, but his numbers are the best basis for an educated guess about how big the Internet is and how quickly it's growing. His most recent survey in mid 1995 counted 6.6 million computers with a Internet connection. Of course that number doesn't indicate how many people actually are on the Internet, because one computer with a direct connection to the Internet may be the network gateway for tens, hundreds, or even thousands of users and their own individual computers. Still, it is from Mark's survey that most estimates, from the conservative to the giddy, are derived.

As I drove I was feeling a bit harried—I was late for meeting Mark and some friends for dinner and I was still thinking about Julia. US 101 took me south out of San Francisco passing Candlestick Park, the airport, and the rim of the Bay with its light-industrial sprawl, which forms the northern reaches of the Valley. The road was wet from a recent, chilly rain, a good sign. It meant more snow up in the mountains. My plan was to pick up Julia in a day or two, then return to the Sierra and a winter that was looking as if it might offer the best skiing in years.

It was shortly after eight o'clock and I was nearly to the Highway 92 overpass, the unofficial northern border of Silicon Valley, when my ringing cell phone broke my train of thought.

"Tsutomu, this is Andrew." He needn't have identified himself, for his voice, with its residual trace of Tennessee vowels, is instantly recognizable.

"Have you got a minute? Can you get to a land line?"

"Not conveniently," I answered. He was spending Christmas vacation at his parents' house in Tennessee. Andrew Gross was a twenty-seven-year-old electrical engineering graduate student at the University of California at San Diego who worked with me on networking and security problems at SDSC (the Center). He had great promise as a computer security researcher, and I'd become something of a mentor to him. As part of his apprenticeship he often watched over my network when I was away. As we talked I got the distinct impression he was really uneasy talking to me while I was using a cellular phone and at the same time had something serious he wanted to tell me. I pressured him to give me a basic idea in some way that wouldn't give anything away.

"Tell me generally what's up," I said. In my harassed mood I wasn't interested in dealing with new problems. He paused. He was obviously mulling what he could say that wouldn't prick up the ears of the few dozen bored or nosy people who were probably at that moment using radio scanners to monitor the local cell phone airwaves the way some people listen to police radio traffic.

"Well," he finally said. "Your log file summaries have gotten shorter."

What he was telling me was that somebody had broken into my computers. I had a queasy feeling, a little bit the way you feel after you realize someone has picked your pocket. In my mind I quickly ran through the implications though my immediate reaction wasn't panic but irritation at one more distraction. We talked for a while and gradually I realized that what he had discovered was not an accounting error. Something was seriously wrong and needed to be dealt with.

My network is set up to maintain an audit file of all the connections made from the outside world—a complete record of who connects and when. Four times a day, a summary of this information is routinely mailed to a remote computer that Andrew monitored. Normally, the summary should get longer between each mailing. If it got unexpectedly shorter, the logical conclusion to draw is that someone had tried to erase the file.

"Oh," I said, "shit," and thought for a moment about the best course of action. "Why don't you dial in and see if you notice anything?" I suggested. "I'll go somewhere and see if I can learn anything as well. I'll call you in a while."

I keep a couple of modems connected to my computers that are convenient for dialing directly into my network. It hadn't occurred to Andrew to connect to our machines this way, but we both knew that if we turned off our direct connection to the Internet, then no one would be able to easily break in again over the network, and the data on my computers would be more likely to stay the way it was when Andrew discovered the shortened log files. He volunteered to mail the summaries of the shortened log files to the wireless electronic mail terminal I usually carry with me.

"Be careful," was the last thing I said before hanging up. "Make sure you preserve the evidence."

Computer security is full of tradeoffs. The art form is coming up with a set of tradeoffs you can live with. It is possible to have absolute computer security: you simply unplug your computer and lock it in a vault, and even the best thief won't be able to steal your data. But this ultimate security solution also means that you won't be able to use your computer. Like everyone else, I have to make trade-offs in the security of my machines and take some attendant risks.

Although the Internet today is, as many writers have commented, like the Wild West, with a lot of real outlaws roaming through it, it wasn't always so. When I was in school at Caltech, and later when I worked as a physics researcher at Los Alamos, the world had not yet awakened to the Net. The culture still showed its roots in the ARPAnet, the Pentagon-funded academic predecessor to the Internet that was established in 1969, and was like a small community where everyone knew everyone else. You greeted your neighbor at the general store and you left your door unlocked.

Today, with millions of people clamoring to connect to the Internet, the rules have changed. The world is plunging ahead, putting every conceivable form of business and private communication in electronic form and shuttling them back and forth over networks that were originally designed for sharing information, not protecting it. There are, as a result, many tempting targets for bandits and information highwaymen.

The vast potential for stealth is one of the most difficult aspects of detecting a crime in cyberspace. In the physical world, if a thief breaks into a bank vault, it's obvious there's been a burglary because the money is gone. In cyberspace, a vault can be stripped without any sign, at first glance, anyway, that a theft has even occurred, for what is stolen is not the original piece of software or data, but a copy that the thief makes. Even commercial software programs worth millions of dollars can be copied in an instant, leaving the original intact. It's all just bits.

There is a school of thought in the Net community that argues that, because a software program is infinitely copyable, then conventional notions of property rights have little relevance. Software should be free, they say, and freely disseminated, and there should be no such thing as software intellectual property rights. A chief proponent of this philosophy is Richard Stallman, who has helped found groups like the Free Software Foundation and the League for Programming Freedom.

I believe that it should be up to the creator to decide whether to give software away or to be compensated for the hard work of writing it. And I certainly have no sympathy for those who pervert the free-software philosophy by reasoning that if it can be freely copied it should be free to steal. There's no justification to illegally break into somebody's computer.

In the last few years, as the Net has become more and more commercial, computer vendors have begun selling security "solutions"—protective hardware and software that is supposed to make it impossible for vandals to break into your computer. The problem with many security products, however, is that they are stopgaps whose claims far outweigh their performance. Their purpose is to make people feel better about security without really doing anything.

One of the most common defenses is called a firewall, which sits between the Internet and your computer and is designed to allow only carefully screened bits to pass through to your own network. Any data that is not recognized as friendly will be blocked. The trouble with firewalls is that while they can be highly effective filters, they can also make it cumbersome to use your computer on a network. In effect, they create a Maginot Line instead of real security. A firewall provides a hard shell but leaves the soft chewy center at the heart of your network vulnerable.

I refuse to be so paranoid that I can't function. My computers are connected to the Net because it's a resource that not only lets me share my work with a community of researchers, but also makes an entire world of information—software, other computers, databases—accessible from my keyboard. Anything of any sensitivity that I intend to send or receive over the Net is encrypted with software that makes it meaningless to anyone without the key to the code. But my computers don't have any unusual electronic walls around them.

Instead, I take other, less crippling precautions, like using encryption, logging activity, and keeping log files, in some cases with alarms. The real secret of computer security is to be aware, to watch the systems carefully, something most people don't do.

When intruders break into computers over the Internet, one of the standard steps they take to elude detection is to erase traces of their presence on the computer they've attacked. They will frequently go into the automatic recordkeeping files, the log files, that are generated by the system and edit out the record of their activity.

But this creates a situation that few computer intruders stop to consider: when they erase the records of their activity, the length of the file suddenly gets shorter. At SDSC and on my machines at home, we have a simple electronic way of noticing this. When Andrew connected to the Net to read his mail from his parents' house in Tennessee, he had checked the summaries of our log files, and realized we had uninvited guests.

It took me another twenty minutes to drive to Mark's two-story townhouse. He lived in a building across the street from SRI International, the research laboratory where the ARPAnet was created a quarter-century ago.

Inside Mark's house, the inventing continues. The place is full of personal computers and workstations, all cabled together into a local-area network. Like the cyber-communes in San Francisco, it has a T-1 link to the outside world. Mark also has the perfect hacker's totem in his living room: a 1950s-style Coke machine, which provides a touch of classic industrial design. Most often the machine is filled with bottled water, but sometimes it actually has Coke.

Mark had been waiting for me. He planned for us to drive to Palo Alto, a few kilometers away, to meet some of my friends for dinner, but he saw that I was clearly distracted.

"Sorry, " I said. "Something's up. I'll need a few more minutes." I explained briefly I'd had a break-in and wanted to assess the damage.

"I hope this won't take very long," Mark said. "I'm hungry."

However, he was sympathetic; the previous fall he'd spent weeks fighting off a determined electronic thief who was trying to steal his cellular telephone software.

I had a sense of urgency to get to things quickly, before the data stored on my computer was lost or altered. Unlike a typical personal computer which until recently could run only one program at a time, Unix computers generally run dozens of programs simultaneously, meaning if data were changed any trail might be quickly erased. Normally I could have easily connected to my computers over Mark's network, but because Andrew was about to shut off outside access via the Internet the only option was using a modem to dial in directly to my computer. I asked Mark if I could go upstairs and use his walk-in closet, a tiny room in which he keeps clothes on one side and an IBM PC and a low-speed 2400-baud modem on the other. Some people hang on to out-of-style suits; Mark refuses to throw away old-fashioned technology if it still has some wear left in it. The security of the telephone was still an issue in the back of my mind, but I decided the need to act quickly outweighed the possible risk.

I sat down in the cramped space and used the modem to connect to my computers in San Diego. From Mark's PC I could control the computers in my small network, both my computers at the SDSC and the ones I have at my house several miles off campus. I browsed around for a while, looking through endlessly scrolling directories of files to see if anything was obviously amiss. On the surface, everything appeared normal, so it was unlikely this was a mere prankster's break-in. As the altering of our log files had indicated, somebody was trying to cover his tracks.

I proceeded gingerly, as any detective would do, careful not to damage any data that might later enable me to reconstruct how the break-in took place. Even something as simple as reading a file can forever obliterate an intruder's digital footprints. I could see from the directories and the system administration logs that Andrew was also connected to my network, making the same kind of survey I was making—but with less care. He had been tromping around, opening files to peek at them, and each time destroying valuable evidence. It irked me, and I sent him a message telling him brusquely not to disturb anything. But he had spent almost an hour snooping around and information had already been lost. Andrew's efforts, though, had led to one particularly significant discovery: some of the packet log files that keep records of our network data traffic had been accessed recently, and then copied to an unknown location elsewhere on the Net. This meant that whoever had broken into my machines now could have any kind of information belonging to other users who had used these machines, including their passwords. If I was the locksmith, the thief now had lots of passkeys. I made a mental note to go look through these data-traffic files later and do damage control. Also, interesting but frustrating was Andrew's discovery that the current network traffic log was invalid, and not helpful to us.

There was a range of information in front of us but none of it seemed to form a complete picture. One hunch was to look at copies of the logs from before they were erased and to see whose records had vanished. From that we might be able to infer who was trying to cover their tracks. We could see that around ten o'clock the night before there had been a flurry of random probes from a network site called csn.org, which was Colorado SuperNet, an Internet service provider from which I had previously seen attempted break-ins. But none of the previous night's attempts from csn.org appeared to have been successful. At roughly the same time, we saw, there had been attempts to connect from two sites with prankish names: wiretap.spies.com and suspects.com. If someone was trying to bait me, these were the type of taunts I would expect to see, although these clues weren't putting us any closer to understanding what had actually happened. We also saw that one of my computers that handled program communication over the network had been started for some reason the night before. This was suspicious, but it might not mean anything at all.

I probed more deeply, very gently looking beneath the surface. The file directories that a computer user sees are actually built from other records a computer maintains at a much lower level. By examining these minute details at the very lowest level of my computer's file structure, I hoped to pick up some hint of the changes that even the most clever interloper might not have thought to erase.

On Ariel, the computer at SDSC that serves as my gateway to the Internet, I could see that the intruder had left some traces. Much of the data wasn't even in English, but rather in the binary representations computers use to communicate internally, and from it I could make out patterns of information still stored on my computer's disk that revealed the ghost of a file that had been created and then erased. Finding it was a little like examining a piece of paper on a yellow legal pad: even though the top page had been torn off, the impression of what was written on the missing sheet can be discerned on the remaining page. The file that had been there momentarily and then copied to some remote point and erased had been named oki.tar.Z.

It was a tiny clue but it was one that pointed in many possible directions. What did it signify? Oki, of course, was the brand of cellular telephone I'd worked on with Mark Lottor; it had been the Oki source code—the programmer's original instructions—that Mark's attackers had been after the previous fall. "Tar" is a Unix utility program that archives and extracts files to and from a single file called a tarfile. A tarfile is traditionally a collection of files on a magnetic tape, but it can be any file. Someone might have gathered software programs I'd written for controlling an Oki cellular telephone, and then merged them into a single file they called oki.tar. The "Z" indicated they had probably squeezed them down in size using another utility program "compress" so that it would take less time to transfer them to some remote place.

The fact that someone had bundled a bunch of files and called them oki indicated a possible motive for why my computers had been attacked: somebody was very interested in the inner work-ings of cell phones. The ghostly shadow of oki.tar.Z also provid-ed me with a set of directional pointers for determining which of my files had been stolen. And because every file that had been bundled together into oki.tar.Z had to be accessed in order to be copied, and the access times had been duly noted by the com-puter, I had a rather detailed accounting of my thief's visit.

On the other side of the country Andrew only had one phone line and so he disconnected and we talked by voice while I con-tinued to examine my network from the computer in Mark's closet.

I told him the next step to take was to call the operations peo-ple at SDSC and have them halt Ariel, the computer that con-nects my network to the outside world and which is housed in a wiring closet next to my office. To halt a computer is very dif-ferent than shutting it down or rebooting it, both of which will wipe out all the data that hasn't already been explicitly saved on the hard disk. A halt command, by contrast, will freeze a com-puter in its tracks, leaving every bit of information in exactly the state it was when the machine was suspended. This step would be crucial to the forensic analysis I now knew I was going to have to perform, which also meant returning to San Diego. Until we found exactly how my network had been attacked I couldn't go back online. I was going to have to examine my sys-tems with the software equivalent of a magnifying glass—or even a microscope. And time wasn't on my side. What I needed to do was in effect analyze footprints that had been left in sand. They stand out, but only as long as they are not covered by others who have traveled the same path.

A little after nine my friends showed up, and finally, after nine-thirty Mark dragged me away from the computer closet. We all drove to The Good Earth, a health food chain restaurant in downtown Palo Alto. They needn't have waited, for all my pres-ence added to the party. I spent some of dinner talking to Andrew on my cell phone, trying to organize things so that we could meet as soon as possible in San Diego. He had already called Jay Dombrowski, communications manager at SDSC, and had con-vinced him that we'd had a serious breach. Dombrowski agreed that the Center would pick up the cost of the plane fare to fly Andrew back to San Diego immediately.

There were few encouraging signs. By halting Ariel quickly there was a chance we would be able to reconstruct some of what happened, but log file information had been erased, and in our brief examination we had not been able to turn up any obvious backdoors, a telltale sign in many network break-ins.

Shortly before eleven Mark and I said good-bye to my friends and we drove back to his townhouse in Menlo Park. I was still distracted, trying to come up with a plan to fly back to San Diego and quickly assess the break-in. Back at Mark's, I connected to my computers again and discovered that Andrew had spent more time prowling through my network again after I had left for dinner. I could see he had done things that were likely to have erased precious forensic data and I called him again, telling him that I was upset that he had blundered around the network. I hung up and realized that when I arrived in San Diego, I was going to need hardware I didn't have to reconstruct the break-in. I asked Mark to call his friend, Lile Elam, because I had cached some disk drives and other equipment in her office at Sun Microsystems several weeks earlier. I've been a consultant at Sun for a number of years and Lile worked there as a technical support person, but the computer maker was closed down for the Christmas holidays. I wanted to know if she was willing to meet us at Sun for a midnight raid to pick up my gear.

Lile was hesitant at first to go into the offices so late at night, but I persuaded her to meet us in front of the building where she worked at the company's Mountain View campus. I pointed out that I knew everyone who mattered at Sun, and promised her that if anyone questioned us, I'd take full responsibility for it. When we arrived in front of Building 18 ten minutes later, Lile was waiting outside.

There was one problem. Parked right in front of the door was a white Sun security pickup. Although the building was closed, it meant a private security guard was probably wandering around inside and might not take kindly to someone walking out with handfuls of disk drives in the middle of the night. Worse, although Lile and I had Sun badges, Mark didn't, and the security guard might wonder what a non–Sun employee was doing with us.

We discussed waiting until he left, but none of us wanted to spend the night in front of the building. We used our badges and began walking down the hallway to Lile's office. Sure enough, two-thirds of the way down the hallway we ran into the guard. As it turned out, we were overly paranoid. He was happy with Lile and me, but challenged Mark. We explained that Mark was a friend of Lile's, though, and that seemed to satisfy him.

Feeling a little as if we'd just crossed a border checkpoint, the three of us went on down the hall to Lile's office where I gathered up my disk drives and some interface cards in antistatic bags. We could see the security truck through Lile's office window and a couple of minutes later the guard left the building, got in the truck, and pulled away. We hurriedly went back down the hall, feeling conspicuous with our hands full of hardware. Outside we walked in front of the video camera and got in our cars and left.

When we got back to Mark's apartment around one-thirty, I booked myself on the seven o'clock Reno Air flight out of San Jose. I'd need to be up by six to get to the airport in time to drop off the Probe at Budget. Mark wished me luck and headed upstairs to bed, as I stretched out on the living room couch to grab a few hours of sleep. I had one last thought before dropping off: *This year, skiing would have to wait.*

CHAPTER 3

Los Angeles has increasingly transformed itself into its own image in the futuristic movie *Blade Runner*—a smoggy, anarchic technopolis.

San Diego, where I live, isn't a pristine Southern California city either, but it has a livable quality I never seem to find in Los Angeles. It appears like an island every time I fly home on a commercial jet dropping steeply over the financial district before landing toward the ocean. Ringed by desert the city evokes a tangible sense of the future drawn from the combination of the hard angles of sterile twenty-first century architecture, lush palm trees, bright green lawns, and ocean. There is no shortage of weird architecture ranging from the abrupt modernist buildings on the University of California campus, where I work, to the surreal Mormon temple off I-5 designed to evoke some mythical European Renaissance church.

When I left San Jose there had been long lines and mass chaos and I was reminded of why I don't usually travel after three-day weekends. On the first working day after Christmas the airport was a seething mass of people all trying to get home. At about eight-thirty on Monday morning, working on four hours of sleep, I made my way out of the airport. I was loaded down with thirty kilos of gear I'd picked up the night before, including the prototype RDI PowerLite. I felt frustrated about being in San Diego instead of on my way back to Lake Tahoe to ski. Andrew was flying in a little later in the day so I walked out to the curb and took a thirty-dollar cab ride directly to the Center and my office.

To describe it as an office is actually being kind. I have a small, windowless room next to an even smaller wiring closet. It is stuffed with several computer monitors, random hardware like disk drives and other spare parts, and a Government security safe, left over from my days as a federal laboratory employee, marked PROPERTY OF LOS ALAMOS NATIONAL LABORATORY. Because I travel so often I work in my office infrequently, but I use it as a storage arca. There are always lots of books and at least one tub of unopened mail that my secretary has set down somewhere. There are also several computer monitors connected by a bundle of video cables to Ariel, the ancient Sun Microsystems worksta-tion that is stuck away in the wiring closet. The closet is also home to a few modems and several other computers including one that functions as a routing computer—a traffic controller for all the Internet data that comes my way.

Several years earlier I had set up Ariel so that the background on its video display constantly showed the most current satellite weather image delivered over the Internet from the University of Illinois at Champaign-Urbana.

I've named my computers after the fallen angels in John Milton's *Paradise Lost.* Unlike *Byte* magazine columnist Jerry Pournelle, who seems to want to breathe life into his household computers by calling them things like Ezekiel in his column every month, I have no intention of anthropomorphizing the machines I work with. To me computers are all basically "its." What I was looking for instead were names that were obviously related but to a casual observer not immediately obvious how. If it's done right it becomes elegant. It also had to be a large set of names because I was always needing more as new computers showed up. Milton's fallen angels turned out to be a useful source of names because I wanted something that offered lots of choices, and also something that would get by the network name censors.

Before we had settled on the angels, Sid and I had had a chat about the naming problem, during which he told me, "I don't want to censor you, but I don't want you to be offensive, either." Some people in the computer network world seem to believe I have an "attitude." Maybe I do, but this was just Sid's way of trying to persuade me not to pick unnecessary fights with the network thought police.

I tend to work on the fastest computers available at any given moment, but I have something of a soft spot in my heart for Ariel, which came with me from Los Alamos. It began life as a Sun-3. Sun began shipping Sun 3s in 1985, which in terms of computer workstation generations makes it an antique. New microprocessor generations tend to come at about eighteen-month intervals. Going back six generations of computer technology would be the equivalent of returning to the era of the horse and buggy.

Ariel has a curious history. Years ago I visited Sun with Brosl Hasslacher, a Los Alamos physicist who has been my mentor over the years, negotiating with Sun over problems we were having with a much more expensive and powerful computer. A Sun executive went out on the loading dock and found Ariel for us as something of a consolation prize. In the years that followed, Ariel has become a vagabond, making its way back at one point to Caltech, where it was used by a student who had worked with me as an intern, before the machine finally wound up in my wiring closet. Today I use it mostly for mail, for storing less-important stuff, and as a jumping-off point to the Internet to give myself net access.

As soon as I got into my office I dropped my bags. I glanced at one of the monitors of the computer that had been frozen the night before by a Center operator. On the display in the console window, the one that reports system status information, was an error message from the XNeWS interpreter, the program that controls the display of information on the computer's screen:

```
process(0x480088, 'teal.csn.org NeWS client', runnable)
Error: /syntaxerror
Command: '.psparse_token'
```

I puzzled over the message briefly but could see no obvious vulnerability. I restarted Ariel long enough to peek at the statistics logs kept in the modem that connected my computers at home to the Center. What I saw was evidence that there had not been a lot of data taken from my home network. The modem log showed it had been connected for five days—about the time I'd been away—and that during that time about four megabytes of data had flowed in each direction. That was just routine house-keeping traffic and the fact that it was balanced in both directions indicated that no one had siphoned files out of my home machines. It was a relief—the principal target had been else-where, probably somewhere among the computers next door in the wiring closet.

I called Sid Karim, the director, about the break-in. He was generally sympathetic to my problem but was unwilling to give me a blank check to solve the problem. He told me that if I was describing the situation reasonably correctly then he was willing to provide some expense money to help with damage control. Translated politely, he was warning I'd better be right about my suspicions. He also declined to pay my usual consulting fees, arguing, "Tsutomu, you're basically on vacation."

I decided that was about all I could hope for under the cir-cumstances, and I went out to my Acura which I'd left in the Center parking lot while I was traveling and drove home.

I have computers both at SDSC and at home connected by a high-speed modem line that always stays open. I'd decided to go home first to examine things because that was where data and programs I really care about are kept.

My house is about a ten-minute drive north of the Center in one of those newish communities of tract housing that dot the Southern California landscape. The commute route takes me past the Scripps Clinic and along what is described as San Diego's Biotech Row. Just as Stanford University served as an incubator for Silicon Valley, Scripps has nurtured a generation of biologists turned entrepreneurs. My neighborhood was largely built in the 1970s and my house is actually a townhouse that fits snugly against its neighbors. It's not my idea of the most desirable archi-tectual style but it's close to campus and it gives me a sense of being out of the city. I can see and smell the ocean and from my upstairs bedroom I can hear waves crashing on the beach at night. I also look out over Torrey Pines State Park where I go when I need someplace to be by myself and think. The beach is out of both wireless computer data and cellular telephone range and sometimes I will just take a pad of paper down there when I need to concentrate.

After parking in the garage I walked inside my house and found it cool and still. By most people's standards my home is spartan. Although it has three bedrooms and a den, I have only a small amount of furniture—a scattering of futons, chairs, and tables. I sleep in the upstairs master bedroom and use the other upstairs bedroom as an equipment room and staging area for various adventures and expeditions. In recent years I have spent time on long backpacking trips, hiked above the Arctic Circle, and followed an eclipse in Baja California.

The absence of furniture is made up for by an abundance of computers. At any one time I might have as many as a dozen machines connected to the Internet at home, depending on what happens to be plugged in at the moment. Many of the machines are stacked in one of my closets, and some of them don't even have monitors, they are simply boxes with processors, memory, and disks. There are a few PowerLites; a SPARCstation Voyager, which was Sun's disappointing experiment in entering the portable computer market; Osiris, a diskless workstation that sits at the head of my bed that I frequently use as a window into the Internet; a pair of servers, Rimmon and Astarte, fast Sun computers with big disks that are good for storing data and crunching numbers; another router; a terminal server; a demo firewall computer—and the list goes on.

While most modern offices today connect their computers with a technology called Ethernet, which was developed at the Xerox Corporation's legendary Palo Alto Research Center during the 1970s, my home computers are linked by fiber optic cables using a technology called ATM, or Asynchronous Transfer Mode. An ATM network organizes information differently than Ethernet. Data are broken down into "cells" rather than "packets." Cells are generally smaller than packets and they're all the same size. That means ATM is better designed for sending video and audio. Moreover, on an ATM network you're always guaranteed the full speed of the network link; you don't have to worry about sharing it with your next-door neighbor.

A lot of people in the computer and the telecommunications industries believe that ATM is going to be the wave of the future. Unlike other network standards it has no single defined speed, and it's scalable, meaning that it can continue to get faster as technology improves. My particular implementation is already fifteen times faster than Ethernet—fast enough to transmit video images that are startlingly clear—much better than anything you see on today's television sets. Already telephone and cable companies are laying the groundwork to replace their existing analog copper wire networks with ATM fiber optic networks. Its supporters are confident that by the turn of the century ATM data networks will be as easily available in homes as telephone jacks and cable outlets are today. That's the vision anyway. I've been quietly experimenting with nitty-gritty engineering details that have to be worked out before any of this becomes a consumer reality.

What fascinates me is the power inherent in high-speed computer networks and what you can do with them as opposed to a single isolated computer. Sun has an advertising slogan, "The network is the computer." When you get past the hype there is a powerful kernel of truth there that is implicit in all of the recent popular interest in the Internet. Single computers are no longer very interesting, but the distributed computer that is emerging out of the web is where the future is hidden. As a result I have orange, white, and beige cables running everywhere. Some of them pass through the walls and some of them are out in the open. These cables carry computer data as tiny flashes of light. Imagine switching a beam of light on and off hundreds of millions of times a second. (As an experiment you can shine a flashlight in one end of a coil of fiber optic cable. When you look at the other end you see this razor-sharp starlike point of light.) One thing is certain—fiber optic cables are much more resistant to being slammed in doors than standard copper cables.

Feeling bone-tired I stood inside my entryway for a moment, glad to be home but frustrated that I wasn't in the mountains. Then I turned off the house alarm and padded upstairs to my bedroom with the intention of taking a nap while I waited for

Andrew to arrive. It was a bright sunlit morning and from my bedroom I could see across the rooftops to Torrey Pines and the ocean. The room was still. There was no noise from fans or whirring disk drives. Although there are three computers in the room I feel strongly that human beings and moving computer parts don't mix.

Nothing had changed visibly, but something was odd. Sitting cross-legged on my bed in front of Osiris's I touched the trackball and the screensaver that was blanking its monitor gave way to a field of windows. I noticed immediately that a large rectangle that sits on the left side of Osiris's screen and that is usually connected to either the outside world or to Ariel at the Center was completely blank. It was all white. There was no sign of life—none of the text that should have been displayed, even if the computer it was connected to was halted.

I thought to myself, this is weird, because even though Ariel was still frozen back at SDSC, Osiris's screen should still register its presence. I sat on my bed and looked at Osiris again and thought some more. Nothing really registered. I halted Osiris. I went and halted its current server computer, Astarte. Then I systematically froze my other computers as well. My entire computer world was suspended, as if it had been frozen in midstep.

I went back downstairs and looked in the refrigerator and realized that there wasn't a lot of food in the house. Not surprising, because I travel so much of the time. I scrounged around and found some Power Bars, which would have to do for the moment.

I returned to my bedroom to try again to analyze the break-in. My first step would be to obtain some forensic tools to examine the intruder's tracks. I switched on my new RDI and began assembling a small toolkit of programs that could collect and analyze data. What I wanted to learn was what files had been read, modified, or created. It's easy to tell precise times when things happen on a computer, because the operating system routinely time stamps any file change. With that information it might be possible to construct a chronology of the intruder's activities. It is possible to alter this information systematically, however, and so I knew it was important not to take any information in the digital world on faith.

I now had a handful of frozen computers, in which the intruder's tracks were hidden as strings of electronic 1's and 0's. My plan was to remove their disks and plug them into a new computer to do the analysis, for by making the disks "read only" it would be possible to avoid any danger of accidentally smudging the data as I explored it. I stared at the portable computer, which was a prototype and might not work. Brand-new machines tend to have glitches that can be irritating. Maybe I'd be lucky. If it worked I'd be able to determine what files the intruder had touched and when. Then possibly I'd also be able to discover how he had broken into my computers.

Shortly before noon I called Andrew, who'd arrived in San Diego several hours after I had and had gone home to drop his gear. He'd taken an even earlier flight from Tennessee than I had from San Jose and we were both feeling pretty trashed. We agreed to meet for dinner that evening to plan a course of action. The last time I'd spoken with Andrew had been at 2:30 A.M., just before I fell asleep. He hadn't slept at all the night before, but he said he was able to doze a little on his flight. Finally, in the early afternoon I lay down on my bed and fell asleep, only to wake later in the afternoon still groggy. But I had this sense the next couple of days were going to be intense and even a short catnap was an improvement.

The ghostly image of oki.tar.Z continued to nag at me. What did it signify? Several years earlier I had helped out Mark Lottor by reverse engineering the software that is built into Oki cellular telephones. Normally the programs that control a cellular phone are hidden in a ROM chip inside the phone. However, most phones have an undocumented interface to the outside world that makes it possible to control the phone remotely from a computer. We examined the software carefully and worked backward from the 1's and 0's embedded in the chip to the original commands intended by the software designers. Reverse engineering software is still controversial, but recent court rulings have generally held that such work is a legitimate activity. Mark wanted to be able to control the Oki phone in order to develop a piece of field diagnostic equipment to sell to cellular telephone companies and law enforcement agencies.

Since we had no help from Oki in figuring out how to control their phones, we had to take their software apart to see how it worked. What we found were lots of undocumented features that cell phone users have no idea exist. A cellular telephone is really little more than a radio with a tiny personal computer, so when we looked closely at the Oki's software it came as no surprise that it had obviously been written by truly clever hackers.

With commands that can be punched into the keypad of an Oki phone, it is possible to obtain all kinds of diagnostic data on how the phone is behaving, such as its signal strength, that are quite useful for phone technicians. Many brands of cell phones also happen to function just as well as the Oki as cellular telephone scanners. Few people realize that if they know the right buttons to push on their cell phone keypads, they can easily listen to all the phone conversations that are going on in their neighborhood—a trick which is, of course, a violation of the Electronic Communications Privacy Act. But since there is no privacy at all in today's cellular telephone system, illegal eavesdropping on cell phone calls has become a popular pastime.

In 1992 I testified before a Congressional hearing held by Representative Edward Markey on the existence of this undocumented cell phone capability. After the committee chairman granted me special immunity, I took a brand-new AT&T cellular phone—actually the same Oki phone but relabeled and sold by AT&T, still in its shrinkwrap packaging—assembled it and pushed a series of buttons. Soon the committee was listening to cellular phone conversations from all over Capitol Hill.

Afterwards a bulky, middle-aged FBI agent came up to me and said, "You have congressional privilege now, but don't ever let me catch you doing that outside this room." His comment confirmed one thing I've noticed in working with the FBI: these guys have no sense of humor.

Oki.tar.Z not only suggested a motive for our break-in, but it also hinted at who the perpetrator might be. A few months earlier in October and November, someone had repeatedly broken into Mark Lottor's computers in an effort to steal the same Oki cellular software that had been pilfered from Ariel.

Mark was in the process of setting up a new cottage business. The Internet was booming, and he had found there was a ready market for publishing pages on the Internet's rapidly expanding World Wide Web. Network Wizards was therefore creating "catalog.com," an inexpensive web site allowing people to display catalog information or whatever else they wanted to communicate. The Web, originally developed as a scientist's research tool by a computer programmer at CERN, the physics research center in Geneva, Switzerland, had emerged almost overnight as a convenient vehicle for permitting electronic commerce on the Internet.

In addition to his Network Wizards fileserver, Mark's home Ethernet network also supported two other computers. Lile, Mark's friend, had created Art on the Net, a virtual artists' gallery housed on a donated Sun workstation that enabled a new generation of digital artists to exhibit their works. Another Sun on his network had been donated as a web site for the League for Programming Freedom, a organization of hackers dedicated to Richard Stallman's crusade to create a world of free, shared software.

For several weeks in early October, Lile had been experiencing strange behavior with her electronic mail account at the commercial Internet service provider Netcom. She would attempt to have her mail forwarded to her art.net Sun from Netcom only to find a short time later the forwarding file had disappeared. She complained to Netcom, but the telephone support person told her it couldn't possibly be a security problem, explaining, "We haven't had a break-in for three weeks."

Then, one Saturday morning in mid-October, Mark woke up and came downstairs to make himself an espresso. He went to his computer to read his mail and was sitting near his fileserver when for no apparent reason it began to make a prolonged *grrrrrr* sound.

That's odd, he thought to himself. The computer, which was linked by a high-speed T-1 connection to the Internet, was supposed to be idle. When he connected to the machine he saw that a long listing of all of his files was in the process of being displayed. He looked further and saw that someone was running a root on his computer.

His first thought was maybe this was the result of some

unusual program he wasn't familiar with. Unix computers have lots of small programs called daemons that constantly run in the background, performing housekeeping tasks. Then he ran a program called netstat, which gives detailed information about what's happening on a local computer's network connection. He could see that someone was connected to his machine from Lile's art.net Sun.

But Lile was sitting across the room from him at her own computer.

"Are you telneting to my computer?" Mark asked, referring to a utility used for connecting to a remote computer across the Net. She wasn't.

His alarm grew until he began to panic when he saw the person logged into his machine begin to tar a group of his files together. Seconds later the cracker began to use ftp—file transfer protocol—a common Internet file transfer utility, to move the tarred file to Netcom.

Mark was horrified. "What am I going to do?" he said to Lile, who had joined him in watching in disbelief as the huge file was copied out of his computer. He looked around his apartment and realized his quickest defense was to take himself off the Net. He ran and pulled his T-1 data cable out of the wall.

Mark and I chatted by phone later that day. He had examined the tarred file after he had pulled the plug from the network and discovered that someone was definitely trying to get the Oki telephone software that we had modified for his cellular telephone diagnostic system. He was able to determine they had been unsuccessful in getting anything of real value, only a small chunk of the file. He warned me to be on guard, and a short time later Andrew and I had seen some probes against our computers which he easily fended off.

The next day Lile and Mark headed down Highway 17 to Santa Cruz to visit a hot tub place near the campus of the University of California at Santa Cruz. While they were driving through the Santa Cruz mountains Mark's cell phone rang.

He answered, and a voice said, "Hi." Mark recognized the caller immediately as someone he knew only slightly but who had links to the computer underground.

"I haven't forwarded my phone and I don't give out my cell phone number," Mark said. "How did you get my number?"

"Let's just say I came across it somehow," the caller answered. "I just wanted to tell you I know who broke into your computer yesterday. "It was Mitnick and his friends, and they were really pissed they didn't get what they wanted."

The name Kevin Mitnick was a familiar one to Mark, as it was to anyone who followed the history of the shadowy world of the computer underground. Mitnick had grown up in the San Fernando Valley in Southern California during the 1970s and had made the transition from the hobbyist world of phone phreaks who tampered with the telephone system, to computer crackers who used networks to break into computers. There seemed to be one significant difference between Kevin Mitnick and the thousands of teenagers who seemed to be imitating Matthew Broderick in the movie *War Games*. Mitnick seemed remarkably incorrigible. Barely thirty-one years old, he had been arrested five times already, going back as far as 1980 when he was only seventeen. Mitnick was currently on the run from a variety of law enforcement agencies including the FBI.

John Markoff, a *New York Times* technology reporter both Mark and I knew well, had co-authored a book called *Cyberpunk,* about computer crime including Kevin Mitnick. He had also written an article about Mitnick in July 1994, saying that he had outfoxed federal and state officials for more than a year. The article reported that Mitnick was a suspect in the computer network theft of software from as many as a half-dozen cellular telephone companies.

Mark remembered that several weeks before his Saturday morning attack, someone he knew as an old friend of Mitnick had called and said he wanted to buy Network Wizards' cell phone software, but he also wanted source code, the original programmer's instructions that would make it possible to further modify the phone's functions. Although Mark declined to sell the source, Mitnick's friend had stayed on the phone for more than an hour wheedling.

There were no more attacks over the weekend, but during the next two weeks, the intruder continued to be a constant pest, breaking into Lile's art.net machine and the League for Programming Freedom computer repeatedly, leaving Trojan

Horses and back doors.

From time to time he would engage her in chat sessions, using a command called talk that permits two users of a Unix system to type back and forth to each other in real time at their keyboards over the Internet.

"Why don't you just give me the software?" her screen read one day. "I'm going to get it anyway."

He also asked for an account on her system, again telling her he would get one anyway. Lile offered him one of her digital artist's virtual studios, but he wasn't interested. He said if she gave him an account he would reveal who he really was.

"I hope you aren't upset with me," he typed

Mark was sitting in the room at the time and he coached her on how to respond. They tried to get him to give away little bits of information about himself, but with little success.

Finally in early December, the invader called Mark on the telephone directly to try to persuade him to give him the software.

"Do you know who I am?" he said. "I want your code," and proceeded to ask Mark if he was upset about the break-ins to his fileserver.

Mark responded that he wasn't, and explained that he had a different philosophy of computer security: if anyone managed to get inside his system, it would just alert him he needed to strengthen his defenses.

"Then I'll just continue trying," the caller said. Mark asked him about why he was so intent on getting the source code to the Oki cellular phone. The anonymous voice responded he wanted to be invisible in the cellular telephone network and he believed that if he was able to alter the behavior of his phone it would put him beyond the reach of cellular telephone tracking and surveillance gear.

They talked three times. The first two phones calls were short, but the third went on more than forty-five minutes during which the caller asked, "You're not taping this, are you?"

Mark said no, but then decided it would be a good idea. He quietly moved across the room and hit the "record" button on his answering machine.

The caller knew who I was and knew that I had helped Mark with the cellular telephone project. He seemed to be probing for more information about me:

Caller: God, so you actually, uh, so he wrote that dis-
           assembler, I see...

Mark: Yeah.

Caller: Why did he write it? For you, or just he hap-
           pened to just write an 8051 disassembler?

Mark: Um ... um, I don't remember just why he wrote
           it. He just hacked it up one evening.

Caller: Shit. just one evening? That's imp...

Mark: Uh, I think it only took him an hour or two,
           actually.

Caller: No way!

Mark: (sigh) (laughs)

Caller: Are you serious?

Mark: Uh huh.

Caller: That guy's a wizard. He should work for your
           company, Network Wizards.

Mark: Uh ... he has better things to do.

Caller: In San Diego still I assume?

Mark: Um, sometimes.

Caller: And Los Alamos?

Mark: Sometimes.

After Mark hung up he called Markoff and played him the
tape to see if he recognized the voice. The reporter had never
formally met Mitnick but had heard his voice on the telephone
and on tapes several times. He said it sounded like him but he
wasn't positive.

Mark next called Jonathan Littman, a Marin County freelance
writer who was writing a book about the computer underground

and who was rumored to have a secret channel to Mitnick. Mark played him the tape and said, "Do you recognize this voice?"

Littman started to laugh. "Of course I do. It's Mitnick."

The possibility that Mitnick was the culprit in my break-in as well as Mark's was an intriguing thought, but one that really didn't lead anywhere useful now, so I put it aside. Lots of people in the computer underground and elsewhere knew that I had worked with Mark on cellular telephone software. At this point the first thing I wanted to do was collect data and find a way to secure our computers as quickly as possible. I began scanning the first of the disk drives that I'd extracted from the computers that had been frozen, using the software tools that I'd gathered. I wanted to find all files that had been read, written to, had their dates changed, or new files that had been created going back to December 21 when I had left San Diego. I sat for a long time in front of the PowerLite. Somewhere in the morass of data I was almost certain to find a clue or a set of clues. No one can be perfect at hiding their presence.

I was also searching for Trojan Horse programs. These are programs often left behind by electronic intruders. They can wake and silently do any number of secret or destructive things. They masquerade as familiar software but could be written to eavesdrop on you, destroy data, or provide a convenient back door security loophole. One way to protect your computers against this kind of tampering is to take a digital snapshot of all the programs that are on your computer—operating system programs, utilities, communications tools, everything. Later you can tell if any files are altered by comparing mathematically generated signatures of the files on the suspect disk against those of your original safely stored copy.

About nine that night Andrew and I met for dinner at a place near campus called Pizza Nova. Andrew is an example of an Easterner who has adapted remarkably well to the California beach scene. With a head of shoulder-length blond hair, a prominent nose, and intense blue eyes, his standard outfit is shorts, T-shirt, and sandals. Andrew is also well known for the fact that he really doesn't like to wear shoes at all, a trait that can sometimes cause trouble when we try to eat in restaurants. He has the hacker-like quality of being able to focus on complex problems for extend-ed periods of time, sometimes aided by several liters of Mountain Dew. I get frustrated with him occasionally because he jumps to conclusions and acts too quickly rather than thinking through the consequences of particular action. But he has a good intuitive grasp of the inner structure of the Internet and we work well together as a team—and I find him a pleasure to work with.

Over dinner we talked about things that needed to be explored. We agreed that for now, it was necessary to concen-trate on actually addressing all the possible vulnerabilities in my network. One thing that puzzled both of us was that the intrud-er had played around with XNeWS, a PostScript-based compo-nent of the operating system that permits you to draw images on your workstation or on a remote computer. PostScript is more widely used as a printer language, giving programmers a set of commands to tell printers where to draw lines, place printed characters, and shade areas. Could that have been a vul-nerability? Maybe the intruders had found a design error in PostScript that would allow them to use it to remotely take con-trol of a computer. I gave Andrew a set of tasks and took a set for myself. We parted with the agreement that we would recon-vene at the Supercom-puter Center the next day.

I drove home feeling emotionally drained and even more exhausted; in fact, things looked bleak. We had a tantalizing set of hints about how my systems had been attacked. But there was no certainty we would be able to make any sense of them, and even if we were able to reconstruct the crime there was no likeli-hood that we would be able to follow a trail back through the Internet if our attackers had really covered their tracks well. It was eating at me, and forcing me to think about things that had been bothering me that went far beyond this particular break-in.

When I got home, Julia called. She was at Toad Hall, and we both had been having a difficult time.

"I'm here and I feel like I'm stuck here," I told her. We talked about the break-in for a while, and then we talked about what she had been doing in San Francisco.

"After John came back, things went well at first," she said, "But things are much more tense now."

It was clear their relationship hadn't been working since I'd met Julia, and it didn't look like anything was changing. On our first wilderness trip together three years ago we'd gone snow camping in the Desolation Wilderness near Lake Tahoe, and she'd told me of her misgivings about her relationship with John. She wasn't happy and wondered aloud whether or not she should stay with it and try to make it work. We'd talked late into the night and she'd told me she thought she should keep trying out of a sense of loyalty to her partner.

Now three years later I could tell she knew the relationship was bad for her, but she didn't seem to be able to get out of it. I knew that she had been trying to end it for some time, but she found familiar things comforting and difficult to part with. It was all making her unhappy and depressed. It wasn't the first time I'd seen her feel this way—a year ago she'd gone to Nepal with John—but he left and she became involved with another man, an American she met while traveling. Their relationship went on for six months, but it ended over her unwillingness to leave John.

It was as if there were two Julias. One was a strong, independent, and adventurous woman who was trying to find what would make her happy and content. But there was another person as well, who was hamstrung by fear and feelings of inadequacy and insecurity. I'd seen her grow stronger and more independent since we'd met, and she was better able to see what was damaging to her, but she hadn't been able to bring herself to make a final break with John.

We talked more about my problems in San Diego. I was unhappy to be here at all, given my skiing plans, and the more I looked at the problem the more apparent it became that it wasn't going to be simple and that I might be wasting my time in a futile search to find out how the break-in had taken place.

Over the past few months I'd already been feeling burned-out by my dealings with NSA. I'd had enough of dealing with computer security for a while, and I'd been looking forward to skiing and working on other problems. But now, as I told Julia, I felt stuck. I was being pulled back to deal with computer security, but without the resources I needed.

"This is the last thing I want to do right now, but I can't walk away from it," I said.

"You sound awful, Tsutomu. I'm worried about you," she replied. She offered to come down and spend time with me.

But I said no, she had enough to deal with without having to come down and comfort me. I was in a foul mood and wanted to focus without interruption, in order to be done with the threat as soon as possible.

"Get some sleep tonight," she finally said. "Between you and Andrew, the two of you will be able to make some progress tomorrow."

It seemed like there wasn't any other option. We said good night, agreeing that we would talk again soon.

Just before going to sleep I remembered that I had forgotten to listen to my voice mail since returning to San Diego. I played back a string of messages that had been left for me at my SDSC office. I listened to four or five routine messages, continually pressing the phone's keypad to zap them out of the system's memory.

Then I heard something that made me sit up in my bed.

"Sent December 27 at 4:33 P.M.," said the prim, electronic female voice.

Immediately came another voice. It sounded like someone who was faking a passable Australian cockney accent. There was no mistaking the message.

"Damn you," said my caller. "My technique is the best. My boss is the best, damn you. I know rdist technique, I know send-mail technique, and my style is much better."

Rdist and sendmail were two garden-variety computer network attacks involving long-known computer system vulnerabilities. This could only be my intruder, calling to taunt me.

"Damn you, don't you know who I am?" he continued. "Me and my friends we'll kill you."

Then it sounded like he turned his head away from the phone in order to sound like another person's voice: "Hey boss, your Kung Fu's really good."

"That's right," concluded my caller in the same Australian accent. "My style is the best."

This time I saved the message. Then I lay back on my bed and stared at the ceiling. This was getting personal, and whoever this was had obviously become pretty cocky. *I don't need this*, I thought to myself. If it hadn't been certain before, now it was. Someone was clearly challenging me.

CHAPTER 4

THE
REAL
WORLD

We frequently call things that we don't understand in the world complex, but that often only means that we haven't yet found a good way of thinking about them.

Throughout my life as a scientist I've been absorbed with exploring and understanding complexity, and I've found that although it might seem that nature could have come up with a complicated way of making things work, there is almost always a very elegant and simple explanation underlying any phenomenon.

That basic outlook has underscored much of my work in fields as diverse as biology and physics, and problems involving computation, which I have focused on for more than a decade and since 1989 as a senior fellow at the San Diego Supercomputer Center. How does the physical world compute its answers? That may seem an impossibly vague question, but it lies at the heart of a radical approach to much of modern science. For example, what ways are there to find a leak in a bucket? On the face of it, a computer would have no simple method of finding the point of the leak. It could iterate over the entire surface of the bucket, point by point, until it found the hole. But there is a better, simpler solution: you fill the bucket and let the water do the work of finding the leak.

It was thinking about such questions regarding the nature of computation that had consumed the legendary physicist Richard

Feynman toward the end of his life. I began taking Feynman's class on the physics of computation when I first entered Caltech as a freshman in 1982, and spent more time with him during the summer of 1984 at Thinking Machines, a start-up supercomputer company in Cambridge, Massachusetts. His outlook influenced my own thinking tremendously. Feynman had a remarkable ability to see the world clearly, and not to be misled by commonly held preconceptions. Throughout my career I have sought to emulate Feynman's approach to science, and I think I have also been helped in gaining this independent perspective through being a scientist and by having grown up between two cultures.

I was born on October 23, 1964, in Nagoya, Japan. My parents grew up in Japan, where they lived through the war. My father, Osamu, was trained as a biochemist, and my mother, Akemi, began work as a pharmacologist. Together they embarked on their careers as research partners, specializing in the study of bioluminescence. In the 1960s the leading institution for bioluminescence research was Princeton University. This period was a wonderful time to do basic research in the United States, and my parents came here when my father accepted a position as a Princeton research faculty member. My mother took time off from her career to raise me and my younger sister, Sachi.

Although I have early memories of traveling back and forth between the United States and Japan, the first times I can remember clearly are the years growing up in Princeton. I particularly recall learning English as a second language in kindergarten and first grade.

Being raised by two scientists permanently shaped my approach to the world. My childhood was spent between my mother's kitchen and my father's lab. From my first steps my family encouraged me to be curious. I was provoked to ask questions, to which I never received "because" replies. My parents' response was often to suggest an experiment through which I could determine for myself the answer.

The value of experimentation was taught to me even in the most commonplace occurrences. Once at dinner I dropped a mushroom on the floor, and when I went to pick it up and eat it my father said, "It's dirty."

"I can't see any dirt here, " I retorted.

The result of this discussion was that my father drove me in to his lab, so that we could examine the dirty mushroom more closely under a microscope.

I was, in general, an argumentative child, though my parents tolerated a remarkable amount from me. I was so quick with rebuttals, even at elementary school age, that my mother threw up her hands one day in exasperation and said, "Are you going to be a scientist—or a *lawyer*—when you grow up?"

In the sixties and seventies Princeton was the quintessential liberal academic community, but I was still an outsider, even though the university had a large Asian population. During this period I returned to Japan frequently, and even lived for the better part of two years there—just enough to ensure that I retained a feeling of being slightly apart from both cultures. I spent my entire fifth grade in school in Nagasaki. In Japan both Japanese and English are taught, and it was interesting to come to know the Japanese view of America after I had experienced it personally.

Because my father's research involved studying bioluminescent jellyfish, I passed many of my summers in Friday Harbor in the San Juan Islands in Washington, where he conducted field research at the University of Washington's marine biological laboratory. I was in my element, let loose with lots of other bored children of academic families. These summers gave me free time to help out in my father's laboratory trying to find something useful to do when I wasn't getting into trouble and roaming the island wilderness. The cool climate, carpets of douglas firs, and crystal-clear tidepools were a wonderful counterpoint to the more civilized and hot and muggy suburban Princeton summers.

When I was twelve years old—because I had skipped several grades I was already in my first year of high school—I began spending less and less time at home. I wasn't getting along particularly well with my parents by then, and I ended up being at the University more and more of the time.

At the time a friend of mine had a job with a psychology professor in a lab that was doing neuropsychological research, and he helped me get work there as well. He was working on trying to get a data acquisition system to function. It was basically a programming job involving a DEC PDP-11/34 computer, which at the time was the standard piece of laboratory computing equipment.

The first time I'd seen a computer was in kindergarten. One of my classmate's fathers, who worked for RCA's Sarnoff Laboratories, brought a computer to school for some kind of a show-and-tell session, and although I didn't get to play with it, it was definitely something I remembered and was intrigued by. I clearly recall that, even at this first encounter, I considered these machines as tools that would help me solve problems.

My real immersion with computing, however, didn't begin until I was ten when, through friends, I stumbled across a quirky and informal Princeton computer club known as the Resistors. Resistors was an acronym for "Radically Emphatic Students Interested in Science Technology and Other Research Studies," and consisted of an anarchic group of teenagers (the average age was probably 15) that met in the E-Quad, Princeton's four-story school of engineering. The first generation of Resistors were influenced by people like Ted Nelson, the visionary social scientist who wrote the book *Computer Lib/Dream Machines* and who was to become the pied piper of hypertext. I was actually a member of the second generation of the Resistors, and what the group gave me was an easy way into the world of computing—in effect, my own personal computer in the era of minicomputers and mainframes. But I was also a little bit of a loner, and I never had any really close relationships with the other Resistors.

The group was actually a result of the same urge that would drive a similar hobbyist club known as the Homebrew Computer Club, which emerged several years later in Silicon Valley. While its members were older, in their early twenties, for the most part, they also were a product of the availability of the first inexpensive microprocessor chips, and their passion to have their own computers led directly to the explosion of the personal computer era. People like Steve Wozniak and Steve Jobs created Apple Computer in the hothouse technological culture that emerged around the Stanford campus in the mid- to late seventies. Other Homebrew members like Lee Felsenstein went on to design both the Sol and Osborne 1 machines.

The Resistors grew up in the thrall of an earlier computer age, with a distinctive East Coast flavor. The mainframe world had emerged during the fifties and sixties at IBM, followed by the minicomputer era of the seventies created by companies like DEC, Data General, and Prime. The minicomputer was the underpinning of the timesharing epoch of computing. A product of MIT hacker culture, timesharing operating systems permitted more than one person to use a computer simultaneously. The trick was to slice computing tasks up into tiny pieces and then have the central processing unit of the computer jump quickly from one task to another in a round-robin fashion. This scheme made computers tremendously more productive and also expanded the power of computing to a vastly broader audience. It was timesharing that also enabled young hackers like me to get access to powerful computers.

AT&T's particular contribution to the computing revolution had been the Unix operating system, a program that was developed by two Bell Laboratories computer scientists, Dennis Ritchie and Ken Thompson, in the late sixties. Operating systems are a combination traffic cop, secretary, and waiter inside a computer. They are the programs that perform all of the basic housekeeping operations and respond to user requests and commands in addition to orchestrating the delicate ballet that goes on between all the different components of a computer system. Operating systems also provide a computer with a distinct personality. Think of them as a language for speaking directly to the computer hardware.

Ritchie and Thompson, who had been aghast at a cumbersome Pentagon-funded operating system development project called Multics, created Unix as an alternative, and it quickly became the programmers' tool of choice for the ragtag army of hackers who were forming a computer culture at various universities and companies around the country. Like thousands of college students at the time, I grew up a child of the Unix revolution.

Unix was a system—created by stripping down many of the features of the big mainframe world and adapted to the capabilities of minicomputers and workstations—unlike the personal computer world, in which operating systems like CP/M and MS-DOS and Apple DOS were built from the ground up. As a result, my generation of hackers expected computers to have certain features that personal computers didn't have, and in some cases still don't have, until more than a decade later. Unix computing concepts like multitasking, hardware memory management, and portability were all part of a gospel that I learned while I taught myself Unix programming between the ages of ten and fifteen. It only made sense that computers should be able to do multiple things at the same time, even for a single user, and utilize hardware memory management, which ensures that a poorly designed program doesn't leave the memory space that has been reserved for it and trample other programs.

I also grew up having no idea that there was any way to use computers other than connected to one another in networks. I first came in contact with the ARPAnet, the Pentagon-funded predecessor to the Internet, in 1976. It was a wide-open, if tiny community—there must have been a grand total of one hundred computers on the entire network—and I loved to explore it.

What I didn't do was spend my afternoons and evenings breaking into computers, a fad that teenagers took up almost a decade later. When I was traveling around the Net in the mid-seventies there were almost no locks, and everything was shared. At various places around the Princeton campus were public dial-up terminals that would allow you to sit down and access the entire Net. I would play games, chat with people, and hop around to places like MIT, Carnegie Mellon, and Stanford.

Although my first programming language was BASIC, a computer language created for education in 1969 at Dartmouth, in the course of playing with it I soon realized I could escape from the narrow confines of a limited programming language to the Unix command shell. The shell—basically the computer's software control panel—broadened my horizon and gave me access to all of the computer's resources, as well as access to the network world beyond. After being confined to the tightly controlled world of Basic, the Unix shell was a little like being on the captain's deck of the Starship *Enterprise*. Reveling in my new freedom I learned to program in C, a language that had been developed by the same crew of Bell Labs hackers who had invented Unix. C was liberating for me. As a language it is obtuse, but once it is mastered, it is remarkably powerful and flexible. C also gave me a skill that put me in great demand, even as a teenager.

A computer science graduate student named Peter Honeyman

offered me my first Unix account at Princeton on the electrical engineering and computer science department's DEC computer. Although it was later taken away when the computer became overloaded with legitimate students, it was my original entry point into a world that was soon to become my passion. The PDP-11/45 was a flaky machine, and Honeyman was obviously smart enough to see that I and another high school student, Paul Rubin, were an untapped source of cheap labor. We soon became the computer's administrators and caretakers.

Occasionally I got in trouble for my computer use. I remember discovering that I could issue commands that would move the head-arm of the magnetic disk drive on our high school minicomputer back and forth in a rapid fashion. The drive was a standard 14-inch IBM frisbee-style monster, whose head for reading and writing magnetic data was controlled by a stepper motor that could be commanded to move in and out and read and write on any of the drive's 203 cylinders. After I successfully moved it to cylinder 0, and then to cylinder 100, I began to wonder, "Gee, what happens when you try to position it to cylinder HEX FFF?" That would be the equivalent of cylinder 4095—unfortunately one that didn't exist.

I issued the command and heard, *Rrrrrr. Crunch.* That was the end of the disk drive. It was a useful lesson, and for me it effectively put to rest one of the canons of computing that are always taught: "Don't worry, you can't hurt the hardware."

High school increasingly became a sideshow in my life, as I spent more and more of my days around the university. At one end of the spectrum I was fascinated with physics, because it explored the fundamental principles underlying everything in the universe, and at the other end, biology, where very simple principles create very complicated systems. In one case you can try to simplify, while in the other, there's no chance of simplifying. I did read in other fields like psychology and geology, but I wasn't intrigued by them, for they were more like botany—in my mind, the art of categorization involving little analysis or understanding.

While I benefited from this sampling of the academic disciplines, it was my computing skills that made me an integral part of the university scene. In 1978 Princeton was facing a growing problem in the proliferation of minicomputers. The school's computing center had earlier tried to maintain a monopoly over all academic computing. It had, in effect, told the various departments, "Since we provide this service, we want you to use our computers." And like any monopolist, they charged outrageous rates. However, Princeton's other departments discovered a loophole that would free them from having to deal with the computing center—special-purpose applications. The various departments all managed to justify buying their own individual minicomputers to carry out odd-ball special-purpose projects that they dreamed up.

The astronomy department had been able to wangle its own DEC PDP-11/60 and wanted to run Unix, but there was no one on staff who knew anything about it. Since I was already hanging around much of the time begging, borrowing, or stealing free computer time, they asked me to come and install some specialized hardware to help them read a particular magnetic data tape.

Through that project, I became the department computing wizard at the age of fourteen. After I wrote a special device driver for them, enabling the computer to reliably talk to some esoteric disk drives, I was invited to work part-time by a young assistant professor, Ed Turner. The tradition in the department then was that computing was the responsibility of the newest faculty member. Ed not only hired me, but introduced me to a remarkable world outside of my claustrophobic high school existence.

Looking back on it, taking that job was one of those watershed events that helped me define who I was at a very young age. It was also an incredible amount of fun, and it gave me access to some of the world's best toys.

I was around the astronomy department constantly throughout the rest of my time in high school, mostly helping with computerized image-processing work. While I learned something about pattern matching and a great deal about systems programming, the job also permanently shaped my attitude toward computing. Trying to solve problems in astrophysics and astronomy convinced me that, if a machine doesn't do what you want it to do, then reprogram it to do the right thing. Early on I learned that a machine does just what you tell it to, and nothing more.

My responsibilities evolved to include designing special hardware for the astronomy department, and in my senior year I was able to help develop a data-storage system for capturing experimental data from a NASA-funded missile launch in which the department was participating. My task was to help design the hardware that would actually collect the bits of data from the flight at the White Sands Missile Range in New Mexico. The problem involved downlinking images from cameras aboard the missile, storing them on videotape recorders, and then trying to convert the data into digital form for computer storage and analysis. It proved to be a successful launch, which brought back data in the ultraviolet range of the spectrum from the fringes of space.

Being around an older community of students and faculty at such a young age, and being essentially precocious, also ultimately got me in trouble. Because I had skipped ahead two grades, I never graduated from junior high, and in the fall of 1980, I was a fifteen-year-old high school senior.

Despite uninspiring grades, I received stellar college-placement test scores, and I was accepted at Carnegie Mellon early in my senior year. I was disappointed, however, that my other choice, MIT, rejected me, even though I had recommendations from a number of faculty at both Princeton and MIT. Throughout my high school years, my attitude had been that as long as I was doing something sufficiently "intellectually" interesting, grades wouldn't matter.

Bored and increasingly resentful of what seemed like silly academic rituals, I would occasionally provoke my teachers. In one English class we were given a list of words that we were required to use in essays to be written over the course of the semester. We were supposed to use the words properly in context, and for each correct use we would be awarded a certain number of points counting toward our final grade.

However, it occurred to me that there was a simpler solution, which I dispatched in a single ten-minute assignment. I wrote a story about a silly English class in which the teacher assigned a list of words, which I included verbatim, as a list. I demanded credit for the entire list, and decided that since I now had enough points to pass I wouldn't show up for the rest of the quarter.

Such stunts didn't endear me to the faculty.

I also didn't fit the stereotype of a computer or science nerd in high school. Although I didn't go out for high school teams, I did love doing all kinds of athletic things on my own. I became an avid cyclist, racing bicycles with a local racing club called the Century Road Club of America. I subsidized my relatively expensive cycling gear by occasionally building bicycle wheels for a local bike shop, Kopp's Cycles. During the winters I began to develop a passion for cross country skiing in the rolling New Jersey countryside.

During the little amount of time I did spend at school, I hung out with a small group of friends, one of whom we referred to as "the terrorist." He was actually a gifted classical pianist, and although the administration would occasionally suspend him, they couldn't really take any more serious steps because they needed him to play at school functions.

He was quite notorious, and his pranks were always dramatic: the stairwell was thermited. The toilets appeared in the middle of the football field. The public address system was once completely fried because he considered it to be a tool for propaganda. It literally smoked.

At the time of the latter prank, I was five-hundred kilometers away, visiting Carnegie Mellon for a college interview, and so had what I knew was the perfect alibi. But I was a known troublemaker, and when I walked back into the school the principal came up to me and said, "You! You did it!"

Later the administration figured out that the PA system had been destroyed when 120-volt alternating current was fed into one of its call buttons with a timer. They discovered this only after they had swapped out the boards and the whole system blew up again, because the timer was on a 24-hour cycle.

The school paper was planning to run an article on this incident, which we knew was full of technical errors. Late one afternoon we went to the newspaper office, took the article from the editor's box, revised it, and then put it back. The finished piece turned out to be quite technically accurate, although no one in the school appreciated how it ended up that way.

"The terrorist" eventually went to Yale, but during high school he never managed to be regarded as anything but a vandal. For his own part, he thought of his actions as political crimes. He was quite well-developed ideologically as a high school student. I'm still not sure where any of my group would have fallen on the political spectrum. Probably antiestablishment—any establishment.

In my own case, I don't know what the final straw was: it might have been grades or it might have been insubordination. But one night during my senior year, I came home for dinner to find that my parents had received three letters from the school. Two of them were commendations for my having won a local math and physics contest, the other was a notice of my expulsion from Princeton High School. Giving up on me as a lost cause for his educational system, the principal had told me earlier that week, "Don't come back, you're persona non grata. If we find you here we'll have you arrested."

My response was, "Okay, fine! I didn't come here when I was a student. What makes you think that I might want to come back?"

When I was kicked out of school, Carnegie Mellon rescinded its offer. They said they would hold my place for the next academic year, giving me another chance to graduate. I ended up in a shouting match with their recruiting officer and told him, "Don't bother."

Shortly afterward, my parents joined the marine biological laboratory in Woods Hole, where my father had accepted a research position. I still had my job in the astronomy department, and my friends were still in Princeton, so I found myself shuttling back and forth between New Jersey and Massachusetts.

Despite my experience in high school, I had always had academic aspirations that focused increasingly on physics, and so I applied to the University of Chicago, Johns Hopkins, and Caltech. When I had first begun the college application process, I had been under the impression that Caltech was too intense, a little like drinking from a fire hose, and so I hadn't applied there. But I had worked for Jim Gunn, a bright young Princeton astronomer who had begun as a astrophysics professor at Caltech, and after my rejection by Carnegie Mellon, he and a couple of others in astrophysics were intent on seeing that I still went to college, and thought that Caltech might actually suit me very well.

With my test scores and recommendations from people like Gunn I was admitted to Caltech for the fall of 1982.

In the summer of 1982, at age seventeen, I traveled to Southern California, planning to study physics and biology when college began a month later. I'd been to Caltech a number of times before, through my work in the Princeton astronomy department, and I took a room in a house just off campus. Compared to Princeton, it has always struck me as a tiny campus. Located in Pasadena, tucked up against the San Gabriel Mountains, it felt claustrophobic; it was too smoggy to bicycle in Los Angeles, and as I didn't have a car, I had no means of escape. It didn't escape my notice that the school motto "And ye shall know the truth, and the truth shall make you free," from John 8:32 in the Bible, was the same motto as the one employed by Central Intelligence Agency.

For my application interview the previous spring, a Caltech faculty member named Jerry Pine had visited me in my office at Princeton. Pine, a high-energy physicist who had made the transition to biology, had suggested I come to California before school started to work during the summer on a project being led by another Caltech faculty member, Geoffrey Fox, a physicist, who had heard from Gunn and others about my reputation as a hacker. Fox was in the early stages of designing a new kind of massively parallel computer known as a hypercube. It was a powerful, novel computer architecture that was in keeping with the trend toward breaking down complex problems into small components and computing them simultaneously. Parallel computing, then being pursued by researchers and companies around the country, would later lead to dramatic increases in the speed of computing, and transform the supercomputer industry.

When I arrived on campus, Fox's team had barely gotten a four-processor prototype working. But since nobody knew how to program the radically new machines, my first job was helping figure out how to use them to solve problems that had previously been solved sequentially. My role was "speed hacking"—trying to figure out clever ways to get more performance for a particular problem—something I had done a lot of at Princeton. One of the things we discovered early on was that the hypercube computers were ideal for computing a set of mathematical problems known as fast-Fourier transformations, which are used in signal processing and have practical applications for everything from hunting enemy submarines, to recognizing human speech, to compressing data.

I worked with Fox full-time for the summer, but after the school year started, my interests moved in other directions, and I quickly drifted away from the project. One factor that led me away was a competing job offer from NASA's Jet Propulsion Laboratory, just up the hill from Caltech. The JPL engineers offered me the opportunity to work in communications systems research, an esoteric area responsible for much of the work involved in building radio bridges to deep-space probes like Pioneer and Voyager that had been sent to other planets. Some of the best communications people in the world were at the lab during this period, and they were looking for students who were adept at stepping in and working on projects in which there were no easy guidelines to follow. My Unix and computing experience turned out to be a much sought-after commodity. The JPL group was trying to build a design system on a Unix machine to help them do gallium-arsenide integrated circuit design, and I soon became the resident Unix hacker and troubleshooter.

At Caltech there is a long hacker's tradition of cleverly manipulating the system. The criteria were that any hack had to be done in good style; it should be clever, amusing, and not a copy of something done before; and most importantly, it should not be destructive or harmful.

I participated in my share of pranks. For example, I had done some rock climbing before I came to Caltech, and once I arrived at school I discovered that the fact the campus was in the middle of a city didn't stop the school's climbers. Scaling buildings is called buildering, and there is even a climber's guide to the architecture of Caltech. Rappeling off buildings at 2 A.M. was one of our favorite sports for avoiding homework. Of course, campus security hated to have people climbing around on their buildings, and so throughout my undergraduate years a running game was waged between the climbers, who were trying to avoid detection, and the guards, who were trying to stop them.

One evening a friend and I decided we would give the security guards something to do. Since there was nothing wrong with simply walking around wearing climbing gear, the two of us slung ropes and climbing hardware over our shoulders, and proceeded to amble leisurely around campus, stopping in front of a few popular climbing routes and many improbable ones. Before long we had collected a following of a handful of guards, who stood and eyed us at a distance with their radios squawking, and continued to follow us around on our tour of great climbing spots, until an hour later we each turned and went home in opposite directions.

On the academic front, I began the school year trying to behave like a normal student, hoping that college would be different from high school. But after the first few weeks I realized that it was much the same experience, and I found I was focusing on what interested me, and ignoring the fact that the school expected me to jump the mandatory hurdles along the way.

There were two classes, however, into which I threw myself with real enthusiasm. One of them was a course taught by Ron Drever, a general relativity experimentalist, who is well known for his work with gravity wave detectors. The problems he's best at solving involve detecting remarkably minute effects in an environment cluttered with larger, more powerful forces. The class, half juniors and seniors, the rest graduate students, except for me, basically focused on how you could measure incredibly small gravitational effects by cleverly setting up your experiments. Much of our time was spent reviewing experiments in theoretical relativity, looking at both effects that had been postulated but not yet measured, and measurements that have actually been accomplished.

One notable thing about the course was that it had no midterm, and the entire grade rested upon designing a laboratory experiment to measure one of the as yet unmeasured effects predicted by general relativity. I came up with an idea for measuring a phenomenon called gravitational frame drag, using a tool called a laser interferometer in a novel way. We all turned in our papers, and Drever started off one of his last lectures by announcing, "I'm very disappointed in you. I only got one original idea out of all the papers, and that was from a freshman."

The other course that had a huge impact on me was a graduate course taught by Richard Feynman; Carver Mead, the father of VLSI, or Very Large Scale Integrated Circuit design; and John Hopfield on the physics of computation. Hopfield, who was one of the inventors of neural networks, a computational model that mimics biological systems, was one of my undergraduate advisers, but it was Feynman's interest in the underlying foundations of computation that particularly intrigued me. Feynman, one of the world's leading theoretical physicists, hadn't taught during my first quarter at Caltech because he was being treated for cancer, but at the end of that quarter I introduced myself, and timidly asked if I could take his upcoming course. He asked me a couple of questions about my background, and then said it would be fine for me to attend. I wound up taking the course both years I was at Caltech.

The seminar focused on the limitations of computing—quantum limitations, communications limitations, coding theory limitations, and thermodynamic limitations—and thus probed the ultimate frontiers. Although I had explored parallel computing even in high school, through Feynman I began to see that while modern computers processed information serially—one instruction and one piece of data at a time—nature computes in parallel. I also began to understand that serial computing actually corrupts the way you think as a scientist. Using serial computers to explore a parallel world often masks the real simplicity of nature.

I spent the summer after my freshman year back in Princeton, where I worked at the Institute for Advanced Study with Steven Wolfram, a physicist who later developed Mathematica, the program that is now widely used in high schools and colleges. It sufficed for summer work, but Wolfram was looking for a professional coder to help him develop software products, which was not something that interested me. I write software, but I do it to solve my own problems.

When I returned to Caltech in the fall, I soon found that I was growing bored by academic drudge work. I began taking more upper division and graduate classes, dabbling in things, hoping to find something in which I could completely immerse myself. In the process, however, I quickly burned out. I was simply losing interest in jumping through academic hoops for no apparent reason. I did increasingly poorly in my required classes, and felt distracted. I was having more fun playing in the graduate classes I was taking, and began to think about doing something else even though I didn't have anything else in particular in mind.

During my first year in Feynman's physics of computation I had met Danny Hillis, the artificial intelligence researcher who had recently founded the Thinking Machines Corporation in Cambridge, Massachusetts. Feynman was a frequent visitor there, along with a range of other scientists and engineers who were intrigued by Danny's radical approach to building a massively parallel computer. At the end of the school year, Hillis invited me to Cambridge to work with Thinking Machines for the summer, so Feynman and I represented the Caltech contingent at what was essentially an MIT start-up company.

The Thinking Machines Connection Machine computer was a dramatic break with what had come before in high-performance computing, a field that had been dominated by Cray Research. Seymour Cray's machines were designed to use a small number of very, very fast, and very expensive, processors. At Thinking Machines, however, the notion was to divide problems so they could be solved by more than 64,000 inexpensive processors working simultaneously.

I was able to work on a number of intriguing projects at the company, but the one that was probably most useful was a simple hack for hooking together an array of small, cheap disks. One of the biggest problems in supercomputing is getting the vast amounts of data used in its calculations in and out of the machine quickly enough. Using a group of inexpensive disks and spreading the data among them, instead of relying on a single fast, but expensive disk, was the perfect complement to the army of inexpensive processors that were actually computing the data. My contribution was to design a "self healing" array of disks— that is, I figured out how data could be arranged across a number of disks, so that if one failed, the data that had been on the sick drive would automatically be regenerated on a spare.

Hillis was a wonderful person with whom to work because he was genuinely more interested in building machines that could *think* than he was in being a successful businessman. He had assembled a remarkable group of engineers and scientists, and things often didn't take place in a predictable fashion.

One Sunday afternoon, for example, Danny and I discovered that we wanted something out of the office Coke machine, but that we were out of quarters. Danny went around the building hunting for the key, which he found, but we both decided that getting the key each time we wanted a soft drink wasn't an optimal answer to the problem. It seemed to us that we could design a more permanent solution: we would simply build an interface to the Coke machine so that you could control it from a computer connected to the Internet. It took us only about half an hour to get a serial interface working that would allow you to control the machine and credit yourself change from your computer's desktop. Our system went one step further than the classic Carnegie Mellon Coke machine hack, which was connected to the Net only in order to provide status information on how many cans were left in the machine and whether they were cold.

I had a wonderful summer at Thinking Machines simply pursuing whatever problem seemed interesting, and when I flew back to Caltech in the fall of 1984, the idea of being a student again was even less inviting than when I'd left in June.

I'd had an offer to work with Steve Chen, Seymour Cray's computer architect, who would later leave to found Supercomputer Systems, Inc. I visited Chen at Cray Research, and toyed with the idea of going there, but locking myself into one company seemed in its own way as confining as school.

At the same time, however, I'd gotten a call from a team of researchers who'd left Caltech for the Los Alamos National Laboratory in New Mexico to build a specialized parallel computer for physics research. Was I interested in coming to work there to join a newly created parallel computing project? It seemed strange that they would pursue an undergraduate when there were so many other people to choose from, but I realized that my breadth of experience in computing was valuable. I thought about my prospects for a while, and went looking for Feynman. I wanted his advice about whether I should stay on as a student.

I found him one afternoon as he was walking across campus. I explained that my grades had put me in trouble with the administration, and I didn't know if I wanted to stay anyway. He told me that if there was anything he could do to help my situation at Caltech, he would be glad to do it. I described the offer I had at

Los Alamos, and asked his opinion. He wasn't going to make any decisions for me, he protested, but I got the feeling he thought I'd do better if I set out on my own. I decided it was time to leave college for good.

I arrived at Los Alamos in late 1984 on a post-doctoral research appointment, even though I had no high school or college degree. At nineteen, I was the youngest staff member to come to the Los Alamos theoretical division since Feynman had joined the Manhattan Project in the 1940s. As the nation's oldest nuclear weapons laboratory the lab was steeped in government bureaucracy, and rife with bureaucrats, some of them my supervisors. At the same time there was a "can do" spirit at the Labs that I found refreshing, and there were pockets of intellectual freedom in which it was possible to pursue interesting science.

Although I had come to Los Alamos in the midst of the Reagan Cold War buildup, within several years the nation's defense budget would peak, and then begin to wind down, forcing the weapons designers, many of them former physics prodigies themselves, to justify their existence for the first time in their careers. I, meantime, took a Young Turk's delight in knowing that I was siphoning funding away from the weapons budget into the far more intellectually interesting area of basic physics research. Instead of puzzling over problems like how to blow up the enemy more efficiently, I worked with a group that spent its time exploring the very fundamentals of computation, which had only theoretical ties to weaponry, and thus put us out of the lab's mainstream.

Although my original mandate at Los Alamos was to help design a new kind of parallel supercomputer, I ended up becoming part of the Theoretical Division's scientific visualization and simulation team, led by a brilliant physicist named Brosl Hasslacher, who was twenty-four years older than me, and in every way my mentor. It was Brosl who recruited me away from Parallel Computer Design and back to physics, and we worked together in a rich collaboration.

Although Brosl had an international reputation as a physicist, many of his superiors at the lab didn't appreciate the significance of his work. One winter, our team was exiled to a virtual Siberia, a trailer gulag outside the main lab building. It didn't bother us that the funky trailer wasn't designed to support clusters of computer workstations and that it needed to be jerry-rigged to ensure adequate electrical power. But because it was essential to stay connected to the outside world, we had to string a coaxial computer cable to another trailer that was already hard-wired to the main laboratory network and the Internet.

It can snow a lot in Los Alamos, so to protect the cable from accidental damage after it was buried in a storm, we placed Day-Glo orange road markers along its length and alerted the maintenance department to its existence. A lot of good that did. The next day a Laboratory snowplow came through and neatly severed it. We strung new cable and called maintenance again, but the next time it snowed, the plow put us out of business once more.

Tougher measures were clearly in order. I had the idea of wrapping the cable in Kevlar, the same rip-proof fabric used for bulletproof vests and for mooring submarines. I took a length of Kevlar cord, anchored one end to a concrete pillar, wound it around the network cable and then fastened the cord's other end to the wall of the neighboring trailer. *So there*, I said to myself.

It worked, but a little too well. The next time a plow ran over our line, the Kevlar caught it, the way the arrester cable snags a fighter plane landing on an aircraft carrier, and the plow yanked the side off our neighbor's trailer. From then on, however, the plow drivers were more cautious.

In the summer of 1985 Brosl spent several weeks visiting the theoretical physicist Uriel Frisch in the French countryside near Nice. The two were collaborating on a fundamentally new approach to computing they called lattice gas automata. In the 1930s the mathematician Alan Turing had proposed a simple sequential device for solving mathematical equations that became known as the Turing Machine. The power of the Turing Machine is that it can simulate every other computational scheme, and as a result it has become the standard tool for thinking about computation.

However, both Brosl and Frisch were physicsts rather than mathematicians, and they came upon a new parallel computational model drawn from a physicist's world view. They realized it was possible to model the flow of fluids in an entirely different way than had been done before, and they began to think about the design of computers that would be needed to simulate such a model. The obvious payoff is that by computing in parallel it is possible to achieve orders-of-magnitude increases in speed. In their model, instead of computing a complex formula sequentially, the flow of a fluid is simulated by a system that is made up of many simple components that interact locally. In other words, an algorithm, or recipe, for sequentially computing a problem is replaced by many independent agents that are called cellular automata.

Traditionally, for example, the flow of fluids has been described by a complex equation known as Navier-Stokes. Now Brosl and Frisch proposed the idea of a hexagonal array at each point of which particles could be represented colliding, and in motion. A set of simple collision rules for each point on the array are enough to model everything that required a complex equation, and it can simulate fluid flow in two or three dimensions.

Frisch and Brosl were good friends and they both realized they were on the edge of a dramatic advance, but Frisch was a Frenchman first, and a quite nationalistic one at that. After several days Brosl realized that every afternoon his friend was going off by himself, and speaking by telephone to a team of four or five programmers in Paris. He was trying to perform an end-run, and give the French a headstart on being the first to implement a working version of the lattice gas automata model!

Brosl decided that two people could play this game, and so one evening he phoned me back at Los Alamos and described his and Frisch's basic theoretical model in detail. I proposed some minor changes and told him that I thought I could implement it quickly. The machine I had to work on was called a Celerity, a Unix scientific workstation with a 1280-by-1024-pixel high-resolution display. I worked at coding for a couple of days to implement Brosl's theory in a program that would graphically display the flow of a fluid as it emerged from the tens of millions of small particle collisions. Because I was just modeling a small set of local rules about the behavior of the particles, the software was dramatically simpler than existing versions. The essential elements of the simulation could be described in several dozen lines of code, and it was far less complex than the several hundreds of lines of code normally required to perform two- and three-dimensional hydrodynamic calculations.

When Brosl came back from France a week later I had something to show him on the display, and it was almost there, but something was not quite right. He came up with a few changes, and then went home while I kept tinkering. About midnight I phoned him.

"Brosl, you better come up here and look," I said. "There's something weird happening on the screen."

On the computer monitor a thin line representing a plate inserted to disturb the flow of the fluid as it passed around it was surrounded by a halo of slowly changing colors. Brosl instantly recognized that we had done it; the image gradually transformed as millions of particle collisions were computed, and vortices were clearly emerging. We left the image frozen on the screen, and the next morning when we came back to the Lab the room was crowded with hydrodynamicists who were startled to see that we were computing something hundreds of times faster than traditional sequential algorithms.

Brosl's theory didn't gain instant acceptance, however. Entire academic empires had been constructed on the old sequential models, and the publication of his paper on lattice gas automata in August 1985 created a nasty spat in the scientific community. Some scientists initially attempted to challenge the accuracy of the technique, but we were soon able to confirm our results. It was remarkable proof that controversial parallel computing techniques could provide dramatic speedups over existing approaches.

Despite his intellectual triumph, Brosl's work still remained outside the mainstream, and in mid-1988 we decided to get away from the politics and infighting of the weapons lab. We moved to San Diego to set up a remote site of the lab's Theoretical Division. With the end of the Cold War the weapons labs were already beginning their decline, and as funding dried up, the bureaucracy was becoming more and more imprisoning. Roger

Dashen, who was a physicist I knew well, was trying to turn the University of San Diego physics department into a lively and eclectic place, and he offered me a research position there. One evening that summer Brosl and I finished loading up an 18-wheeler semitrailer with our computer gear and headed west, through the cool desert night.

CHAPTER 5

On the morning after Andrew and I arrived in San Diego following the break-in, Room 408 of the Supercomputer Center became our war room.

A large room on the top floor, it once offered a view of the ocean, which had been recently blocked by the new School of International Affairs building, and further obscured by a pair of monitors, a camera, and other videoconferencing aparatus partially covering the windows along that side of the room. But otherwise the room's various features—a long conference table, whiteboards on its walls, and network connections for our portable computers—were perfect for our purposes.

Around midday our impromptu force began to assemble. Even though it was Christmas week and school was out, there were always some researchers, students, post-docs, and even the occasional administrator and technician around the Center, and we were able to assemble an instant detective team for our effort to recreate the break-in. To add a little incentive we had lunch ordered from the Thai House, one of our regular spots, about ten kilometers from the campus. I had decided that if Sid was going to spring for expense money we ought to do something truly useful with it—like feeding people.

I had managed to round up with several phone calls an eclectic squad of people who were willing to volunteer some of their time. Because it was short notice it was something of a rag-tag

army, and while some of the members of the group took a specific task, others were there just to lend moral support, or out of
curiosity. Rama Ramachandran was a former UCSD undergraduate who was now in business school at the University of Chicago
and was visiting for the holidays. I was still puzzled by the strange
syntax error message from the X-NeWS PostScript interpreter
that had been on Ariel's console display the previous day, and
since Rama was a real PostScript wizard, we immediately set him
to work examining the interpreter to see if it had been exploited
to gain entry.

Among those joining us were John Moreland, a scientific visualization programmer; and Henry Ptasinski, a grad student in
electrical and computer engineering at UCSD. At the time,
Henry was also one of the system administrators at CERFnet, an
Internet service provider that is closely affiliated with the Center.

And then there was a manager of network security at the
Center. Tom and I usually get along well as long as we don't have
to work together, but he likes to get involved in everything, and
sometimes I refer to him as a roving speed bump. I may seem
cruel in this regard, but I've never been able to figure out how to
be tolerant dealing with the people who are responsible for main-
taining the needless red tape and regulations that seem to make
any large organization run. Julia says that my favorite word is
"bozo," and argues that I should work on being a little more
diplomatic. I tried to do so now, when he showed up to see if he
could do anything useful. I gave him a chunk of code called the
"remote procedure call ToolTalk database server daemon," or
rpc.ttdbserverd—which facilitates the communication of some
programs across a network of computers—and asked him if he
would go off and analyze it for vulnerabilities we didn't know
about. We had become suspicious that it might have played a part
in the break-in, because one of our activity log files had recorded
an unusual access to it one Christmas night.

When he left the room, one of the graduate students turned to
me and said, "Why did you give him something like that to do?
You're always complaining about him."

Andrew and I looked at each other, and I replied, "Basically to
keep him out of trouble and out of our hair."

"You know he's not going to stay out of your hair," the student
said.

"So?" I said. "This will keep him busy for a while, at least."

We were still doing data collection at this point, and things were looking pretty bleak, which made me even grumpier. I had already taken data off Rimmon and Astarte, my machines at home. At this point we could tell that Osiris had been tampered with, but not how. On each of these computers we had checked to see if any files had been altered and if any questionable programs had been left behind. When we didn't see any immediately I began to worry even more, for it suggested that our interloper knew some other way to get in, and that he thought he'd be able to return undetected. I couldn't consider going back on-line until I assessed what our risk of another break-in was. Everybody went off to his individual task, leaving Andrew and me working at the portable computers we had set up.

Progress turned out to be sporadic. Thanks to Ariel's age, getting useful data out of the computer was frustrating and took us much of the day. Most of the components in a modern computer are connected by a bundle of wires known as a data bus. Microprocessors, computer memory, disk drives, graphics displays, and assorted peripherals all plug into this main highway or backplane, which is really just a set of parallel wires that enables information to shuttle back and forth with incredible rapidity. Ariel was so old that it used a bus called VME which was originally invented for minicomputers back in the 1980s. Its disk drives were also based on an outdated standard so there was no way that we could hook Ariel's disks directly to my portable computers, which used more modern SCSI disk drives. As a result, we first had to copy all the necessary data off Ariel before we could work with it safely.

The two of us went rummaging around the building trying to borrow some extra disks to accommodate this huge amount of data until finally, late in the afternoon, we managed to scrounge up a two-gigabyte drive from the folks at CERFnet. (To understand just how much information two gigabytes represents, think of one of these drives as having the capacity to comfortably store the entire *Encyclopaedia Britannica*, both pictures and text—all in the palm of your hand.) More hours were taken trying to figure out how to move all the data so that it would be organized exactly as it was stored on Ariel.

It wasn't until 10 P.M. that I had the data from Ariel transferred to the hard drive and ready to be examined on my RDI portable. By that time almost everyone else had left the Center, and Andrew and I felt the need for a dinner break. We took the elevator downstairs and drove off campus to Rubio's, an inexpensive fish-taco restaurant, where neither of us was particularly happy to be. "Look, we're on someone else's expense account and we really should be getting better meals than this," I told Andrew. "I don't want to present Sid with a dinner bill for $4.95." But after ten o'clock in that part of San Diego, there aren't too many choices. We ate quickly, eager to return to the Center and see what Ariel's data would tell us.

Back in Room 408, it took me about an hour to run the forensic-analysis programs that, as with Rimmon and Astarte, at home, revealed which of Ariel's files had been accessed, modified, or corrupted. For the first time I knew what had actually been stolen from Ariel: virtually everything in my directories. Much of it was valuable to me and my work, including tens of thousands of my e-mail messages, source code for programs I had written, and sensitive proprietary data. There were no conclusions to be drawn from this bill of particulars, however, because the thief or thieves were so indiscriminate that they had also spent hours copying programs that are freely available elsewhere on the Net, including various tools that I myself had downloaded from the Free Software Foundation.

Our analysis of Ariel's data did turn up one piece of news: the intruders had been stealing files only two hours before Andrew discovered the break-in. So now we had a fairly complete picture of what had happened, and some indication of when. But we still couldn't answer the question that, to me, was the more important one: *How did they do it?*

I knew that Osiris, the machine at the head of my bed, had been accessed before Ariel, at my SDSC office, but I didn't know how they had gotten to either machine, or if they had used one to get to the other. And then there was that XNeWS PostScript interpreter error message on Ariel, which seemed to indicate an attempted probe from Colorado SuperNet. Significant—or a false clue? If our attacker really knew what he was doing, disinformation was a possibility we had to be aware of.

There were also other bits and pieces that made up a puzzle I still couldn't assemble. One of them was a mysterious program, Tap, that I had seen when I peered into Osiris's memory the day before. It was a transient program that someone had created and placed in my computer's memory for a specific task. When the computer was turned off or rebooted it would vanish forever. And what about the ghost of the file oki.tar.Z, whose creation suggested that someone was after cellular telephone software, despite the otherwise indiscrimate nature of the looting?

There was another crucial discovery from looking at Ariel's data; the intruder had tried to overwrite our packet logs, the detailed records we keep of various packets of data that had been sent to or from our machines over the Internet. The erased log files revealed that in trying to overwrite them the intruder hadn't completely covered over the original file. It was as if he had tried to hide his footprints in the sand by throwing buckets of more sand on top of them. But here and there, heels and toes and even a whole foot were still visible. It appeared that we had our first clues. We might not have the entire getaway path, but at least we'd know in which direction to start tracking.

In fact, while none of the puzzle pieces fit yet, the packet log gave us a potential way to start putting our clues together. The intruder's alteration of the separate activity log had first alerted Andrew to the break-in. Now the clumsily overwritten packet log file could potentially help us recreate it, thanks to the technology used for routing chunks of data—packets—over the Internet.

This technology is called "Packet switching," and like the Internet itself it is the direct outgrowth of an idea conceived in the early 1960s by a Rand Corporation researcher named Paul Baran. In those days, at the height of the Cold War, the military was obsessed with the problem of surviving a nuclear war, and so one of the assignments they handed to their think tanks was inventing a communication system that would continue to operate even if some of its nodes were destroyed.

Baran hatched the idea of a computer network that could automatically reroute traffic. The technique, packet switching, involved breaking each message up into lots and lots of small packets. Each packet contained only a small portion of the message, accompanied by a "packet header" that contained enough

information so that at each waypoint in its passage through the
network, each of these little data parcels could be rerouted if necessary and still arrive safely at its final destination. The routing
computers were given enough intelligence so that even if the
packets took different routes and arrived out of order, or were
even lost, it was possible to reassemble the message in the correct
order and request that lost packets be resent.

Baran's was a brilliant concept, and in the late 1960s the
Pentagon's Advanced Projects Research Agency, or ARPA, funded an experimental project to develop such a network. The first
"Watson, come here. I need your help" message was sent between
Stanford Research Institute in Menlo Park, now SRI
International, and a group of computer researchers at UCLA in
1970. Since then, things have gotten a little out of hand: from
the original two ARPAnet sites, the Internet network had
expanded to more than 6.6 million machines and was still growing at a geometric rate.

But while the multitude of machines and users are overbur-
dening the Internet in various ways, and providing cover for people intent on mischief, each of the billions of packets flowing
through the network still has that informative header, telling not
only where the packet is going, but where it supposedly came
from. And because I knew that a packet filter can duly note all
this information, I was hoping that the Ariel's packet logs might
eventually help recreate the intruder's actions.

But there was a complication: although the intruder had
failed to overwrite the packet-log file, his effort to erase it was
going to make reading the data difficult. The way computer
data is stored on a hard drive is similar to the way a library organizes its holdings. What you really want in a library is to be able
to go and ask the librarian for a particular book, and then be
handed the book—you don't care where it's actually stored. In
the same way, information about the files that you create on a
computer is all stored in one place on the hard disk—think of
it as a library card catalogue—but the information itself is kept
somewhere else, usually scattered in little blocks all over the
disk's surface.

Like librarians, computer operating systems take care of the
tedious grunt work of storing and hunting for the information.

When the operating system erases a file, what it actually does is erase the pointers to the information, the file card in the catalog, rather than the information itself, which remains until all available space on the hard disk is filled up and the erased data eventually gets written over by newly stored data. (Trying to prevent such write-overs was one of the reasons I had Ariel and the other machines halted as soon as possible after learning of the break-in.)

So even though the packet file had been erased, it was actually possible that its data could still be reconstructed from the disk— it was just that the task was a little bit like the one the king's men faced with Humpty Dumpty. As a first step in how we would proceed, Andrew said, "I think I can write a program that will find the spot in the file where the corruption ends and then look for the place the real data begin." This would be a useful start, but it wouldn't necessarily let us find all the disparate pieces of the data we were looking for—as this would only turn up data written to the file after it had been tampered with.

It occurred to me that there might be a better, less obvious way to find the same data. As a physicist I think a lot about concepts like entropy and chaos, and I have spent a lot of time building tools that look for patterns that might not be otherwise apparent. A body of data may appear to be noise, but in fact may have a hidden structure. The challenge is to extract that structure, which may exist in a clear form, or in some form that requires the right filter to see.

In a way I was facing the same problem that a Roman cryptographer might have confronted in attempting to break an ancient coding scheme known as a Caesar cipher. In this procedure, military messages were written on the surfaces of parchment that had been wrapped around a cylinder or cone. The only way to decode the message was to find an object of the same size and shape and to keep wrapping the paper around it until the writing lined up.

Likewise, I needed to find a pattern in the tiny pieces of data scattered across the surface of our disks. Like all computer data, it was in the form of binary code—strings of 1's and 0's that can represent digits, letters, and other types of information. Each piece of string was a link in a chain of information; the problem was to discover the pattern by which these individual links had been scattered, so we could find them and reassemble the chain. I had put off doing this, because it seemed like a long shot. But we hadn't learned enough from our other analysis thus far, so it now seemed like the necessary next step.

"Let's see who can do this first," I told Andrew at about 1:30 A.M. We agreed that Andrew would write his conventional program for retrieving the packet information, while I would write one to look for patterns on the disk and then attempt to reassemble them into something that resembled the original file. We settled in front of our workstations at a conference table, facing each other, Andrew tapping away at his RDI portable, and I at my newer version of the same computer, a machine in which I was growing increasingly confident, despite its being an unproven prototype.

I wrote a program I called Hunt to search the disk that I ran for the first time at about 2:45 in the morning, and a second program called Catch, which was designed to organize what Hunt found. I actually won the race by a nose, with my programs finishing their tasks at nearly 4 A.M., just ahead of Andrew's. In the end, we both succeeded in retrieving data, and Andrew's partial file was a useful check of my catch of relevant data: 14 million bytes that had been scattered among nearly 2 billion others and which might now finally enable us to recreate our intruder's actions.

Savoring the moment, I sat back and casually scanned through our reconstituted packet-log file. With this information, we might have a chance to replay his actual keystrokes, much like rewinding a videotape to watch a television show. We now had a chance of putting the puzzle back together. It was the first time that I had been able to feel good in three days.

My intruder had assumed that by overwriting the data he would make it disappear. He should have known better. "He's probably an MS-DOS user," I grumbled. If he was trying to be invisible he shouldn't have been sloppy. I began to wonder how good he really was. One of the standard strategies in the computer underground is to share "cookbook" recipes for attacks, and then use these step-by-step programs against targets over the Internet. There's a lot of that: someone steals a hardware or software company's source code, or stumbles upon garden-variety computer-security software like the type that had been among my stolen files, or studies computer science journals and figures out a way to break into a system. If he succeeds he passes word around the network to his friends, or posts the how-to details on any of the various underground bulletin boards that function as rogues' hangouts on the Internet. Maybe our intruder was just an anklebiter who had learned how to read technical manuals or bulletin board postings, and hadn't realized that covering your trail in the digital world isn't always as easy as it seems.

However promising our leads, I was on my third night of little sleep, so we agreed to quit the search. I drove home, and as my Acura glided through the deserted streets I took satisfaction in knowing that even if we didn't find enough information in the packet log file to start chasing our intruder in earnest, at the very least we should be able to figure out how he broke in, and so find ways to improve our locks. When I got home the first hint of sunrise was filtering through my bedroom, but despite my physical exhaustion, sleep eluded me. I sat crosslegged on my futon bed in front of Osiris while looking through our systems for other clues. I played with rpc.ttdbserverd. Why had it been left running on the night of the break-in? Did the attacker have some clever program that spanned an entire computer network to break security? It nagged at me, but after another hour of fruitless searching, it looked like a dead end.

Late that morning, as my car climbed the hill to SDSC, instead of feeling dread, I was anticipating the challenge ahead. Andrew had already arrived in Room 408, as had most of the others, and lunch had been brought in again. While we were eating, the phone rang in the conference room.

It was Mike Bowen, someone I knew at CERFnet. Mike, a technical support person and a wizard with a type of digital technology known as ISDN telephone technology, also kept his ear to the ground for rumblings from the computer underworld. I had talked to him the day before on the off chance he might have heard something about our break-in. He had told me he knew a guy named Justin Petersen, whom I'd heard of, who was in prison in Los Angeles for credit-card fraud and was trying to strike a deal with Federal prosecutors. Petersen had been trying to persuade

Mike to use his contacts in the computer-security community to see if someone could persuade the Feds to listen to his alibi—that he had been set up by Kevin Mitnick while he was trying to help the FBI find Mitnick. Maybe I'd want to chat with Petersen? "Sure," I had told Mike. "Why not?"

Now Mike was calling back, saying he had set things up. Because Petersen was in prison he was allowed phone calls only from a restricted list of people. For him to speak to anyone else, a person from this list would make the phone call and then three-way the other party into the conversation. That was about to happen, Mike said, and told me to stand by. He hung up.

A few minutes later, the phone rang again. "Hi, I'm here with the person who you were expecting to hear from," said a voice I didn't recognize.

"Who are you?" I asked.

"Why don't you call me Eric," another voice on the line responded. Petersen had decided to use one of his many aliases, although another, Agent Steal, was the best known.

Justin Tanner Petersen was a strange character. A Southern California native, he had originally been arrested in Dallas in 1991 and charged with credit-card fraud and other computer crimes. In a plea bargain, he arranged with the Secret Service and FBI to be released to work under Federal supervision to help agents track down computer criminals, while other charges against him played out in the California courts. Petersen had supposedly put the FBI on the trail of Kevin Mitnick in 1992, forcing Mitnick to go on the lam. And he had also helped law-enforcement officials assemble evidence against Kevin Poulsen, a Silicon Valley programmer who had been arrested in 1991 and who finally pleaded guilty in June 1994 to electronically taking over a Pacific Bell central office telephone switch to rig contests at two Los Angeles radio stations, from which he won two Porsches, more than $20,000 in cash, and at least two trips to Hawaii. (If you are in control of the telephone company's central office switch, you can be lucky caller number ninety-five whenever you want.) Meanwhile, the FBI had an extensive dossier against Poulsen for other computer and telecommunications activities, such as listening to the phone calls of his former girlfriend, tapping into conversations of telephone company security officials investigating him, and even monitoring the electronic communications of FBI agents who were tailing Imelda Marcos's daughter in Woodside, California.

But while working for the FBI, Petersen had allegedly returned to computer crime himself. In an October 1993 courthouse meeting with a prosecutor for the Los Angeles district attorney's office, he admitted to credit-card fraud. Then, in the middle of the meeting, he told his attorney he needed to take a break, walked from the room, and fled. He lived on the run until being recaptured in August 1994, and now, more than four months later, he was about to be sentenced and was hoping that I could help him make a deal for a lenient sentence in exchange for his helping us catch Kevin Mitnick. Although he'd been trying to negotiate with the Justice Department, his prospects seemed grim. Because I knew Scott Charney, the Justice Department's chief computer crime prosecutor, Petersen seemed to hold out some hope I could help him in making a deal.

He believed it was Mitnick who had turned him in to the Feds in his most recent arrest, and he didn't sound happy about it. He had a flat Southern California accent and I had the distinct sense that he wasn't being very sincere.

"I don't even know if it was Kevin Mitnick who broke in to my computers," I said.

"It sure sounds like Kevin's M.O.," Petersen responded.

I was skeptical. There were potentially thousands of people who could have gone after my machines. "What would you need to find him?" I asked. "I understand that you're in a difficult situation, given that it seems you screwed over the Feds at least once."

He was vague. "I know things that I obviously don't want to say over this phone line," he replied.

Petersen began proposing that we meet in person, and then he would be able to tell me more. He said he thought he was very close to catching Mitnick, that it would take maybe a month. He proposed expense money. He was hard to read, and I kept trying to figure out whether he actually had something or not.

After we talked for about forty-five minutes I finally said, "If I get a chance I'll mention this to to law enforcement people, but I don't think it will lead anywhere." I added that if I was in Los

Angeles I would come visit him in prison. We hung up, and I called Mike Bowen and said, "Should I believe any of this?"

"I don't know, maybe," Mike answered. Perhaps Mitnick really had set up Petersen. "But there's another possibility," he continued. "Maybe Justin is worried that Kevin Mitnick has the goods on him, enough to put him away for a long time."

I decided that for now, at least, I might be better off analyzing Ariel's data than relying on people like Justin Petersen.

Shortly after 5 P.M. Andrew and I were ready to begin recreating a second-by-second chronicle of the events of the break-in on one of the large whiteboards along the wall. We had attracted a small audience of curiosity seekers who had heard about our project, including Jay Dombrowski, the Center's manager responsible for networks and communications.

We were at the crux of our investigation, and doing it so publicly was something of a risk: it wouldn't look very impressive if we came up empty-handed. But the opportunity for us all to learn something outweighed the risk of embarrassment.

During the afternoon I'd massaged the reassembled packet log file with a program I'd written called Cook that threw out anything extraneous. I'd also assembled the various forensics data we'd collected—primarily, our records of the files that had been accessed—and merged it into one file, organized chronologically, that gave us a single timeline of all events. The packet log was already organized chronologically. Everything we had done over the last several days had been preparation for this: we would now systematically compare the packet logs, which would show us exactly what the attacker typed or transmitted, with the forensics data, which would reveal the consequences of each of these actions.

Andrew stood at the whiteboard with a magic marker, and I sat in front of my RDI workstation. I began calling out each event as I extracted it from the lists we had compiled and merged.

I began with the afternoon of Christmas day—shortly after I had wandered by the computer in the entryway at Toad Hall and thought about checking mail on my network.

"14:09:32," I called out. From our reconstructed packet data we saw that Ariel received this command over the Internet, an exploratory probe:

```
finger -l @ariel.sdsc.edu
```

Finger is a standard Unix utility that displays information about each logged-in user, and Ariel responded by giving basic information, telling the prober that there were current connections to Astarte, Rimmon, and Osiris, and that my computer had been unattended for several days. Over the next three minutes in our computer timeline, I called out six more probes, each targeting a different aspect of my network.

"14:11:49," I read. "Hey, they've run a remote procedure call on Osiris."

Andrew walked around the table and studied the screen of my portable. He was an expert on remote procedure calls, RPC's, an operating system function that lets programs ask a remote computer to do something. The result he was studying was displayed in hexadecimal format, the base-16 numbering system that good hackers learn to read as a second language. "That's a showmount -e to show exported file systems," he said. In other words, it was a command that allowed the person executing it to determine which hard disks were shared by the other computers in my network. Someone was trying to build what is known as a trust model of my network, to see which computers had special relationships, with few security barriers between them. It was an attempt to see which computers in my network "trusted" each other, as Osiris and Rimonn did, for example.

I looked more closely at the probes and made a striking discovery: *They all came from toad.com.*

"This is very strange," I said to Andrew. "I was at Toad Hall when these probes were made, not ten meters away from the machine they came from." I could see that the RPC had come from source port 721 at toad.com, which meant it had been issued by someone who was root on Toad. I knew there had been no one else physically present at Toad Hall at the time but Julia and myself, and I realized that the attack could have been staged from anywhere on the Internet. Still, I couldn't help wondering whether the intruder was someone I knew.

I was puzzled, but there was nothing to do but plunge ahead.

Six minutes later in the data stream we saw evidence of someone attempting to initiate an Internet connection—a request called SYN, for synchronize.

"14:18:22," I said. "I see a remote log-in connection from 130.92.6.97 to Rimmon . . . wait, there are a whole bunch more!" I was struck by this. Normally, a SYN request should have initiated a single computer handshaking sequence—the brief greeting and interrogation between two machines before they agree to communicate over the Internet. This requires the pair of computers creating and exchanging a sequence of one-time-use numbers to ensure that this conversation isn't confused with any other simultaneous coversations that either computer may also be having.

But in this case, it was as if this remote machine was saying "hello," "hello," "hello," "hello," in rapid succession, without listening to Rimmon's reply. Why would that happen?

I stopped and tried to find where these rapid-fire SYNs had come from. The digits 130.92.6.97 were the remote computer's Internet address, and it took several queries to various Internet databases, but I finally got an answer: currently, there was no such computer. The messages to Rimmon had appeared to come from a network in Switzerland:

```
University of Berne (NET-UNIBE)
Institute of Informatics and Applied
  Mathematics
Laenggasssstrasse 51
CH-3012 Berne
SWITZERLAND

Netname: UNIBE
Netnumber: 130.92.0.0

Coordinator:
Buetikofer, Fritz (FB61) btkfr@ID.UNIBE.CH
+41 31 65 3843
Domain System inverse mapping provided by:
ARWEN.UNIBE.CH 130.92.9.52
SWIBE9.UNIBE.CH 130.92.1.1
SCSNMS.SWITCH.CH 130.59.1.30
```

That network existed, as indicated by the first five digits: 130.92. But it appeared that the computer that had tried to connect to Rimmon, the machine designated by the complete address, 130.92.6.97, didn't answer, or didn't exist, at least not now. The computer could have been turned off since the attack, I supposed, and so would not be showing up in the database. Or there was another possibility: The address could have been a forgery.

I resumed the chronology: "14:18:25." It was just three seconds later, in our data timeline. And now there was another SYN, this time to Osiris from a computer called apollo.it.luc.edu. I queried the Internet database again and found out that luc.edu was Loyola University in Chicago. As had happened to Rimmon from the mystery Swiss machine, Osiris was now receiving a series of remote log-in connection requests from the Loyola machine.

"This is very weird," I muttered. What was going on? Osiris was receiving a series of SYNs, each with a sequence number to initiate the handshake. But when Osiris sent back its acknowledgment—SYN-ACK, which included a second sequence number—the Loyola machine was not taking the normal next step. Instead of replying with a third sequence number, the Loyola computer would start the process over by issuing the command RST, for reset. This happened twenty times in rapid succession. Why?

I continued to hunt through the data, and then I saw something that at first didn't make any sense at all. All of the packet data that we were analyzing were packets that had come in from the Internet through Ariel, which was sitting in the wiring closet here at the Supercomputer Center. But now, our records had begun showing traffic that seemed to be flowing directly between Osiris and Rimmon, inside my house. "Wait, I shouldn't be seeing these packets!" I said. "Why am I seeing local traffic between Osiris and Rimmon?"

But suddenly it came to me—the answer I had been pursuing around the clock for the last three days. The remote computer had seized on the fact that Osiris trusted Rimmon and had forged a one-way connection to Osiris that appeared to be from Rimmon, but was actually coming directly from our intruder.

"Ah, I understand," I said. The room fell quiet, as I looked at Andrew. "So that's how they broke in."

All those aborted handshakes now made sense. The attacker had needed to be able to predict the sequence number that Osiris was sending out with each SYN-ACK. A sequence number in this case was simply an authenticator, much like the number they give you while you're waiting in line at the delicatessen, so that when it's your turn to talk to the man behind the counter he and everybody else recognize your right to proceed. Our intruder planned to masquerade as Rimmon, a computer that Osiris trusted, and in order to do it successfully he needed to be able to send Osiris back the sequence number, the delicatessen number, that it, Osiris, would expect Rimmon to present.

And now I understood why the intruder had sent that first flurry of messages to Rimmon. They had filled up an input queue, in effect gagging Rimmon so that it couldn't respond when it came time to present its sequence number. Once Rimmon was bound and gagged, the attacker had then sent that series of twenty SYNs to Osiris, to learn the formula by which Osiris generated its sequence numbers—each was 128,000 larger than the previous one—and thus be ready to slip into Rimmon's place in the deli line and respond with the appropriate sequence number. The intruder then gave the sequence number Osiris was expecting, and used it to open a communications channel.

Andrew had come over from the whiteboard and was watching my screen over my shoulder. Now that they had broken in, *what did they do?* Pretending to be Rimmon, the attacker at the Loyola computer had sent the following short message through the one-way channel: "echo + + >/.rhosts." That simple command caused Osiris itself to drop all of its defenses and made it possible for anyone to connect to it without a password. The intruder had convinced Osiris that it was opening up a digital conversation with its trusted file server in the next room, Rimmon.

It was now almost six in the evening, and Andrew had returned to write up the sequence on the whiteboard. Jay Dombrowski, who was following some but not all of the chronology that we created, politely excused himself to go home for dinner.

I thought about it for a minute and realized that the style of attack was a familiar one. With a deft sleight-of-hand the attacker had made packets coming from outside our network appear to be coming from the safety of the inside. This was an "IP spoofing" attack, a type that had been described in theory in the computer science literature but which, as far as I knew, had never before been carried out as a hostile attack.

The attack was based on a weakness in the set of technical communications instructions for Internet traffic, known as the Transmission Control Protocol/Internet Protocol (TCP/IP), which had been developed in the late 1970s and early 1980s. IP spoofing, manipulating the handshake sequence numbers to impersonate another computer, was possible because the handshake procedures, created in an era when nobody worried much about Internet security, had been designed merely to clarify who was who on the Internet, not verify.

I was familiar with a technical paper on TCP/IP security problems, written in 1989 by Steve Bellovin, a computer security researcher at Bell Labs, in which he had described how an IP-spoofing attack might play out. But the potential to use IP-spoofing to pose as a "trusted" computer had first been brought to the research community's attention even earlier, in a 1984 paper that a student named Robert Tappan Morris had written while a summer intern also at Bell Labs. On the final page of his report Morris had given a cookbook description of how such an attack would work. More than ten years later, his paper appeared prophetic: "Bell Labs has a growing TCP/IP network connecting machines with varying security needs; perhaps steps should be taken to reduce their vulnerability to each other."

As night fell, Room 408 was bathed in cold fluorescence as we continued following the attack's digital trail. One of the things I'd discovered on Tuesday was that on both Ariel and Osiris the intruder had inserted a program directly into the computer's operating system memory. Sun Microsystem's Unix has a standard feature that permits you to modify the heart of the operating system, while it is still running, to add new functions. These programs are called "kernel modules" and they can be directly placed in software "slots" in the operating system while the computer is still running. Typically you might use one if you were adding some new peripheral to your computer. The one on Ariel just seemed to be garbage, but I had tried to take the one I found in Osiris's memory apart and had not been able to immediately tell very much about what it was designed to do. It did have a suggestive name however, Tap 2.01.

At the time I'd wondered if it was a "sniffer" program, to enable

the intruder to subsequently monitor the traffic over my network, looking for things like passwords that might abet subse-
quent break-ins to my machines or the computers of other people who communicate with me. But now in the traces of our
packet data I could see what had happened. After installing and
running a backdoor program on Osiris, the intruder returned
through his backdoor network port, a separate channel that happened to be one that our packet logs weren't monitoring, and so
we lost direct traces of his keystrokes. But during this blind spot
in our packet-log data, we could still follow his activities, the consequences of his keystrokes, by consulting our forensics data for
this same time period.

We could see that he had inserted a kernel-module program
called Tap into a slot in Osiris's operating system. Almost immediately afterward we could see his activity jump from Osiris at my
home to Ariel at the Center. Although Osiris and Rimmon had a
trust relationship that made them vulnerable to IP spoofing,
Osiris and Ariel didn't. Initiating a communications session with
Ariel would have required a much more elaborate set of procedures, including a password. He had needed another strategy, and
this is where Tap came in. As he could see with finger, my home
machine already had an open session to Ariel running on its
screen. It appeared that Tap had allowed him to literally hijack
this open window on Osiris's screen, and use it to control Ariel.
Tap was a program that gave my thief the power of a puppet master, sending keystrokes through the portal just as if he had been
sitting on my bed.

It was after midnight, and Andrew and I were once again the
only ones working late in Room 408. The inactive videoconfer-
ence terminals along the windows stared at me opaquely, and
suddenly I recalled how the blank window on Osiris's display had
puzzled me two days earlier. It was now obvious: my trespasser
had broken through that screen portal in much the same way a
burglar would jimmy open a window and then climb through it.
And once he was inside Ariel, he had been able to help himself to
my software and e-mail messages, and then carry them away to
who knew where on the Internet.

CHAPTER 6

In the days immediately after I unraveled the IP-spoofing attack my life didn't return to normal, for there was too much cleanup and reconstruction work to be done. But I did find time for skating in the Southern California winter sunshine and talked with Julia regularly by telephone, as we discussed the possibility of her coming to visit me in San Diego. Much of my time was given over to building a more secure router for my network that would not only keep attackers out but would also keep detailed log files and alert us quickly if we were attacked. Andrew also worked long hours, deciphering the programs that had been left behind by our data thieves, and together we spent several days mopping up final details and trying to make certain that we understood exactly how our security had been violated.

I called Toad Hall to ask John Gilmore about the early probes from toad.com. He had become increasingly uncomfortable about my contact with Julia. It was a strained conversation. I told him about the attacks on my computers and the initial probes from his computer. He looked at the accounting logs his computer kept, reporting there was no suspicious activity.

"You know as well as I do that if somebody broke into toad they could have doctored your log files to hide themselves," I said.

Later, I spoke with Julia and we both decided the attack was an amazing coincidence. We knew I hadn't been involved, but I had been just upstairs from the computer, and we realized that in raising the issue we might be opening a can of worms. Was somebody trying to frame me, or for that matter, to frame John? Or was it something else entirely? We decided it would be best not to make a point of it, as there were so many erroneous conclusions that people might jump to.

While I was in San Diego both Andrew and I began working on refining my network's defensive perimeter. For many people, security in the Internet today is simply a matter of going out and buying a system called a firewall, a black-box solution that just restricts the type of data packets that can flow from the outside world. I've never believed that merely building thicker castle walls will offer a better defense, so instead we set traps and built alarms into the network, making it easier for us to detect and respond to future intrusions. Ariel was upgraded yet again, this time with the installation of more modern disk drives. We also wrote software that would protect against any future IP spoofing or similar attacks. We wanted to be automatically notified if someone attempted a spoofing attack in the future, and we began to modify our network software so that it would be impossible to fool our machines with a forged Internet address.

Our new security router was designed to look at the address of each packet that flowed from the Internet to my network. If it found an address that appeared to be coming from the inside it would say, in effect, "Wait a minute, this shouldn't happen," and then not only reject the packet but also set off an alarm at the same time.

I scrounged around and salvaged a bunch of spare parts, and configured the secure routing computer to sit on the network between the outside world and my piece of the Supercomputer Center network. It was built out of a Sun SPARCstation we commandeered for the task, which took up residence in the wiring closet next to Ariel. We actually gave it three names. If you wanted to send packets to the outside world you sent them into "chaos." If you were sending packets to my computers then you leave them to "chance" the whole router we named the "Abyss."

At the heart of our defense was a basic computer network technology called packet filtering. The ability to scrutinize and capture individual packets as they moved by on a wire first emerged in the early 1980s, because network designers needed a diagnostic tool to monitor and tune their systems. More recently, however, packet filtering has become a powerful tool with great potential for abuse. Neither the first Ethernet local area network nor the first Internet computer networks were built with privacy or security in mind. They were simply research projects designed to let computer scientists and engineers explore the idea of hooking computers up within offices and between cities and states. But between the late 1960s and today, computer networks evolved from being research tools to the point that they've become an integral part of the fabric of our society. Ethernet works by broadcasting every packet along the entire wire. Normally, computers on the network listen to the packet broadcasts and simply take the packets addressed to them. The problem with Ethernet technology is that someone can take over a computer on the network and simply scoop up all the packets, whether they are addressed to him or not. This data is usually not encrypted and it is a tremendous security loophole because sniffing is a passive activity. There is no way to know for certain whether packets bound for your computer are being illicitly snatched up and scanned by someone else.

As more and more data began to be transferred over computer networks, somewhere along the way the bad guys began using packet filters, or "sniffers" as they became known, to watch all the traffic flowing over a network, saving it to later extract passwords and anything else that moved between two computers.

But just as packet filtering can be used to invade privacy, it can also be used to protect privacy and security by network operators who would otherwise be defenseless against those who are breaking into their systems. One of the projects I've undertaken over the years has been to build better packet filters to keep up with increasingly faster computer networks. As a result, I've been criticized by privacy rights advocates for improving technology that can be dangerous in the wrong hands. People have even suggested that I was building technology for Big Brother. Obviously, like many technologies in the world, packet filtering can be misused and abused, but by itself, it's just a tool. And tools are tools are tools. The possibility of its misuse is not enough to dissuade me from developing a tool, particularly when it has such a vital role.

The first opportunity I had had to put this technology in play against a live opponent on the Net came early in 1991 when I received a call from Castor Fu, a former Caltech classmate. Castor had worked with me at Los Alamos and had gone on to become a graduate student in physics at Stanford. In January of that year he noticed that Embezzle, one of the workstations in the Stanford physics department, was exhibiting strange behavior.

Investigating, he discovered that a long-dormant account named Adrian had been taken over by an interloper who was using it as a staging area for attacks on all sorts of government computers. Often coming in to the Stanford network by telephone, the cracker would then use the Internet to launch his forays from the university's computers. Irritated, Castor went to notify the university's computer security administrators. He learned they knew about the attack but had decided not to take action because they felt it was better to let the intruder continue, and thus have some idea of what he was up to, rather than to be left totally in the dark.

The university's lack of concern upset Castor even more, and he asked me to help him in his own vigilante action. We set up monitoring software on his network, and I wrote software permitting us to reconstruct the packets we captured during his raids in a videolike presentation. Replaying the data, we could see exactly what our Adrian interloper saw and watch all of his keystrokes just as he typed them.

At the time Stanford had a wide open bank of dial-in modems, which enabled anyone to connect to the university's computers. We ultimately discovered the intruder was a young Dutchman who seemed to have a remarkable amount of free time to sit and attack a variety of mostly military and government computers around the Internet. Castor guessed he was Dutch because he used the word *probeeren*, Dutch for "try," as a new password he created for the stolen account. We also noticed that the attacks came at times corresponding with programmers' hours in Europe. For several months we monitored his activities and tried to see that he didn't do anything harmful. When he did break into other accounts on the Net, we would warn people of the attacks.

As it turned out we weren't the only ones keeping an eye on

Adrian. About the same time we began tracking him, Bill Cheswick, a Bell Labs computer security researcher, noticed that someone was using Embezzle at Stanford to snoop around Bell Labs' system in Murray Hill, New Jersey. Rather than simply locking the attacker out, Cheswick decided to play with him, cat and mouse style. He built a phony computer, which he and his compatriots at Bell Labs referred to as their "jail." He set up the special gateway computer outside of the Bell Labs firewall machine and created a software "playroom" in which the intruder's every move and keystroke could be watched.

The Dutchman whom we called Adrian was known as Berferd to Cheswick's team, named after the account he had commandeered at Bell Labs. (The account name itself was a bit of Bell whimsy: in an episode of the old *Dick Van Dyke Show*, Van Dyke's real-life brother, Jerry, had called Dick "Berferd," because he "looked like a Berferd." By the same logic, the Bell Labs' researchers decided it was a good name for their cracker.) For several months Cheswick studied Berferd's activities, fed him phony information, and attempted to help computer-security people elsewhere who were trying to trace him. Meanwhile, Cheswick indulged in a bit of his own mischief: in the software he wrote to masquerade as a Bell Labs system he inserted several "wait" states designed to simulate a busy computer system. The Dutch attacker must have frequently been left tapping his fingers on his desk while he waited, but he apparently never caught on.

Occasionally the intruder did something that was outright destructive. Once Cheswick saw Berferd type the command "rm-rf / &"—perhaps the most devastating command in the Unix vocabulary. When issued from a root account it causes a computer to systematically walk through all its directories, erasing every file. Apparently Berferd wanted to cover his tracks and didn't care how much damage he did. Within the confines of the Bell Labs "jail," this command could do little harm. But Berferd's willingness to use it confirmed for Cheswick that he was far from harmless. In a paper about the attack written some months later Cheswick wrote, "Some crackers defend their work, stating that they don't do any real damage. Our cracker tried this with us [unsuccessfully to erase our files], and succeeded with this command on other systems."

Adrian and the several compatriots with whom he seemed to be working appeared to be members of a shadowy computer underground who shared information about various bugs and vulnerabilities in the computer systems they were attacking. Ironically, their forays did have the benefit of revealing the poor state of many computers that should have had real locks on their doors. On one NASA computer Adrian tried to log in as "news"—an account on many Unix computers to handle Usenet transactions between different computers on the network. The computer responded that news didn't have a password and asked him to create one of his own!

Another time we watched as he successfully used Robert Tappan Morris's notorious "sendmail" bug. Sendmail is the Internet's standard mail-handling program, and in 1988 Morris had written a worm program that exploited a flaw in sendmail that affected more than six thousand computers on the Internet. That flaw had been widely known for three years, and Sun had distributed software patching it. It was apparent that some system administrators were just too lazy to secure their machines and suffered the consequences.

Yet another time, we watched as Adrian broke into the computers of the Pentagon's Pacific Fleet Command and read mail. He used a search command to hunt for all occurrences of the word "Golf." We guessed he was actually looking for the word "Gulf," because it was at this very point that the U.S. military was mobilizing its forces in the Persian Gulf region. In fact late one night Castor was stalking Adrian as he poked and pried his way through the Internet when someone popped his head into his office at Stanford and said, "You know, there's a war on."

Castor looked at him blankly for a second and then said, "I know, it's just like a war."

The guy seemed just as baffled. Finally he said, "No, it really *is* a war. The Allies just started bombing Baghdad."

Despite the fact that Adrian was now even reading the military's unclassified e-mail with impunity, it was hard to get the bureaucrats in various government agencies to do anything about the problem. The more Castor and I watched, the more we realized that Adrian/Berferd wasn't really a skilled Unix hacker, but simply persistent. He once sat and typed "mail -a," "mail -b," "mail -c," all the way to "mail -z," and then repeated the process in upper-case, hunting for a particular vulnerability that he never found. A lot of what he was doing also fell into the "monkey see, monkey do" category. Since he didn't appear to know that much and was simply copying techniques he saw, I decided to stage my own experiment. We spent some time "teaching" Adrian new vulnerabilities by purposely lowering some part of a computer defense he was probing to briefly allow him entry. Then we would patch it, in effect locking him out. Unaware of the ruse, he would repeat the same trick all over the network; though he failed everywhere else, he gave us a distinct signature with which to identify him when he was in action.

One night I left a telnet session running on Embezzle at Stanford. I had telnetted to a computer at the Los Alamos National Laboratory and then logged off the session. This left the path to the lab still visible for Adrian to retrace, although it was a pointer to a place I was pretty sure he would be unable to break into. Tipped off by Castor and me, Los Alamos had been interested in Adrian, but needed an official reason to take action.

The next day when Adrian ran the ps command to see what programs were running on the Stanford computer he found my abandoned telnet to Los Alamos—lanl.gov—and took the bait. He began attempting to break into the weapons laboratory computers. I called the security officers at the Lab and told them Adrian was attacking their network. Although he was unsuccessful, Adrian had become an official Department of Energy security concern.

Ultimately telephone tracing proved impossible, because at the time there was no computer crime law in the Netherlands, and the Dutch telephone company would not assist with the trace requests from U.S. officials. However, in April, Wietse Venema, a Dutch computer security expert, contacted security experts in America and told them he'd tracked down a small group of Dutch programmers who were breaking into computer systems in the United States. He was able to identify Berferd, including his name, address, phone number, and even his bank account number. Around the same time I received a call from John Markoff, the *New York Times* reporter. We had never met, but Markoff had heard I was monitoring the Dutch intruder. I described our surveillance, and on April 21 Markoff's story appeared on the front page of the *Times.*

Dutch Computer Rogues Infiltrate American Systems With Impunity

By JOHN MARKOFF, Special to The
New York Times

Beyond the reach of American law, a group of Dutch computer intruders have been openly defying United States military, space and intelligence authorities for almost six months. Recently they broke into a United States military computer while being filmed by a Dutch television station.

The intruders, working over local telephone lines that enable them to tap American computer networks at almost no cost, have not done serious damage, Federal investigators say. And they have not penetrated the most secure Government computer systems. But they have entered a wide range of computers, including those at the Kennedy Space Center, the Pentagon's Pacific Fleet Command, the Lawrence Livermore National Laboratory and Stanford University using an international computer network known as the Internet.

While the information on these systems is not classified, the computers store a great variety of material, including routine memorandums, unpublished reports and data from experiments. Federal officials said the group had tampered with some information stored on systems they have illegally entered.

United States Government officials said that they had been tracking the interlopers, but that no arrests had been made because there are no legal restrictions in the Netherlands barring unauthorized computer access. Telephone calls to Dutch Government officials in the Netherlands and the United States seeking comment were not returned.

Although Markoff agreed not to name me, deep in the story he included a reference to my involvement:

The Dutch group was detected last year after an unusually skilled United States Government computer researcher at a national laboratory tracked its every move using advanced computer security techniques. He notified Federal authorities of the break-ins.

The researcher has been able to make computer records of the intruders' keystrokes as they have electronically prowled through United States military, NASA, university and dozens of other computers. It has then been possible to play this information back and gain an exact picture of the computer screen as it appeared to the intruders in the Netherlands.

The newspaper article and the ensuing clamor it created generated interest in my work within the government, and I eventually gave a number of presentations about Adrian and his attacks to various agencies. As part of these lectures, I prepared a videotape of some of Adrian's sessions so that people who weren't familiar with computers could understand exactly how system crackers worked, and to experience what it was like to watch a computer screen from over a cracker's shoulder. They would be able to see and hear, down to the bells that sounded on his terminal, what he saw and heard in real time. I had originally planned to use the extra soundtracks on the tape, one for snide comments on Adrian's techniques and the other for a laugh track. Unfortunately I never found the time or the budget.

The Adrian incident also provided me with a useful civics lesson. In the fall of 1991 I was in Washington, D.C., scheduled to show my Adrian tape to researchers at the General Accounting Office, whom Congress had ordered to investigate the break-ins. Just before I was to begin my presentation, however, Justice Department attorneys learned about the talk. They phoned the GAO and demanded I not present my tape, claiming it was part of their evidence in the case they were pursuing with the Dutch government. While I sat and waited inside a windowless conference room, three Justice Department attorneys sped across town in a taxi and confronted GAO lawyers, apparently concerned that I was about to embarrass the bureaucracy. I found the whole thing ridiculous—bureaucrats trying to coverup their lapses. In the end I was not allowed to give the presentation until several months later—and then only with officials from the Justice Department and FBI standing by.

The uproar over the Adrian incident helped push me toward computer security research, which in turn led me on a quest for better tools. One of the tools I modified for my work was a sophisticated piece of software called the Berkeley Packet Filter. Originally written by Van Jacobson and Steven McCanne at the federally funded Lawrence Berkeley Laboratories in 1990, it was designed for the simple task of monitoring computer network performance and debugging. The drawback was that it had been created for the existing generation of computer networks. Most businesses and research centers still use Ethernet. However, Ethernet is an aging standard, and by 1994 I found it necessary to create software that would be able to deal with much more advanced computer networks, such as those that use fiber optic cables and can reach speeds at least an order of magnitude faster than Ethernet. Today, most large commercial online services have internal fiber optic networks to handle the billions of bytes of data that circulate daily between their machines. The modified version of the BPF that I wrote was able to filter more than one hundred thousand packets a second, even when it was running on a Sun workstation several years old. Unlike the original BPF, my version was designed to bury itself inside the operating system of a computer and watch for certain information as it flowed through the computer from the Internet. When a packet from a certain address, or for that matter any other desired piece of information designated by the user flashed by, BPF would grab it and place it in a file where it could be kept for later viewing.

I had developed my initial version of the faster BPF in the expectation that I would receive additional research funding for the work from the National Security Agency. The Agency had begun supporting my work under a Los Alamos National Labs research grant in 1991, and had promised to extend their support for my work, but the funding was never forthcoming. I developed the tool, but after I completed the work, in early 1994, the bureaucrats in the agency reneged on funding.

The idea of working with the NSA is controversial in the community of security professionals and civil libertarians, many of whom regard the NSA as a high-tech castle of darkness.

Libertarian by inclination or by the influence of their colleagues, the nation's best computer hackers tend to possess a remarkable sensitivity to even the slightest hint of a civil liberties violation. They view with deep distrust the work of the National Security Agency, which has the twin missions of electronic spying around the globe and protecting the government's computer data. This distrust extends to anyone who works with the agency. Am I contaminated because I accepted research funding from the NSA? The situation reminds me of the scene in the movie *Dr. Strangelove* where General Jack D. Ripper is obsessed by the idea of his bodily fluids being contaminated. I think the idea of guilt by association is absurd.

My view is very different. First of all, I don't believe in classified research and so I don't do it. The work I was undertaking on packet-filtering tools was supposed to be funded by the agency for public release. The tools were to be made widely available to everyone, to use against the bad guys who were already using similar tools to invade people's privacy and compromise the security of machines on the Internet.

But even more to the point, I believe that the agency, rather than inherently evil, is essentially inept. Many people are frightened of the NSA, not realizing that it is like any other bureaucracy, with all of a bureaucracy's attendant failings. Because the NSA staff lives in a classified world, the government's normal system of checks and balances doesn't apply. But that doesn't mean that their technology outpaces the open computer world; it just means they're out of touch and ponderous.

In any case, I feel strongly that tools like BPF are absolutely essential if the Internet is to have real security, and if we are to have the ability to trace vandals through the Net. If people are concerned that individual privacy is at stake, they should probably worry less about who should have the right to monitor the networks, and instead focus their efforts on making cryptographic software widely available. If information is encrypted it doesn't matter who sees it if they can't read the code. Cryptography is another example of my point that a tool is just a tool. It was, after all, used primarily by kings, generals, and spies until only two decades ago. Then work done by scientists at Stanford, MIT, and UCLA, coupled with the advent of the inexpensive personal computer, made encryption software available to anyone. As a result, the balance of power is dramatically shifting away from the

NSA back toward the individual, and toward protecting our civil liberties.

In San Diego, while we prepared to go back on-line, our intruder continued to bait us, placing a second call on the afternoon of December 30. When I returned to my office and played back my voice mail, my antagonist was there again. The voice mail system told me that the message had been left only minutes earlier, at 2:35 P.M. It began with a howling sound, a little like a yowling cat—or was it a rooster crowing?—which then trailed off into an odd-sounding whine.

"Your security technique will be defeated," the message began, in a voice that sounded as if it might be a different person from the first caller. "Your technique is no good." A garbled sentence followed. I listened to it over and over again, but could make no sense of it.

It seemed the intruder had now figured out that we were off the Net, and he was trying to taunt us into making ourselves accessible. "These guys are being pretty cocky," I said to Andrew when I played the message for him. "Why don't they get a life?" Whoever it was—he, they—was trying to bait us, but I wasn't sure why. It seemed childish. At the same time I was relieved, for they obviously thought that they had gotten away clean, and it seemed possible that their overconfidence might increase their vulnerability in the future.

On New Year's Eve the two of us were at the Center working on the security router. We took a brief break to drive back to Andrew's apartment where his wife, Sarah, and a small group of friends were celebrating. The television was on, the champagne was passed, and finally the clock struck midnight. We stayed for a short while longer and then headed back to work. I coded laboriously for a couple of more hours and then at 3 A.M. went home to sleep, my part of the routing filter essentially complete.

I had been growing concerned about Julia, who was sounding more depressed each time we spoke. She hadn't left Toad Hall for days, and although she had been saying she was coming to visit me, she had missed a couple of flights. So the next day, because

Julia was still arguing with John over the idea of her coming to San Diego, I decided to fly north.

At around 8 P.M. Andrew drove me to the airport and I left him with a list of items to finish and loose ends to attend to. He told me he had hopes of going back to work that evening and pushing on. In the end, however, our pace caught up with him, for we had both been running on as few as four hours of sleep for five days. Andrew went home and directly to sleep and then slept the entire next day.

I flew to San Jose where I picked up a rental car and drove to San Francisco, stopping by Mark Lottor's on the way to pick up the skiing stuff I had left there on the morning of the twenty-seventh. My thought was to get Julia outdoors, whether it was for a day hike or a ski in the mountains, hoping that away from Toad Hall, she would have a chance to think about things from a fresh perspective. She had been a close friend for a long time, and I'd once made her a promise that if she was ever in a rut or feeling down, I would come and we would spend time together away from the city. She'd made the same promise to me.

By the time I got to the city it was past 11 P.M.. Julia and I met at our prearranged rendezvous point: Dan Farmer's flat on the Panhandle in the Haight-Ashbury district. Dan and I had been friends for a long time and we both had little respect for the established computer security world. He is a controversial security expert who would gain international attention in 1995 while he was working as a security specialist for Silicon Graphics, Inc., a Mountain View, California, workstation maker. The controversy was due to a security testing program named SATAN (Security Administrator Tool for Analyzing Networks) he coauthored with Venema, the Dutch security expert. SATAN was designed to automatically check for widely known computer system vulnerabilities so that system administrators would have a quick way of identifying and assessing the weaknesses of their own networks. Hoping to force computer security professionals out of their complacency, Dan was planning to make the program generally available over the Internet. This meant that all the crackers would have an easy way to prowl the Net looking for weak spots, and that all lazy computer system administrators who had not patched their systems would be at risk.

The imminent release of the final version of his program over the Internet, scheduled for April 1995, would create intense debate. Keeping computer security information closely held versus distributing it widely has always been a heated issue in computer security circles. Dan had obviously hoped to raise the heat by giving his program so demonic a name: SATAN.

Dan, an ex-Marine, also has a personal style that tweaks the more buttoned-down managerial types in Silicon Valley. Slightly built, but with bright red curly hair that falls past his shoulders, a penchant for black T-shirts and leather clothes, and studded with a variety of metal objects piercing various parts of his body, he does not match the stereotype of a computer geek. In early 1995 Silicon Graphics, in a fit of corporate cowardice and short-sightedness, decided to fire Dan just before he released the final version of SATAN. Several weeks later he was rehired by Sun, SGI's competitor, but the whole affair made such a big splash in Silicon Valley that SGI managed to lose doubly by getting bad press and losing Dan.

Julia and I talked late into the night; and she shared the depth of the anger and pain between John and her. Things had gotten much more stressful in the past week. It was becoming clear to Julia that things weren't working, yet I started to wonder whether there was something self-destructive in her unwillingness to end her relationship with him.

We were planning to hike in the Marin Headlands the next day, but John called in the morning looking for Julia. After talking to John she seemed even more unsettled and tense. The two of us walked over to a burrito shop on Haight Street, where I thought we were going to get food for our hike, but Julia insisted on taking lunch to John. We got the food, drove to Toad Hall, and I waited in the car and ate my burrito. Before long both of them emerged to go on our hike.

I had thought the point was for Julia to get away from the environment that she was feeling trapped by, but this was defeating the purpose of going hiking. It looked like the three of us were going to have to spend an awkward afternoon together, and I wondered, *why is she doing this?* On the way over to Marin I drove while Julia sat next to me and John sat in the backseat. The two of them kept snapping at each other, and I finally interrupted and said, "Will you two please cool it."

To an outsider the situation must have seemed very odd, but jealousy was never an issue for me with Julia. Despite the deepening frost in our friendship, John had long claimed that he himself wasn't jealous, but I had come to dismiss this as an effort to be politically correct because I thought he was acting possessive. It had been clear to me for a long time that nothing I did would change the ultimate outcome of their relationship. I wanted Julia to be able to decide for herself what she would do with her life. If I honestly didn't feel threatened, it was because in my heart I believed that it was Julia's decision to make, not mine.

When we reached the Headlands we parked the car and walked out the Tennessee Valley Trail to the beach. Julia and I had hiked there many times before, and I now stood by myself watching the waves crash, and listening to the surf, while John and Julia walked along the beach. It was foggy, windy, and chilly, adding to the gray mood that seemed to pervade everything. At the end of the day I went back to Dan's for the night, alone.

Over the next couple of days, however, Julia and I spent a lot of time together. One day we hiked near the Cliff House at a place called Land's End, a wild spot on the edge of the ocean with rocks, sea lions, and majestic cypress pines. We enjoyed each other's company, and she began to get away from the situation she had felt trapped by. Still, I could see she was afraid of antagonizing John, and I also realized that there wasn't much more that I could do to help her. I still wanted to go skiing, and so I made arrangements to catch a ride back to the mountains the next day with Emily Sklar.

That night I drove down to Menlo Park to visit Mark Lottor. He met me at San Francisco Airport, where I dropped off the rented car, and then we went hunting for nongreasy and relatively healthy fast food. I had been intending to do a lot of cross-country ski racing during the winter and so was trying to eat reasonably well, even while I was traveling. But after 10 P.M. on the Peninsula, that turned out to be an impossibility. We finally found a Jack-in-the-Box in Redwood City. I looked for a fish sandwich, which I will eat under duress, but it was not on the menu, so I ended up settling for french fries—not very healthy, but by that time it didn't matter. When we got to Mark's place, I was exhausted, but he wanted his own security router to protect against the type of IP-spoofing attacks I had described to him, and I had agreed to help him. The two of us worked into the early hours.

The next morning, Thursday January 5, I woke with a start at about eleven and saw that my pager had several messages from Emily, who lives in Palo Alto. She was panicking because she couldn't find me and wanted to get on the road to Truckee where she was scheduled to teach cross-country skiing that weekend.

Emily showed up ten minutes later in a pickup truck loaded with wood to heat the cabin. We threw my skis in the back and headed for the Sierra. For the moment I was free from being concerned about Julia, and free from my intruder. As friends, Emily and I were comfortable talking about all kinds of things, and as the daughter of two therapists, she had useful insights about relationships. Her suggestion in this case was that I get away from the situation for a while—advice that seemed reasonable, and, under the circumstances, easily practicable.

It was raining on the way up through Sacramento, and by Auburn, in the foothills, the rain had turned to snow. Chain control was in force, but the storm was starting to let up. We stopped for supplies in Auburn at Ikeda's, the funky roadside fast food restaurant/natural food grocery store that has hamburgers, which I don't eat, but also has good milk shakes, french fries, and fresh and dried fruit and nuts, which I do. When we got to Truckee, I bought a pizza for dinner in town, which ended up being stone cold by the time we got to the cabin fifteen minutes later. Because it was late, we unloaded only our essential ski gear and computer equipment. Inside, the cabin was freezing, and so I lit a fire, then heated the pizza in the oven and ate it while Emily, who was allergic to dairy products, made her own dinner.

We skied only a little bit on Friday, but when the storm finally passed on Saturday, we took advantage of the fresh snow by spending the day on the trails. It was a great workout after a long period of no exercise and little sleep, and I was grateful to be able to forget the past two weeks.

I hadn't been checking my San Diego voice mail regularly

because the phone in the cabin had been flaky when we moved in, but when I finally did call in, there was a phone message from Becky Bace, a computer scientist at the NSA. At that point the agency had zero credibility with me because of its total failure to come through with funding for a computer security group they had encouraged me to establish. But Becky, my main contact in the information security section of the agency, who seemed to have been caught in the middle of an unresponsive organization, was still trying to make it happen.

For months she had also been trying to persuade me to come to the Computer Misuse and Anomaly Detection (CMAD) Conference, an annual conference on computer security and intrusion detection that the agency cosponsored each year with the Air Force Information Warfare Center. I'd been refusing, for I didn't want to speak and I was fed up with dealing with the agency. But she had kept sweetening the offer, and this year, instead of being held on the University of California at Davis campus, as the previous two had been, the conference would be at the Sonoma Mission Inn Spa and Resort.

Usually I quickly become bored with academic and theoretical discussions of computer security, but now, in the wake of the break-in, it seemed there was a chance to talk about something that was more interesting, and better yet, to use our data to describe exactly what had transpired. One of the areas of computer crime detection that is still in a relatively primitive state is methodology. For hundreds of years people have been investigating physical crimes, and while some of forensics is still a black art, there are well-established methods for investigating crime scenes and finding evidence. In the digital world, however, there is still very little in the way of formal detection methodology.

I called Becky back and she again offered an invitation to the conference. "Why don't you just come and hang out in the hot tub?" she said. "You don't even have to give a talk, just chat with people." I told her I wasn't interested in freeloading, but said that I now thought that I might be interested in attending, and speaking, after all. She was delighted, and she closed the conversation by saying she hadn't given up on the idea of the computer security research team, adding they were on the verge of getting the funding approved. "Yeah, sure you will," I responded.

But she had been prepared, at least, to pay my conference expenses, and throw in an honorarium. I hadn't told her what I planned to speak about, but the last thing I said was that I would bring "a surprise."

Later that day there was another message on the UCSD voice mail system. This one consisted of a haunting melody, as if someone were playing the soundtrack to a suspense thriller I didn't recognize. It continued for thirty seconds and then ended abruptly. It was the kind of music that is designed to make you cast a glance over your shoulder to see if anyone is stalking you. Was someone? Was my intruder still waiting out there for me to let my guard down? I had no way of knowing, but he seemed to be reminding me he was still in the hunt. If so, he would have to find an even more sophisticated trick for sneaking into my system.

After I left San Francisco, Julia and I spoke often and it was easy for me to see that she needed to get away from the setting she was trapped in, so I invited her to join me at the CMAD conference. A hot springs resort would give her an opportunity to unwind. The conference began during the midst of the biggest California floods in a century, particularly in Sonoma County. We arrived at the Sonoma Mission Inn on Tuesday January 10, in time for an evening reception and wandered around sampling food from a Mexican buffet and chatting with people I hadn't seen for some time. In addition to computer security professionals there were contingents from the military and the government intelligence community. Being around people in the spy world is always an odd experience, because you're never certain they are actually who they say they are. In the rest of the world there usually are sanity checks that tell you when you're off base, but in the classified, fantasy world of intelligence, such cues often don't exist, and it's easy for some of these people to stray far from reality.

I introduced Julia to Blaine Burnham, who manages in the information security section of the NSA. He shook Julia's hand and intoned meaningfully, "I've heard a lot about you," as if somebody who worked at a Big Brother agency might reasonably be expected to have a dossier on all in attendance at a cocktail party. She was immediately on guard and paranoid, and we quickly moved on.

The computer security world is actually a remarkably close and inbred community, and many of the big names in the field were at the conference. It's not a world I'm directly a part of but one in which I like to show up every once in a while, drop a few bombshells, and leave. The problem with conferences like CMAD is that they're emblematic of the generally sad condition of computer security. At any of these events the attendees are more often than not inclined to put their heads in the sand and refuse to acknowledge they're seeing an increasing sophistication in the attacks.

A lot of users who have old computer systems have decided that, rather than fundamentally redesigning them to make them more secure, they will purchase a black box to sit between their computers and the outside world, giving them the illusion of protection. As a result, a lot of money is spent on building automated "intrusion detection" systems, which are derived from artificial intelligence software that looks for what it suspects is "anomalous behavior" on the part of users, and then sets off alarms. Much effort is also directed toward trying to replace very expensive security officers who actually look through records, with a program that tries to do the same thing.

We ran into Bill Cheswick, the Bell Labs researcher who had monitored Adrian/Berferd several years earlier and who is a recognized expert in computer firewalls. I knew him through phone conversations and e-mail, but we had never actually met. He has a round face, curly hair, and is slightly portly without actually being heavy. I teased him about showing up at this posh resort, and he responded this was more fun than being stuck in his office in New Jersey in the middle of winter.

I've always had a great deal of respect for Ches, as he's called, who has a great sense of humor and enthusiasm. Both of us had grown up in the computer hacker world, where an adventure game called Zork was one of the first text-based games that emerged on mainframe computers in the late 1970s. Like many such games, Zork created a series of imaginary underground caves through which you hunted by typing commands at the keyboard representing East, West, North, South, Up, and Down. It had no graphics, but that didn't really matter, since the best graphics are in your head. The currency of Zork was Zorkmids, and it was Ches who had introduced me to the idea of thinking of Zorkmids as the generic representation for money, rather than dollars. There is usually too much emotion tied to dollars, he reasoned, but not to Zorkmids. People might be greedy with dollars, but never with Zorkmids. Ches had noted (only partly in jest, I think) that for hackers the point of large corporations was to provide enough Zorkmids so you could continue to play the game.

Ches was also the author of the definitive computer security text on firewalls, written with Steve Bellovin, who ironically, was also the author of the influential paper that described IP spoofing in 1989. Ches told me that in his own presentation earlier that day he had mentioned spoofing, noting that it had never been seen "in the wild."

One of the other people I ran into that first evening was Tom Longstaff, who is one of the best technical people at the Computer Emergency Response Team, a government-funded organization at Carnegie Mellon University in Pittsburgh. CERT, as it is known, was set up in 1989 in the wake of the Robert Tappan Morris Internet worm episode. It's mission is to gather and disseminate timely information about security problems around the Internet, but they tend to work with a bureaucratic caution that belies the "emergency" in their name. I've always had the sense is that he is a person who wants to do the right thing but frequently has his hands tied by the organization for which he works. I had tried to contact him in December after my break-in, but we had missed making connections. As I described the IP-spoofing attack to him he was clearly intrigued, and I promised I would give the complete technical description in my talk the following day.

I showed up downstairs the next morning with my RDI PowerLite and my ice ax. The laptop had the notes for my talk, and I was actually going to use the ice ax as a pointer, to drive home my point that tools are tools. I wasn't going to actually refer to the ax but instead hoped that its mere presence would make people wonder what this tool was for, and maybe they'd get my idea.

I had wanted to connect my computer directly to an overhead projector and the hotel's audiovisual system, but the conference organizers hadn't been able to find any audiovisual equipment on short notice. I was scheduled to speak after the first break, and during the break I scrambled around and created transparencies to talk from, although most of them were just screen shots of directories or lists of commands.

I titled my talk "What I Did During My Christmas Vacation," a tongue-in-cheek joke for those who knew me. I'm not a person who attaches much importance to Christmas, which I usually refer to as "winter break."

Even though the topic of IP spoofing was potentially a dry one, I could feel the level of interest in the room pick up, because I was the first one at the meeting to describe a real break-in and not some theoretical computer security problem. I wanted to show how the investigation was actually carried out, describing in detail how I followed the trail. I noted that the attack appeared to be scripted or automated, based on the timing of events. That was a significant factor, because if the attack was packaged as a program, it was likely that it could be used by people with no special technical skills who were simply part of the network of underground bulletin boards and Internet conferencing systems that traffic in this kind of information. It's not that there is a tightly knit conspiracy out there; it's just that crackers talk to each other and they are not bound by the rules of a bureaucracy with a cover-your-ass mentality. Their existence ensures that any new flaw or security loophole that is discovered is known by the computer underground much more quickly than by the computer security establishment, where people don't communicate as effectively.

The fact that it had taken a great deal of detailed analysis for me to reconstruct the break-in was something that clearly hit home with the audience. The situation I was describing was the type of attack that might have been going on undetected beneath their own noses all along. The implication of my talk was that people might have doors with huge locks, but there's a small space between the door and the floor that bad guys can just slip right through.

I then played the two voice mail messages I had stored as digital files on my notebook computer. When my computer speaker emitted that cheesy accent, it was so distorted that it was difficult to make out the exact words, but people got the idea that someone had singled me out. Many computer security types have gotten their heads buried so far in the sand that they've forgotten there are real enemies out there. *Me and my friends, we'll kill you.* In front of an audience of computer professionals the voice was chilling. There was silence in the room while I waited for questions.

My point had been that this was a general vulnerability affecting much of the Internet, because so much of it relies on address-based authentication—electronic mail, for example. If I send you an electronic mail message, for example, how do you know it's really me? It's the same as if you received a postcard in the mail—you might recognize the handwriting, but that is the only clue you have as to whether the message has been forged. The addressing scheme that underlies the Internet had never been intended to be used for authentication. It is possible to fool it in many ways by masquerading as a trusted computer. The Internet's job is simply to make sure that packets get from here to there, not to provide authentication, and this attack showed the system was all too vulnerable to subversion. You merely trust that the address is accurate and the sender is who he or she claims to be. The attack on my machines demonstrated that low-level Internet protocols, the basic packaging for network communications, are wide open and can be exploited. To guard completely against this kind of subversion would require an exhaustive reengineering of these basic protocols of the Internet.

The last question from the audience was, "Do you have any idea who did this to you?"

"Not really," I replied.

After the panel a woman came up and introduced herself to me as Martha Stansell-Gamm. I remembered her from a law enforcement event a few years earlier. With her blond hair tied back in a bun and very conservatively dressed, Marty looked businesslike. She worked in the Justice Department computer crime unit and asked me if I had told the FBI about the break-in. I told her I hadn't and explained that in the past I hadn't had very good luck dealing with the Bureau. Things had gotten dropped, and so I hadn't even considered calling them this time.

"Tsutomu, I'm surprised to hear this," she said. "I'll make sure that we're more responsive in the future." She promised to have someone call me about the incident. Although she said she hadn't been able to follow all of the technical details of my description, I got the sense that she had a sharp mind and wasn't going to act like a bureaucrat.

After chatting with Marty I bumped in to Jim Settle, a stocky, square-shouldered FBI agent who had once run the Bureau's computer crime squad. He'd left the Bureau and was now working for I-Net, a computer security contractor in the Washington, D.C., area. In 1991, while Settle was still with the Bureau, I'd lectured at one of his agent-training sessions and showed my Adrian tapes to give them some idea of what an attack looks like. At the time I got the impression he was slightly put off or didn't know what to make of me. Now he was friendly and said he thought he might have some idea who was behind the attack. I mentioned the Oki phone software and said we had some suspicion that it might be Kevin Mitnick, because we were pretty sure he'd tried to steal it from Mark Lottor. But Settle doubted it was Mitnick, because of the technical skill involved, and instead he suggested it might be some crackers that he had heard of operating out of Philadelphia.

After the panel, as I spoke with members of the audience, I began to realize the attendees at the conference seemed to take this vulnerability seriously, but I sensed there would be no easy way to get their organizations to do the same thing. I had a long chat with Tom Longstaff who acknowledged that IP spoofing was a significant problem, but said that he thought it unlikely that he could persuade CERT to issue an advisory because of the politics surrounding the situation on publicizing vulnerabilities. As a government-funded agency, CERT has always been tremendously conservative and afraid to step on anybody's toes. If they issued an advisory warning about the danger of IP address spoofing they would have to list the names of the manufacturers whose equipment was vulnerable, a step that was politically very sensitive.

Later, after dinner and lots of wine, I was talking to Bill Cheswick and Marcus Ranum, another skilled computer security specialist, about CERT's passivity, and Marcus came up with the idea of not waiting for CERT, but going ahead and publishing the details of the vulnerability on our own. I saw Longstaff and we went over to him.

"What would you do if we released a forged CERT advisory, detailing the problem and warning about it?" I asked him.

"I guess we'd have to print a retraction," he replied, and then added with a laugh, "If it's a really good posting maybe we'd just distribute it."

He explained it would be very difficult to create an accurate forgery because CERT digitally signed each advisory with an authentication number generated using Pretty Good Privacy (PGP), the free encryption system written by Philip Zimmermann. I pointed out that even if everyone knew that it was a forgery, a faked advisory would accomplish the same purpose of alerting people to the problem. By the end of our conversation I had the feeling that Longstaff wouldn't have minded us trying to pull off a forgery, but there was no way he was going to encourage us.

Julia and I spent much of the last day of the conference playing hookey, because a conference at the Sonoma Mission Inn was too good a junket to waste by spending the entire time in a darkened meeting room. I did stop in for one talk being given by Marty about how the Digital Telephony Act, which President Clinton had signed into law the previous October, had given on-line service and Internet providers the ability to monitor the keystrokes of the people communicating over their systems. It was anathema to privacy rights groups, but an important tool that was absolutely vital for tracking intruders.

In the afternoon we decided to go out to soak in the hot tub, and we bumped into Marty again. At this point there was nothing businesslike about her, in her one-piece blue bathing suit. Initially she was a bit sheepish because she, like we, knew the conference wasn't over yet, but like us, she was probably bored stiff. She explained that she was taking a hot tub to be fully relaxed, because she was flying directly home to Washington, where she would have to deal with her children, including a sick baby, and her husband, who was tired of taking care of the family in her absence.

It was raining lightly, which gave the whole hot tub area a wonderful misty quality. We chatted about the day's presentations. Marty said that in February the Justice Department was planning a seminar in San Diego on the legal issues relating to computer crime. The department wanted to round up all of the assistant United States attorneys who had been given responsibility for the area. She invited me to the training session, and I said I would be glad to come and speak about technology.

Although rain began falling quite heavily, we were too content to move and through the Sonoma mist we began talking about my break-in. Marty couldn't understand why we weren't being more aggressive in tracking down what we had from packet traffic we'd logged from Ariel. "We had interesting pointers leading back to places like Colorado SuperNet and Loyola University in Chicago," I told her. "But we don't have any resources, so I haven't been able to follow up and pursue anything." I explained that I'd been trying to put a computer security research team together for months but had been stalled entirely by NSA's delay in funding us. "I'm tired of banging my head against the bureaucracy and getting nowhere," I said. "I'm burned out."

"But Tsutomu, this is a new area of law," she replied. "It's important that we find test cases and play them all the way out."

The conference was almost over and we all decided we should make a final appearance as things broke up. As we were getting out of the tub I turned and said, "I'd love to push this thing further but I don't have any really strong leads. Based on the data taken I suspect that Kevin Mitnick might be behind this. But I don't have any hard evidence. And from what I know, this kind of an attack is really beyond his technical capability."

CHAPTER 7

Late Thursday afternoon Julia and I left the CMAD conference, and stopped to visit a friend of hers in Fairfax on our way back to San Francisco. The rain kept falling, and I kept regretting the snow in the Sierras that I wasn't getting to ski, but for the moment I was distracted by the fact that the world around us had been transformed into a fantastic, mist-shrouded landscape. For anyone who has grown up in the East, much of California always has this arid desert quality except in places like Marin County where, at the height of the rainy season, the world turns a shimmering emerald green.

On the hour-long drive down to Fairfax I was still thinking about the discussions I'd had with Tom Longstaff about whether CERT should issue a security advisory on IP spoofing. By keeping this kind of information secret from computer systems managers, whom did these guys think they were helping? It was likely that within a month the details of the break-in would be widespread in the computer underground anyway, making copycat attacks inevitable. The only people who wouldn't know about it would be those responsible for actually protecting the security of computers on the Internet.

This is stupid, I thought to myself, even though there didn't seem to be anything I could do about the situation. And, in a sense, it wasn't my problem. I'd gotten up in front of some of the nation's leading computer security experts and given a report on the exact mechanism of the attack. Now CERT was being CERT, slow-moving and cautious, and if I was frustrated, it was in the face of an unfortunately typical situation.

After a Mexican dinner in Fairfax, we drove back to San Francisco to pick up Julia's car, a 1987 Mazda hatchback, which had sat in front of Toad Hall for several months while she had trekked in Nepal. She followed me down to the airport to drop off our rented Oldsmobile, and on our way back the Mazda's engine began making an ominous grinding noise. We limped home and spent the night at Dan Farmer's.

In the morning I checked the oil, which didn't even register on the dipstick, and so we eased the car to a quick-change oil place on Divisadero. We learned later that John had loaned the car to a number of people while Julia was away, and no one had bothered to maintain it. She was livid. Although it had more than 135,000 miles on it, she'd always taken good care of the car, but now the engine sounded as if it might be permanently damaged.

Afterward, the engine sounded sick, but was still functioning, so we loaded the car with ski gear and took off, hoping to beat the Friday ski traffic to the mountains. At the cabin the driveway was full of new snow, and although it took a half hour of shoveling before we could get the car parked, I was glad I was finally going to get some skiing in.

The next three days were a pure escape, as Julia and I skied and talked, and spent the evenings making large dinners with Emily.

On Tuesday night, however, I had a phone message from Tom Longstaff. The next morning I returned his call, and he told me that there had been more break-ins around the Internet, using the IP-spoofing trick.

"What were the targets?" I inquired.

"Tsutomu, I'm sorry, you know that's information that CERT keeps confidential. I can't tell you."

"Well, let's approach this differently," I said. "Why don't I tell you *where* I think the attacks came from."

I checked my notes and said: "I'll bet that your new attacks have come from apollo.it.luc.edu at the Loyola University in Chicago."

I was right—it matched—and I asked how it had happened.

As with the open portal between Osiris and Ariel, someone's session had been hijacked. But in this case the user had actually been sitting at his machine and could see that someone had taken over his session. His network manager, who had been alerted that the attack was unfolding, was able to capture the intruder's every data packet. This information had allowed him to precisely reconstruct the attack.

I asked Tom if this new incident had changed CERT's mind, and if they were now actually ready to put out an advisory. He would say only that they were still considering it, but the implication was that there might finally be enough ammunition with which to act.

After we hung up I pondered what the new attacks might mean. It seemed clear that IP spoofing presented a significant vulnerability to the entire Internet community. There were thousands of computer sites where trust between two computers in a local network was a convenient, established fact, and now all of them were at risk. I couldn't stand by any longer and wonder when CERT was going to take action. This was something that people should know about. But how to do it? It occurred to me that John Markoff at the *Times* had asked me to call him when I heard about things that might be significant stories. Since we had first talked in 1991 about Adrian, Markoff and I had exchanged information regularly about computer security and the Internet. We had actually met face-to-face several years earlier at one of the Hackers' conferences and discovered we both liked being in the wilderness, and we had gone on a couple of long backcountry ski trips together. Markoff had come to rely on me for technical expertise in his writing about the Internet and cryptography, and I found him a useful source of news and gossip. Markoff had told me he wasn't interested in garden-variety computer crime stories, only in cases in which some larger issue was involved, as in the case of the Dutch computer cracker who was operating beyond the reach of United States law. IP spoofing, which was an insidious weakness in the basic fabric of the Internet, seemed to be a perfect candidate. Even if CERT was bound by its organizational guidelines, I figured I was free to talk about my presentation. There were more than fifty people who had listened to my talk at CMAD, and any one of them could have told a newspaper reporter about it. I might as well call one myself.

I reached Markoff at his office and told him about my CMAD presentation and gave him a brief explanation of IP spoofing. I warned him that CERT was still considering producing an advisory, and that he should probably call them to ask when it was going to be released. We agreed that he wouldn't tell the CERT people who had told him about my paper, but since he knew at least a half-dozen people who had been at the conference it wasn't likely to be an issue.

Two days later, on Thursday January 19, Marty Stansell-Gam called to say that she had instructed the FBI to contact me. The next day, Richard Ress, an FBI agent from Washington, left a long message asking about the break-in and apologizing for my past problems with the Bureau. When I returned the call, he resumed where his message had left off, delivering a five-minute monologue about how the FBI had run into difficulties in dealing with computer crime, and how they were going to change the way they dealt with it. He acknowledged that the Bureau realized that it had been unresponsive to me before, and now they wanted to do everything possible to be more helpful in the future. It sounded great, but I'd heard such promises before.

Later that day Andrew spoke with Marty and then to Levord Burns, the FBI's top computer crime field agent. I'd worked with Burns in the past on previous break-ins, and thought of him as a good law enforcement agent in the wrong job, for he knew little about computers or technology. In his call Andrew had described the particulars of our situation to Burns and then sent him a fax outlining generally what we had learned about it.

Markoff had been working on his story during the week and had been negotiating with CERT over when it would be printed. In the end, he agreed to postpone his story, after CERT officials argued that publishing on Friday would give intruders an entire weekend in which to experiment while network managers were away from their systems.

I went skiing late on Saturday. It was growing dark, and the snow was icy, which meant very fast skiing. Only the stragglers were still on Tahoe Donner's winding, dipping trails, and I was alone for much of the time. As I skied it occurred to me that the NSA would likely be dismayed by the *Times* article, because any publicity tends to offend them. I stopped briefly at a warming hut and I called Becky Bace to alert her, figuring that with her independent streak, she might be amused by the whole thing. In a field that is notable for its lack of women, she sometimes refers to herself as the "mother of computer security." At thirty-nine, she seems to have been around long enough to have become a fixture of sorts and to know everyone.

I reached her at home, and as I had suspected she *was* actually amused by the prospect of CMAD's getting some attention. Here, she remarked, was this obscure academic conference that never gets any consideration outside of a tiny community of academics, military, and intelligence people, and now one of its presentations was going to be written up in the *New York Times*. In the fading afternoon light I skied home wondering how things would unfold.

Markoff's story, which the *Times* first released on its newswires on Sunday evening, was given prominent placement on the front page of Monday's paper.

Data Network Is Found Open To New Threat

By John Markoff, Special to The New
York Times

SAN FRANCISCO, Jan. 22—A Federal computer security agency has discovered that unknown intruders have developed a new way to break into computer systems, and the agency plans on Monday to advise users how to guard against the problem.

The new form of attack leaves many of the 20 million government, business, university and home computers on the global Internet vulnerable to eavesdropping and theft. Officials say that unless computer users take the complicated measures they will prescribe, intruders could copy or destroy documents or even operate undetected by posing as an authorized user of the system.

For computer users, the problem is akin to homeowners discovering that burglars have master keys to all the front doors in the neighborhood.

The first known attack using the new technique took place on Dec. 25 against the computer of a well-known computer security expert at the San Diego

Supercomputer Center. An unknown individual or group took over his computer for more than a day and electronically stole a large number of security programs he had developed.

Since then several attacks have been reported, and there is no way of knowing how many others may have occurred. Officials of the Government-financed Computer Emergency Response Team say that the new assaults are a warning that better security precautions will have to be taken before commerce comes to the Internet, a worldwide web of interconnected computers that exchange electronic messages, documents and computer programs.

The article went on to identify me by name and refer to my CMAD talk. While several years earlier this kind of story would have been buried in the back pages, if it appeared at all, the Internet had now become big news.

Although CERT had told Markoff that its own release would be issued early Monday morning, the advisory document, which told of the attacks and summarized the defensive steps that computer systems managers should take, wasn't actually circulated until 2:30 P.M. Eastern Standard Time—almost nineteen hours after the *Times* story hit the newswires. That delay led to a great deal of consternation on the part of many systems managers, who were upset that they were first learning about Internet security flaws from the news media. Still, the fact that a relatively arcane matter like IP spoofing was suddenly a page-one story had a beneficial side effect: usually, CERT advisories go to system administrators who typically are too busy to deal with the problems but in this case the highest corporate executives were hearing about the vulnerability in a form they could understand, and so there was pressure from the top down.

I later found out the reason for the CERT delay. The group had decided to circulate a draft of the advisory before making a public release about the problem and it had been confusing to many people who weren't able to figure out how IP spoofing differed from another class of problems referred to as "source routing attacks." Source routing involves a similar vulnerability to IP spoofing that enables an attacker to specify a path through the Internet to ensure that each data packet returning from a target machine is first routed through an attacking computer. Because it is such a well-known weakness, many traffic routing computers on the Internet no longer permit source routing. So CERT had taken extra time to rework the final release.

The CERT document, which thanked Bellovin, Cheswick, me, and three other people for contributing to understanding the problem, began with a three-paragraph introduction:

January 23, 1995

IP Spoofing Attacks and Hijacked Terminal Connections

The CERT Coordination Center has received reports of attacks in which intruders create packets with spoofed source IP addresses. These attacks exploit applications that use authentication based on IP addresses. This exploitation leads to user and possibly root access on the targeted system. Note that this attack does not involve source routing. Recommended solutions are described in Section III below.

In the current attack pattern, intruders may dynamically modify the kernel of a Sun 4.1.X system once root access is attained. In this attack, which is separate from the IP spoofing attack, intruders use a tool to take control of any open terminal or login session from users on the system. Note that although the tool is currently being used primarily on SunOS 4.1.x systems, the system features that make this attack possible are not unique to SunOS.

As we receive additional information relating to this advisory, we will place advisories and their associated README files are available by anonymous FTP from info.cert.org. We encourage you to check the README files regularly for updates on advisories that relate to your site.

The day the *Times* story appeared, SDSC was flooded with telephone calls. When Robert Borchers, the National Science

Foundation's program manager for the five supercomputer centers—SDSC's patron saint, in other words—called to find out what was going on, the person answering the phone didn't know who he was, and so routed him to the public relations contact, who didn't recognize his name, either. Borchers was passed to a series of SDSC employees who had all been instructed to say nothing, before he finally got in touch with Sid. Borchers was not pleased, but luckily he has a sense of humor.

By mid-morning, SDSC had received more than forty calls from the news media alone, and I ended up spending much of the day in my cabin responding to reporters and people in the Internet community anxious to learn more about the incident. I talked by phone to the Associated Press, Reuters, *USA Today*, *The Wall Street Journal*, and the *Philadelphia Inquirer*, and by e-mail with CNN, a news organization I've always admired because it's difficult to slant your coverage when it is being viewed everywhere in the world. I handled these inquiries and several others, and asked Ann Redelfs, SDSC's public relations person, to deal with the rest. Steve Bellovin, the researcher who had written the original paper describing IP-spoofing attacks, sent e-mail asking for more details. But I also heard from many clueless makers of computer security products, who, even though they had no idea what IP spoofing was, were quite certain that their hardware or software would protect us. It's very easy to propose solutions when you don't know what the problem is.

From what I'd heard, a lot of the staff at the Center were very uptight about the situation, believing that the worst thing in the world was to have your security breach reported on the front page of the *New York Times*. Sid, too, was concerned about the negative publicity, but he generally took the matter well, telling me the only thing he regretted was not having notified Bob Borchers ahead of time. As far as I was concerned, it was a good thing we had been able to figure out what had happened, as opposed to the many sites that had probably been broken into without the system administrator's even noticing.

I got out for a short ski in the afternoon, and when I returned Julia and I decided that with her assistance—technical writing is one of her talents—I should write something that described the attack in technical detail. The cabin was filled with the gray light of a midwinter late afternoon. Outside a gentle snow was falling, diffusing the lights from the ski lift across the valley, discernible through the living room picture window. Neither of us had bothered to get up to turn on what few lights the cabin had, and I sat at the dining room table huddling over the soft glow of the screen on my portable.

My pager buzzed, which surprised me, because it had never received a page at the cabin before, and in any case I had always assumed it was out of range. I reached over, picked it up, and in the gloom peered at the display.

The digits read 911911, the emergency code, repeated.

"Odd," I said to Julia, showing her the tiny screen. I set it down. Seconds later it buzzed again, and the same six digits appeared again.

Why would someone page me with 911? We looked at each other, through the deepening gloom. Almost no one had my pager number, which changes frequently, but among my stolen files was a back-up "image" of the memory inside my cell phone, which contained a directory that included my pager number. Was this another message from the same person who had been leaving me the cryptic voice mail? I set the pager on the table, and watched as every half-minute or so it buzzed on the hard surface like a rattlesnake for ten or fifteen seconds, each time producing that same eerie string of digits, 911911, as if someone were warning me to call for help. Here we were, deep in the Sierras, in a remote cabin: If they knew my pager number, what else did they know?

I called PageNet, the pager company to which I subscribed, and told them someone was harassing me, and asked them to attempt to trace the phone calls. Julia and I watched the pager continue to jitter on the table, until I finally reached over and shut it off. I didn't feel fear, just the spooky sense that someone could now really badger me if they wanted to.

We didn't get started on our writing project until about 10 P.M., after dinner, but by 3:30 in the morning we had a detailed document, which I planned to post on Usenet. Unlike the CERT advisory, which carefully left out any of the names of organizations who had suffered break-ins, I was not going to change the names to protect the guilty.

The Usenet, which predates the Internet by a few years, began as an anarchic messaging system for many of the world's Unix-based computers, which were originally linked mostly by regular telephone lines and modems. From the beginning, the Usenet was organized into news groups where people could post and read messages pertaining to the group's designated subject matter. Now there are more than twelve thousand different groups where people can discuss every subject imaginable. I planned to post my report to three news groups where security issues were discussed regularly—comp.security.misc, comp.protocols.tcp-ip, and alt.security—when I got back to San Diego.

The title of my message was "Technical details of the attack described by Markoff in NYT." It began: "Greetings from Lake Tahoe. There seems to be a lot of confusion about the IP address spoofing and connection hijacking attacks described by John Markoff's 1/23/95 NYT article and CERT advisory CA-95:01. Here are some technical details from my presentation on 1/11/95 at CMAD 3 in Sonoma, California. Hopefully this will help clear up any misunderstandings as to the nature of these attacks." The posting then detailed the attack blow by blow, starting with initial probes from toad.com, the computer in John Gilmore's basement, and winding up with the hijacking of Osiris.

While Julia and I were working I called Andrew in San Diego. We talked about his work improving our software security perimeter, and his conversations with Levord Burns of the FBI, and I told him about the flurry of 911 pages.

There was a long pause on the other end of the line.

Finally, Andrew said quietly: "Tsutomu, that was me. I just added you to the list of alert phone numbers. There was a bug in the filtering router code I was setting up that made it trigger when it shouldn't have." He had been building alarms in our defensive software to automatically send pages if a break-in was attempted. The digits 911911 were his unmistakable way of indicating an emergency.

In one sense it was a relief to know the reason my pager had been behaving like a rattlesnake, but I was exasperated, and thought to myself, *Andrew, that's why I'm the adviser, and you're the graduate student.*

Early Tuesday morning, after getting about three hours of sleep, Julia and I drove to the Reno airport in miserable weather. She was taking the United Express 9:35 flight to San Francisco and I was flying Reno Air to San Diego at 11:20. It had been an enjoyable ten days of working, playing, and sharing each other's company, but now we had to make our farewells at her departure gate. She was heading back to see John because she had promised to speak to him that morning. But she was reluctant to go and told me she was feeling scared, yet she felt she needed to honor her commitment. I had no idea when we would see each other again, and I felt concerned, since the last time she had gone to Toad Hall she had been miserable and it had been very hard for her to get away. As she walked to her plane, I waved to her through the large plate glass window and watched her plane taxi onto the runway.

After her flight had left I went to check in for my own flight and while I waited I pulled out my RadioMail terminal, the wireless modem connected to my Hewlett Packard 100 palmtop computer that allows me to send and receive electronic mail in every major city in the country. It took almost an hour for the RadioMail unit to suck in the unusually large number of messages that had been queued for me. One was from a mailing list that I'm on for a bunch of my former Caltech classmates, and it mentioned that there was an article about a Shimomura on the front page of *USA Today*. Then somebody else sent me a note saying, "Are you the same guy?" I sent back a note: "Yeah, I'm the same guy, and finding your name in the *New York Times* like this is a lousy thing to have happen in the middle of your ski vacation."

When I got to San Diego I made an appearance at a meeting of the senior fellows at SDSC, and then spent some time returning more calls from reporters. Andrew meanwhile was dealing with campus security people and had also contacted the FBI to see if we could get a trap-and-trace order on my office telephone. We figured that our intruder was likely to call again, and if he did, we wanted to know where he was calling from.

On Tuesday afternoon I realized I'd been sitting all day and decided that if I couldn't ski, at least I'd go skating, and went for a 25-kilometer skate around Lake Miramar, where an informal group of in-line speed-skaters gathers every evening. Whatever kind of privacy I'd enjoyed in the past seemed to be vanishing, but among this pack of two dozen skaters I could remain anonymous.

When I got home later that night, I decided to add one final touch to my break-in report before posting it to Usenet. I had previously made digitized files of the "We'll kill you" and the "Your technique is no good" voice mail messages left by my intruder, and now I was going to make them publicly available. SDSC operated an Internet site permitting ftp computer file transfers. The site contained free software available under a variety of headings and I had Andrew put the voice mail messages in a directory that we named pub/security/sounds/—a not so veiled reference to Usenet distribution categories of similar redeeming value like alt.sex.sounds. He named the two files tweedledee.au and tweedledum.au, the "au" indicating audio files for downloaders' listening pleasure. I added a note about the files in my "Technical details" report, and finally posted it to Usenet at 4 A.M.

Tweedledee.au and tweedledum.au enjoyed a brief popularity on the Internet audio charts. The *San Jose Mercury News* created a World Wide Web page link to the files from their *Mercury Center* Internet service, and *Newsweek* included quotes from them in its article about the break-in. I was guessing that my intruder, like many people, read the newspapers and news magazines, and would probably be feeling pretty pleased with himself about the attention his handiwork was receiving. Maybe I could bait him into calling again, and if he did, maybe we could spring our telephone tracing trap on him.

I had been playing phone tag with David Bank, a *San Jose Mercury News* reporter who covered telecommunications, and I finally talked to him in the afternoon. He told me he was having trouble finding my Usenet posting, so I sent him a copy via e-mail, and thought nothing more about it. Several days after he read my report about the initial toad.com attack, he called John Gilmore to ask about it. John told Bank I'd actually been at Toad Hall when the attack on my San Diego machines occurred. Bank began to investigate a scenario in which, as part of my funding dispute with the NSA, I had broken into my own computers to generate material for the CMAD talk. The premise was that a phony attack of my own invention would give me an opportunity to show off my skills to my potential sponsors. The flaw in the theory was that everyone knew that I was friends with Julia and John. Why would I be stupid enough to fake an attack, then publish information that would point almost directly back to me? But Bank, who was a persistent former metro reporter at the *Mercury News*, began to dog my trail, calling all kinds of people who knew me, in an effort to prove his hypothesis.

The real trail lay elsewhere and gradually the first indications of it were starting to appear. On January 17, while I was at Truckee, SDSC received an e-mail from Liudvikas Bukys, a computer system administrator at the University of Rochester. The last paragraph of his note warned that the Center might have severe problems if it didn't already know about the break-ins, for security managers at Rochester had found pointers back to my network while they were investigating a break-in of their own. Andrew had talked to the Rochester group and then to security staff at Loyola University as well, which had had a similar break-in and had also been notified by Rochester.

Andrew had called me at Truckee and told me that somehow my files had been transferred to a computer at the University of Rochester from Loyola so that the security managers there could examine them. The Rochester administrators were concerned that they had lost some source code from Silicon Graphics's IRIX operating system during their own break-in. However, when the computer administrators at Rochester examined the stolen files that had been found at Loyola, they realized they were my files. Andrew had initially been confused, and for a while we believed that my files had been stashed at Rochester by the intruders as well, which wasn't true.

We also learned that over the weekend somebody else had discovered that my files had made their way to Rochester, possibly because of the newspaper articles that reported the break-in there. Whoever it was had again broken into the Rochester machines using the same IP-spoofing attack, stolen the files again, and then deleted them. The spoofing attack was successful at Rochester a second time because although the network administrators at the university had configured the university firewall to defeat such attacks, they had unfortunately made a configuration error when they were changing their router's software.

On Wednesday, Andrew and I looked at the files that had been retrieved from Loyola University. There was one interesting clue:

whoever hid the stolen data on the University computer had gone through my files to see what he had taken. One thing that caught our attention was that a digitized picture of Kevin Mitnick had been pulled out of my compressed files and stored separately. Why, I wondered aloud, of all the material had the thief left the photo of Mitnick lying about?

Was Mitnick our intruder?

"Nah," both Andrew and I said almost simultaneously—it was too obvious. Besides, in a March break-in into SDSC's computers, an intruder had planted information to make it look as if the attack had been performed by someone else, and so we were both extremely wary about attributing too much significance to such an obvious clue.

I'd thought the press attention would begin to die away, but instead it continued to build up throughout the week. That afternoon, two reporters working on a story for the Gannett papers in Rochester had listened to the recordings at the ftp site and called me at SDSC, asking how it felt to receive a death threat. I told them I didn't take it seriously. On Thursday, several publications sent photographers, essentially wasting the entire day. Adding to the media frenzy was the fact that the new university athletic center next door to SDSC was being dedicated that day, and Hillary Clinton was attending the ceremony, surrounded by reporters and camera crews. A *Newsweek* photographer showed up at my office with an array of photo gear and lots of lenses and special gels, and told me his editors had instructed him to shoot pictures "in the style used by *Wired*," the San Francisco magazine about Net culture that is known for its bizarre graphics.

We took pictures at the Center for a while and then the photographer suggested we drive up to Torrey Pines State Park and shoot pictures there. But we arrived just after the gate had been closed, and so were forced to park outside, where the photographer posed me on a clump of rocks. I'd been a photographer in high school, and now for the first time I realized what it was like to be on the other side of the lens, feeling entirely silly as I sat there pretending to play with one of my portable computers. A group of people walked by and stopped to watch. I heard one ask, "What's going on here? Are they shooting a computer ad?" The published "photo" was obviously the art director's idea of being avant-garde; for it was a bizarre picture of me sitting cross-legged with my laptop, with an inset picture of me erupting from my own head.

That evening Julia called, and although things were unpleasant at Toad Hall, she sounded better. We had only spoken briefly during the last couple of days because I had been so busy. I told her about my adventures in the face of the media onslaught, and how silly I'd felt playing model for the photographers earlier in the day.

"This time, things started out badly and got worse," she said. "I can see that what is going on here is bad for me, and that I need to make some hard choices."

This was something that I hadn't heard before from Julia. Previously she had been fearful of leaving her familiar surroundings.

"I would like to be with you and I know that means leaving John," she said a quiet voice. "But this is going to be very hard because we've been involved for a long time."

She still wasn't certain how she was going to make the break, but I was elated.

"I'll do anything I can to help you," I told her. We had missed each other and agreed to meet as soon as possible.

The following night I went on the Friday night skate that convenes each week at 7:30 P.M. at a bike shop in Mission Beach. There are usually only fifteen or twenty people along—a much smaller version of the Friday "Midnight Rollers" night skate in San Francisco, which often attracts more than four hundred people and which I try not to miss when I'm in the Bay Area. The San Diego skate, a leisurely social event called the Dinner Roll, usually goes for about 20 kilometers over a course that ends up in a part of the city with lots of restaurants.

At around 9:30 we had just started the return leg of the route when the cell phone in my fanny pack rang. My phone has a combination earplug-microphone so I can converse and skate at the same time, and I listened as Sid told me that he had checked the *New York Times* service on America Online, and found an early copy of Markoff's article.

"You're not going to like what it says," Sid told me, and began reading it aloud, with sarcasm: "It was as if the thieves, to prove their prowess, had burglarized the locksmith," he began. "Which is why Tsutomu Shimomura, the keeper of the keys in this case, is taking the break-in as a personal affront—and why he considers solving the crime a matter of honor."

I couldn't help smiling at Markoff's melodramatic prose as Sid continued reading and I kept rolling: "Mr. Shimomura, one of the country's most skilled computer security experts, is the person who prompted a government computer agency to issue a chilling warning on Monday. Unknown intruders, the agency cautioned, had used a sophisticated break-in technique to steal files from Mr. Shimomura's own well-guarded computer in his home near San Diego. And the stealth and style of the attack indicated that many of the millions of computers connected to the global Internet network could be at risk. There have been at least four other known victims so far, including computers at Loyola University of Chicago, the University of Rochester and Drexel University in Philadelphia."

The article quoted me at several points, including: "Looks like the ankle-biters have learned to read technical manuals. . . . Somebody should teach them some manners."

When Sid finished, I told him I actually thought the article was reasonably entertaining. But he was upset, and he feared that the effect of the article would be to make SDSC a huge target. "Tsutomu, this is deliberately inflammatory and challenging," he fumed. "You're clearly trying to provoke them."

As I headed back, we talked about the article for more than ten minutes, concluding that we would have to wait and see what happened.

Later, after midnight, I went down and picked up a copy of the *Times* at the Circle K, a local convenience store about a five-minute drive from my house, to see for myself how provocative the article actually was. As I read it over, I realized Sid was right, it was inflammatory, but it was still entertaining.

The next morning I was up fairly early because my landlord was thinking about selling the house and came by with his wife to look things over. It was the first low-key morning since the CERT story had appeared. Life seemed finally to be returning to normal, and I was looking forward to a calm weekend.

I was standing in my living room talking to my visitors, Markoff called, and I told him I'd call right back. Five minutes later I phoned him at the *Times* San Francisco bureau.

"I've got bad news," he began. "Your stolen files have been found at the Well."

CHAPTER 8

On Friday night, January 27, when he logged into his account on the Well, a popular computer conferencing service in the Bay Area, Bruce Koball had made a puzzling discovery.

Koball, a Berkeley-based software designer, is an organizer of the annual Computers, Freedom and Privacy conference, and the Well had given Koball an additional free account to help in his preparations for the 1995 gathering. Because he hadn't used the CFP account for several months, he was surprised to log into his personal Well account on Friday evening and see a message from the Well's system-support staff warning him to remove the 150 megabytes of material currently stored in the CFP account, or they would delete it for him.

Such messages are common at the Well, whose staff routinely runs an accounting program to uncover "disk hogs"—people who take up inordinate storage space on the service's computers—and Koball was simply one of several Well subscribers to receive such a warning that day. But since Koball had barely used the CFP account, the message made no sense until he looked at its directory. The account had clearly been taken over by an intruder and filled with mysterious compressed files and batches of electronic mail:

```
well% ls -l
total 158127
```

```
-rw-r--r--  1 cfp       128273 Dec 26 23:02    bad.tgz
-rw-r--r--  1 cfp       547400 Dec 26 23:07    brk.tar.Z
-rw-r--r--  1 cfp         6620 Dec 26 23:07    clobber.tar.Z
-rw-r--r--  1 cfp         2972 Dec 26 23:07    clobber.tgz
-rw-r--r--  1 cfp          734 Mar 14  1991    dead.letter
-rw-r--r--  1 cfp       704251 Dec 26 23:11    disasm.tar.Z
-rw-r--r--  1 cfp      4558390 Dec 26 23:31    file.941210.0214.gz
-rw-r--r--  1 cfp      1584288 Dec 26 23:39    file.941215.0211.gz
-rw-r--r--  1 cfp      2099998 Dec 26 23:47    file.941217.0149.gz
-rw-r--r--  1 cfp      1087949 Dec 27 10:09    kdm.jpeg
-rw-r--r--  1 cfp       275100 Dec 27 10:09    kdm.ps.Z
-rw-r--r--  1 cfp      1068231 Dec 27 10:10    mbox.1.Z
-rw-r--r--  1 cfp       869439 Dec 27 10:10    mbox.2.Z
-rw-r--r--  1 cfp       495875 Dec 27 10:10    mbox.Z
-rw-r--r--  1 cfp        43734 Dec 27 10:10    modesn.txt.Z
-rw-r--r--  1 cfp      1440017 Dec 27 10:11    newoki.tar.Z
-rw-r--r--  1 cfp       999242 Dec 27 10:12    okitsu.tar.Z
-rw-rw-rw-  1 cfp       578305 Dec 28 09:25    stuff.tar.Z
-rw-rw-rw-  1 cfp    140846522 Dec 27 11:28    t.tgz
-rw-r--r--  1 cfp       146557 Dec 27 11:28    toplevel.tar.Z
-rw-r--r--  1 cfp      3967175 Dec 27 11:31    tt.Z
-rw-r--r--  1 cfp          307 Dec 20  1990    xmodem.log
-rw-r--r--  1 cfp       187656 Dec 27 11:31    ztools.tar.Z
```

The directory listing showed the total amount of disk space the files occupied as well as their names, modification dates, and other details. Among the files were three named "mbox," standard Unix nomenclature for the file that holds a user's mail. When Koball looked in some of the mail files, he found that all the messages were addressed to the same party: tsutomu@ariel.sdsc.edu.

Although Koball and I had attended a number of annual gatherings of computer industry pioneers called Hackers' Conferences together, the name Tsutomu didn't immediately click. He was baffled and still wondering what to do about his discovery when he heard the next day's edition of the *New York Times* land on his front doorstep later that evening, as it does before midnight at many homes in the Bay Area. Koball brought in the paper, browsed through it, turned to the front of the business section, and there it was—Markoff's article and a photo of me sitting in the the operations room of the San Diego Supercomputer Center.

Early the next morning Koball phoned Hua-Pei Chen, system

adminstrator for the Well, which is based in Sausalito in Marin County. He reported his discovery, told her about the connection to me, and asked her to delete the files and kill the CFP account.

A short time later Koball received a call from his friend John Wharton, a freelance chip designer and a principal organizer of the elite Asilomar conference on microprocessor design attended each year in Monterey by many of the "graybeard" pioneers in the semiconductor and personal computer industries. Wharton, who was driving up Highway 101 to the Cow Palace in San Francisco on his way to a model-railroad show, wanted to know if there would be a demonstration of a digital model train sound-effects system that Koball had developed with Neil Young, the rock star, who is also a model-train fanatic.

Koball is a pioneer in an industry that is injecting computer "intelligence" into all sorts of consumer products, and has developed software for particularly neat gadgets like the Avocet cyclometers used by serious bicyclists and altimeter watches favored by climbers—myself included. (When Julia was in Nepal she'd noticed that Koball's watch is the definitive status item among the Sherpas who accompany Western climbers in the Himalaya.)

Koball told Wharton that no, his model-train sound system wouldn't be on display, but then he quickly turned the conversation to his Well discovery. Wharton was fascinated, and as the two discussed the matter, he agreed that killing the CFP account seemed the reasonable approach. After the call ended Wharton began to wonder if either of them really knew enough to reach such a conclusion, and it occurred to him that a good person to consult would be his friend Marianne Mueller, a systems software programmer at Sun Microsystems who was far more knowledgeable than he about Unix, the Internet, and security issues in general. He tried phoning her home and work numbers, but was unable to reach her.

I had in fact encountered both Mueller and Wharton a year earlier in Las Vegas at the annual convention of the computer underground, called Defcon, a bizarre gathering of anklebiters, telecom industry security people, and undoubtedly a few cops, that I had somehow let Markoff drag me to. One of the few high points was a talk Mueller gave about female hackers, in which she introduced her own digitally outfitted version of a Barbie doll, which she called Hacker Barbe, deliberately misspelling the name to avoid copyright problems with Barbie's maker, Mattel, Inc. It was all quite funny, though the humor was lost on the teenage and college-age boys attending the conference, who seemed primarily interested in juvenile pranks like defeating the hotel's microprocessor-controlled door locks.

By this time Wharton was approaching the turnoff for the San Francisco airport, and he remembered that Mueller had mentioned on the previous day that she would be seeing a friend off to Tokyo around noon on Saturday. He took the airport exit, drove to the top of the parking garage, spotted Mueller's MR2 in the international departures area, and was able to park right next to it. As he ran into the terminal Wharton saw from a departures monitor that a JAL flight was just leaving. He stopped in the concourse, and began to scan the crowd.

Wharton, with his long, bushy, graying hair, wire-rim glasses, and Birkenstocks, hadn't been standing long in the airport concourse when he spotted Mueller, dressed in black motorcycle leathers and a Cypherpunks T-shirt, and ran up to her. Milking the clandestine possibilities of this encounter in an international air terminal, Wharton swore Mueller to secrecy before telling her what he'd just heard from Koball.

"Nothing should be done to the files!" Mueller said, alarmed. She insisted that they not be erased or altered in any way, for any changes might tip off the thief that his presence had been discovered. Instead, she explained, the Well's security staff should put monitoring software in place and keep a log of everyone who tried to access the files. Wharton, still enjoying this cloak-and-dagger plot, but now more conscious of the seriousness of the matter, called Koball back with his cell phone.

"Red Dog Leader," he began, when Koball answered. "This is Cosmic Whiner. I just reconnoitered with Cyber Mama; she says you should leave them files alone!"

After speaking a short time later with Mueller over a regular phone, Koball called the Well back to countermand his prior instructions. As it turned out, worried Well officials had already discussed the situation among themselves, and had decided not to take any action yet that might risk alerting the intruder. Koball then phoned Markoff, who in turn called to alert me and give me Koball's number in Berkeley.

It was nearly noon when Bruce Koball and I spoke. He described the files he'd found the previous evening in the CFP directory, and read me the access dates, not all of which were useful because he had already read some of the files. But there was no question that they consisted of material stolen from Ariel in December—the programs I'd written, the extraneous free software that had been pointless to steal, and, worst of all, megabytes and megabytes of my mail, which felt like a tremendous invasion of my privacy.

He briefed me on his conversations earlier that morning, with Pei at the Well, with Wharton and Mueller, and then with Pei once again. It was a great plot, but I wasn't interested in any spy stuff no matter what Markoff's article might have said about my considering "solving the crime a matter of honor." It was my electronic mail that was being scattered all over the Internet, and I told Koball I wanted the files erased. He gave me Pei's cell phone number, and I called to tell her the same thing.

Pei explained that the Well officials were uncertain about how to proceed, since they were concerned that erasing the files would not only give notice to the person who had taken over the CFP account, but might also provoke the intruder into some sort of retaliation.

"I want those files off your machine," I said again. From what Koball had told me, the intruder had set the "permission" parameters on the CFP account to "world readable," meaning that anyone with access to the Well could look at the files it contained. I wasn't comfortable with making my mail public under any circumstances, and I especially didn't want any of my personal or professional files becoming the popular literature of the computer underground. In any case, I also understood the Well's qualms, so I began talking Pei through a set of steps that would make it look as if Koball had simply responded to the disk hog warning and cleaned the files from the CFP directory without taking note of their content.

I didn't know very much about the Well, at that point. Several months earlier, when I had been consulting at Sun Microsystems, I had briefly met the Well's owner, Bruce Katz (pronounced cates), who was in the market for new computers. I had only a hazy recollection that the Well was an electronic hangout for everyone from hackers' conference regulars to Dead Heads with modems.

Pei, for her part, seemed rather hazy about the Well's security vulnerabilities. Like many people, she had been reading about the San Diego break-in, and as of that morning she knew that at least one Well account had been cracked, but she hadn't connected the two events.

"Ah, that makes a lot more sense," she said, after I explained to her how my files had ended up on her system. She acknowledged that the Well knew it was probably under-equipped to handle this problem, and said that during that morning's frantic round of phone conversations, one of the Well's board members, John Perry Barlow, a Grateful Dead lyricist and one of the founders of the Electronic Frontier Foundation, had suggested that the Well invite me to Sausalito to help them.

I was scheduled to speak at a computer conference in Palm Springs the following week, where I had arranged to meet Julia, and told Pei I was already overcommitted. But how about, I suggested, if I had my student Andrew Gross fly up to Sausalito and take a look around?

I spent several hours making the arrangements. Andrew and his wife, Sarah, a doctoral candidate in chemistry at UCSD, were in the process of moving to another apartment because the mold in their student flat had become intolerable, even to someone with Sarah's fascination with organic matter. They agreed, however, that he could spring free by Tuesday for a flight north. I next persuaded Sid to continue Andrew's Supercomputer Center salary, and even kick in some expense money, while he was in the Bay Area. I still wasn't intent on tracking the intruder, but I thought that if Andrew went up to the Well we might be able to discover additional useful information about the Ariel break-in and what had happened with my files afterward.

Koball had by now e-mailed me the file-creation and access times for the contents of the CFP directory (and added a message saying he'd been glad to see that I was wearing one of his Avocet Vertech altimeter watches in the *Times* photo). Once I knew when the files had been created I was able to determine that copies of my material had been deposited at the Well within twelve hours of their removal from Ariel. While it was possible that the files could have made one or even several stops elsewhere on the Internet before landing at the Well, the timing suggested that the Well's cracker was someone with a fairly close link to the person who had stolen my files—or was the thief himself.

On Wednesday afternoon, before I left for the Palm Springs conference, I received a phone update from Andrew, who had gotten to Sausalito the previous evening. Anticipating the arrival of a computer commando, the Well had rented him an imposing Jeep Cherokee, with which Andrew was quite taken, since his own car in San Diego was a thirteen-year-old Honda Accord. Otherwise he was frustrated: so far his entire stay had been taken up in meetings with Well officials about nondisclosure agreements they wanted him to sign before letting him peer into their system; he had spent no time yet actually looking at their problems. Because he is typically much more accommodating and diplomatic than I, Andrew's unhappiness struck me as a bad sign of how muddled things might be at the Well.

After flying to Palm Springs, I checked into the Westin Mission Hills Resort, where the conference sponsors were picking up expenses for Julia and myself. It was late afternoon, and Julia hadn't arrived yet from San Francisco, having missed her flight. She had become embroiled in another agonizing discussion with John, who vowed that if she went to Palm Springs with me, their relationship was over. She had told him that she was going anyway, but she didn't want to end things in anger. As a compromise she had agreed that they would meet the following weekend to say goodbye.

I went off to the speakers' reception, leaving a note at the front desk for her, and she finally caught up with me at the conference dinner at around 9 P.M. She was stressed out and exhausted from having spent hours on stand-by in Los Angeles until she could get a flight to Palm Springs. But she had made it, and we were delighted to see each other.

This event was a Vanguard Conference, one in a series of seminars that the Computer Sciences Corporation, a high-tech consulting firm, conducted throughout the year for high-ranking corporate executives responsible for information technology at their companies. The attendees included representatives from a long list of businesses like AT&T, American Express, Federal Express, Morgan Stanley, and Turner Broadcasting.

The speaker list was also impressive and varied, and included Bill Cheswick, the Bell Labs computer security expert; Whitfield Diffie, father of a widely adopted technique for computer privacy called public-key cryptography; Clifford Stoll, the itinerant astronomer who in the mid-eighties tracked down some young German computer vandals and then turned the story into a bestselling nonfiction book, *The Cuckoo's Egg;* Mitchell Kapor, the founder of Lotus Development and cofounder of the Electronic Frontier Foundation; and Nicholas Negroponte, founder and director of the MIT Media Laboratory.

I had been invited as a last-minute replacement for another speaker by one of the conference organizers, Larry Smarr, director of the federally financed National Center for Supercomputer Applications in Illinois, one of SDSC's sister organizations. I had assumed that my sudden celebrity had a lot to do with the invitation, though I wasn't sure whether to be flattered when I learned that I was actually taking the place of Mark Abene, a convicted computer felon from New York, better known as Phiber Optic, who had to cancel when his parole officer refused to let him leave the state. But I felt better when I ran into Bill Cheswick at the speakers' reception; Ches joked that he and I now seemed to be regulars on the computer security rubber-chicken circuit.

People kept coming up to me remarking, "I saw your picture in the paper," so often that I developed a standard response: "It's better than having your picture in the post office."

My well publicized break-in had engendered a striking degree of paranoia among the corporate types in attendance, many of whom were responsible for their companies' networks. They had apparently concluded that if "one of the country's most skilled computer security experts" could get attacked with impunity, then they were obviously even more vulnerable. "It's a sad day when you have to learn about security problems first in the pages of the *New York Times*," someone from Morgan Stanley, the big investment bank, had written me in an e-mail message after

Markoff's CERT story appeared early the previous week. Now executives at the conference were approaching me and asking if I would be willing to come to their companies to do a security review and to consult.

On Thursday, I gave an only slightly more polished version of my CMAD presentation, demonstrating what an IP-spoofing attack looked like "in the wild," but I'm afraid my attempt to underscore the complexities of real computer crime only had the effect of bewildering many of my listeners. That Friday, though, on a panel with Ches, I took the audience through my Adrian video from the 1991 government and military break-ins, and the group not only followed along but seemed to take satisfaction in seeing a case where the "good guys" had been able to detect, and then contain, the villains.

After the talk Julia and I skated on the bike paths and streets of Palm Springs, marveling at the immaculately maintained lawns here in the middle of the desert. By the time of the outdoor reception Thursday evening, serenaded by a country-and-western band, we had finally started to have fun and were not looking forward to leaving the next day. And yet the nearby snow-capped San Jacinto peaks served as reminders that we would be heading back up to the Sierra Nevada, to pick up the skiing we had interrupted nearly two weeks before.

Early Friday afternoon, Larry Smarr and I became engrossed in discussing the possibility of a joint computer-security research project between SDSC and Smarr's Center. Too much of what passed for computer security, we had decided, was simply a defensive duck-and-cover posture; we wanted to develop a much more aggressive model for confronting the enemy, drawing upon military war-game theory, and discovering the extent to which it could be applied to the electronic realm. If computer intruders were routinely hunted down and identified it would dramatically lower the incident rate.

Losing track of the time, I realized that I had to find Julia, who I discovered talking shop with a group of systems professionals. I pulled her away so we could make our commuter flight to Los Angeles, where we were to catch a connecting flight to Reno. As it was, we barely made it, getting delayed in Palm Springs rush-hour traffic, and ending up charging through the terminal, a light brigade of portable computers, skate tote bags, carry-on luggage, and ski gear.

The next morning we drove to Mount Rose, 20 kilometers southwest of the Reno airport for a ski-patrol training session. It was a beautiful day, sunny, clear, and cool, and it was wonderful to be back on the snow. We spent the day conducting drills with avalanche beacons, the signal transmitters that skiers wear to help rescuers find them if they get buried by a slide. One group would go out and bury a set of beacons, and others would then practice locating them and digging them up. There were other exercises, too, including working with pulley systems, rescue sleds, and medical gear. On Sunday, we went off for a long ski on our own, and when we got back to the cabin that night we were both exhausted from our weekend's exertions.

I spent an hour or so returning phone calls and checking in with friends, hearing several times that David Bank, the *San Jose Mercury* reporter, was still pursuing the theory that I had staged the break-in as publicity stunt. I also heard that Bank had dined with John Gilmore on the same evening that Julia had flown to meet me in Palm Springs, and I began to wonder what John had told the reporter. Certainly, the nature of the attack on Ariel indicated a sophisticated perpetrator familiar with TCP/IP and Unix. And those initial probes had, after all, come from toad.com.

As I mused aloud about my suspicions as we ate, Julia and I concluded that no matter how angry John might be with either of us, he was too principled a crusader for electronic privacy to have anything to do with a computer break-in. Still, the rumors and the continued questioning of my motives made me curious about where this train of events would lead, and we decided to write up a chronological record of events to help us understand and explain what had happened.

Around 11 P.M. Andrew called. We had been in touch briefly several times since Wednesday, but this was my first opportunity for a full update. "What have you found so far?" I asked him, still hoping that he could handle things at the Well on his own.

"Tsutomu, I think you should come down here and help me," he said. "I'm in over my head."

After having spent several days wading through the Well bureaucracy, Andrew had finally begun to examine the stolen software stashed on the Well system on Sunday morning, and it turned out to contain much more than just my collection of files. He had spent the day creating an inventory of the stolen material, growing increasingly alarmed by the value and sheer volume of the contraband. "It's clear we're dealing with something other than your average high school or college system cracker," he said.

The software was located in a number of illicit accounts on the Well, and my stolen files, so carefully deleted a week earlier, had shown up again, in a different account. This fact alone suggested that whoever had commandeered the Well's computers was cocky enough to believe he could come and go, moving things around with impunity. Andrew began rattling off a list of what he'd found, but I interrupted, saying I wanted to go through it systematically. Rich Ress of the FBI had told me during that apologetic phone call back in January that the Bureau assigned priority to its cases by dollar value. I decided that if they wanted dollars, I would now give them dollars.

As Andrew began once again to itemize his findings, I started to respond by estimating the worth of each stolen program, whether in market value or in development costs. Besides my software, there was cellular phone software from Qualcomm, a San Diego technology firm; lots of programs from an East Coast software house called Intermetrics, which makes software development tools; Silicon Graphics source code, the 3-D workstation software used in creating most of Hollywood's movie special effects; plus the computer security software that was supposed to keep the company's programs from being stolen; sniffer logs from Motorola's Semiconductor Products Sector Internet gateway computer, which had captured information flowing into Motorola's network, including passwords; various stolen passwords captured by other sniffer programs; an entire password file from apple.com, Apple Computer's gateway to the Internet; and sundry software tools for breaking into computers in various ways.

At the end of my tally the dollar count reached millions of dollars in software development costs, a figure that didn't include perhaps the most remarkable trophy, whose potential value I couldn't begin to estimate: a long data file named 0108.gz, containing more than twenty-thousand credit card account numbers of the subscribers to Netcom On-Line Communications Services Inc., an Internet service provider based in San Jose, California. Many online network companies ask their subscribers to provide full credit card information when they establish their accounts, though such information is generally not stored on a computer connected to the Internet.

Credit card information wasn't Netcom's only loss. The thief had also pilfered its subscriber password file, another parcel of information that ordinarily should not have been accessible. The version of Sun Microsystem's operating system installed at Netcom takes some measures to protect that file: the passwords in the file are encrypted, which theoretically makes them useless to anyone who might stumble upon them, and the file containing the passwords is inaccessible except to someone who has root access to their computers.

Still, possessing a copy of that file would enable a thief to unscramble some poorly chosen passwords. The method of encryption used to encode them is well known. Given this, it would simply be a matter of using that method to encrypt each word in a large dictionary, then comparing the scrambled dictionary words with the encrypted passwords in the file. For any matches, the cracker could backtrack to the unencrypted dictionary word and presto! a valid password. A break-in artist can use a computer to run this kind of codebreaking attack quickly and successfully against people who are careless enough to use ordinary words as passwords.

Andrew then turned to another category of stolen goods: e-mail. Besides the contents of my mailbox, the thief or thieves had rifled two other people's mail. Andrew and I both recognized the name of Eric Allman, who was the author of sendmail, the standard Internet mail program. My guess was that Allman's mail had been scoured for reports of new security flaws in sendmail, but Andrew, sensitive to privacy issues, had not read the stolen mail. The other name, which neither of us knew, was that of a Stanford student named Paul Kocher, whose e-mail the thief had squirreled away for reasons unknown to us.

The Well's monitoring had narrowed the intruder's comings

and goings down to a forged account called dono, using the password "fucknmc"—which in itself sounded like a clue. In the Unix and Internet world there is a grand tradition of using the initials of your first, middle and last names as a log-in name, and we wondered who was the "nmc" against whom the thief seemed to bear a grudge.

Andrew and the Well staffers on the case could see only what went on locally when the thief connected from a remote computer, but by tracing dono's activities on the Well, it was possible to see a definite pattern of activity emerging and to make some reasonable guesses about what he was doing elsewhere. Because the burglar tools and stolen goods constituted evidence that no clear-thinking criminal would want to leave lying around on hard disks at home, the dono cracker was apparently using the Well as an electronic storage locker. For each sortie against a computer on the Internet, dono would fetch copies of his tools from the Well in a predictable sequence.

First he would come and take a garden-variety break-in program that enabled him to get root on a less-than-vigilant computer system somewhere on the Internet. Then, a short time later, he would come back and pick up a "cloaking" program, which would hide his presence on the raided system, at least from the casual observer, by deleting traces of his activities from the system logs. After finishing his nefarious tasks, the intruder would return to the Well to pick up a sniffer program, which he could leave behind at the raided site for gathering passwords that might make it possible to break into other machines later.

This was a very methodical criminal.

But Andrew had also seen that the cracker, true to the form displayed in our San Diego break-in, was being sloppy. Once he had run his cloaking program on a particular computer he'd broken into, which removed evidence of his presence from accounting files, he didn't bother to cover his tracks as he proceeded to carry away his stolen files. Records of the actual file transfer, for example, might be left elsewhere on the system. A casual observer might not notice his activities, but anyone looking for such behavior could probably track it easily.

It took three-quarters of an hour for Andrew to describe all that he had observed. "This is huge, Tsutomu," Andrew concluded.

"We don't even have enough computers to provide adequate monitoring." Worse, he continued, even though he had caved in and signed all the nondisclosure documents the Well had placed before him, his activities were still being narrowly circumscribed by a woman named Claudia Stroud, the administrative assistant to Bruce Katz, the Well's owner.

"I've been here a week, I've collected data," Andrew said. "I've got some idea of where these guys are coming from, but now I'm in over my head. Now it's your turn."

He told me that Well executives wanted to have a meeting the next day with a small group of people to discuss how to respond to the attacks. I assured him that I would be present, but asked him if he could get it postponed until the evening; I wanted to get in one more day of skiing before leaving the mountains.

In the meantime, I told Andrew he should gather some more information. I wanted data on the time and date of each file's access, and asked him to make a timeline of the cracker's connections to the Well. I also suggested that he make a more thorough search for backdoors and Trojans. It was important that he and the Well's monitoring squad not prematurely narrow the scope of their surveillance. We didn't want to be like the drunk in the classic joke, who upon losing his keys looked for them only under the streetlight because "that's where the light's best." He had brought one of the RDI computers with him from San Diego and I asked him to pick up the second one I had lent to Soeren Christensen, a friend who worked at Sun, once he arrived in the Bay Area. I was bringing a third machine to give us enough resources to both monitor and analyze the data.

After we hung up I sat on the floor of the cabin and for many quiet minutes watched the fire dancing through the glass of the potbellied stove. Despite his protestations that he was in over his head, Andrew had uncovered a great deal of evidence. Real crimes were being committed, with no sign of letup, and there was now a hot trail to follow.

PART TWO PURSUIT

CHAPTER 9

BOTANY

On Monday Julia and I woke midmorning.

I sat up in the low bed in the center of the A-frame's loft and stretched. The loft filled the back half of the cabin, and I could see nothing but gray light filtering through the curtains that covered the picture window at its front. I thought again about Andrew's call for help the previous evening. There clearly was a case to pursue, and I could no longer in good conscience hope that someone else would take care of it. That's why, after talking to Andrew, I'd stayed up late dealing with voice mail and e-mail—a ritual to prepare for reimmersing myself in the outside world. There was yet another threatening message, and I forwarded it to Andrew and attached a message asking him to contact the authorities to trace the call.

Even though it didn't look like a great day to ski, I was determined to get out once more. A light snow was falling, whipped by a gusty wind until it blew sideways, and occasionally even straight up into the air.

I didn't have a particular plan, but it seemed logical to spend a couple of days at the Well to size up the problem. There were growing reasons to think that our intruder might be Kevin Mitnick, not only the Oki and Qualcomm cellular source code that had been stashed at the Well, but also other random indications— including the tip from the cracker Justin Petersen. But there were also still reasons to rule out Mitnick as well, particularly the sophistication of the IP-spoofing attack and the voicemail taunts, which I was fairly certain were not the work of a single person (although Mitnick, of course, could have been part of a conspiracy). If it was actually Kevin Mitnick, there would certainly be a lot of interest from law enforcement types. Levord Burns, the field agent with whom Andrew had been talking, worked for Rich Ress in the FBI's computer crime squad in Washington, D.C.. The Bureau gave every appearance that they were going to be helpful this time, but ever since I'd talked with the FBI about computer crime at their Quantico training center, my impression was that even if they had decided to be helpful, it was no guarantee of success. I have respect for the integrity of the agents I've met, but even they admit that they are usually outgunned when it comes to computer crime. The average field agent has usually taken a training class so that he knows how to recognize a computer at the crime scene, but he probably won't know how to turn it on.

I had no doubt, on the other hand, that the Bureau does understand a great deal about the psychology of the habitual criminal. At Quantico I also learned about techniques for tracking and catching serial killers, and how easy it is to get away with serial homicide. FBI serial crime experts believe that there are similarities between computer crime and other more violent kinds of elaborately repeated crimes. It's a controversial idea, but the FBI experts argue that the same compulsive behavior, and the same craving for power drives both kinds of criminals. These behavioral scientists theorize that in each of the cases the criminals have a need for a fix, which becomes increasingly frequent. More relevant for my work is their assumption that in either type of serial crime, the major investigative problem is information management—organizing and marshaling the accumulated facts. Frequently, they say, when they backtrack in a serial crime case, they discover they already had the solution to the case much earlier but didn't recognize it.

Before I left the cabin I asked Julia if she wanted to come along, even though I had no idea what might develop or where the trail would lead. I thought that her organizational skills might be useful in our investigation. She said that she didn't know much about computer security issues, and it was a chance to learn more about them. She decided to come to Sausalito, but took a final look at the poor conditions outside and opted to skip the ski.

I finally headed over to the Tahoe Donner cross-country center, around noon. Few people were on the trails, and the grooming machines had left the course fast. It was well into the afternoon, and the light was already beginning to fade when I called Julia to pick me up. I didn't have time to change from my lycra cross-country clothes before we headed for the Bay Area in her Mazda.

The weather was turning worse, and chain control was in place on Interstate 80, making things even slower on our way out of the mountains. It was merely raining by the time we got closer to San Francisco and took the back roads north of the Bay to Marin County. Around 8:30 P.M. we arrived at the Buckeye Roadhouse, a trendy restaurant in Mill Valley, near Sausalito, where the Well is located. We had planned a dinner there as an opportunity to meet several of the Well's board members and other friends of the Well in order to reach a consensus about how the on-line service was going to handle the attacks. Andrew, who was staying in a spare room in Pei's home, had already arrived and before we sat down he brought me up to date. More cellular telephone software and a variety of commercial programs were discovered stashed in other places on the Well. Today he had found the software for a Motorola cellular telephone.

He also told me of an odd but intriguing discovery. One of the things he had come up with was a peculiar backdoor communication channel the intruder was using on the Well. Because the attacker could become root on the Well whenever he wanted, he could freely examine any other user's electronic mail. The monitoring team watched him check a number of mailboxes, including that of Jon Littman, the Marin County freelance writer, who had a legitimate Well account. Littman was working on a book detailing the exploits of Kevin Poulsen, the Bay Area computer cracker whom Justin Petersen had helped implicate in the radio station scam and who was still in prison charged with espionage for possession of classified military computer tapes. He had also

been assigned a piece about Kevin Mitnick the year before by
Playboy.

While Andrew had been monitoring the network, he had
watched as the intruder became root and copied a file from a
remote computer, a letter written by Kevin Ziese, an officer in
charge of the Air Force Information Warfare Center in San
Antonio, Texas. The intruder then logged in as Littman and,
within Littman's own account, began to compose a message that
he addressed to the writer, with a note in the Subject line: "Here
you go :-) A vision from God." He then attempted to copy the
Kevin Ziese file into the Littman message, but got stuck when
he apparently could not figure out how to use the Well's mail-
editing software.

He then abandoned the mail program and instead returned to
the Well as root once again and simply added the Ziese file to
Littman's mailbox file. The Ziese letter contained a long discussion of the dangers inherent in the IP-spoofing attack, and it
referred to a conversation that Ziese had with me at the CMAD
conference. At the bottom of the letter, above Kevin Ziese's signature line, the intruder inserted a single line which said "****
Hey john [*sic*], Kevin is a good name :-)".

Andrew was certain that this was the final clue pointing to
Kevin Mitnick. I was still hesitant to jump to that conclusion.
After all, there is no shortage of Kevins in the world. But clearly,
we both wondered the same thing: was Littman aware of this private channel the intruder had created? There was no evidence
that he knew, or, if he had noticed, that it was anything more
than a taunt by the intruder, not a sign of complicity.

We went inside to meet Bruce Katz and the Well board. A
large table had been reserved for us in the back. Bruce Koball,
the Berkeley programmer, had been invited, as well as several
other longtime members of the Well community. An old friend
of Julia and John Gilmore, Koball gave her a quizzical look
when she showed up with me. But there was such a din in the
Buckeye you could barely hear the person next to you, so there
was little chance for Julia to quietly explain what had happened. In any case, I was preoccupied by my dissatisfaction
with this noisy meeting spot, which was hardly conducive to
holding a confidential group discussion. It seemed we were vio-

lating basic operational security principles at the outset of the investigation.

The Buckeye was Bavarian in an antlers-on-the-wall sort of way. I ordered salmon and Julia a shepherd's pie, while Andrew opted for some remarkably large slab of meat, obviously taking advantage of the menu.

Bruce Katz sat next to me. An entrepreneur in his mid-forties who had founded and run the Rockport shoe company before buying the Well, he had thinning long hair and informal dress that made him look more like a veteran of the 1960s than a businessman. Over the din, I tried to brief him on what we'd found. As if to underscore the urgency of the situation, shortly after we sat down a Well employee who was monitoring the system back at the office called to tell Pei that the intruder had just used the Well as a jumping-off point to break in to Internex, another commercial Internet service based in Menlo Park, California.

I knew Bob Berger, the computer engineer who was Internex's founder, because he had provided ISDN Internet connections for Sun Microsystems at various times. I also knew something else about Internex: it was Markoff's Internet electronic mail provider. It occurred to me that this might be the reason for the attack, but I decided not to voice this suspicion until I could investigate. When Andrew and Pei decided they would call Internex in the morning, I tried to persuade them that the company should be alerted immediately. But, nobody seemed anxious to give up dinner and track down an Internex system administrator, who would probably be hard to locate at this hour, anyway.

Katz wanted to know whether the intruder was a person who could potentially damage the Well's system. Since we still weren't sure who it was, we didn't have a good answer, and since we had no idea how he might respond if he detected our monitoring, I told Katz the possibility of retaliation could not be ruled out.

The damage question cut to the core of the issue. It's a common argument in the computer underground to say that breaking into computer systems is morally defensible because all the trespassers are doing is looking, not tampering. Crackers also like to claim that they are in effect helping make systems more secure by revealing vulnerabilities to system operators.

To me these are ridiculous claims. Once upon a time such behavior might have been defensible, when computer networks were research systems used only by engineers and research scholars, although not many engineers or professors I know would agree. In any case, today, when companies and individuals are using computer networks as essential elements of their businesses and lives, the cracker rationale is tantamount to my saying that it would be permissible for me to break into your house and walk around as long as I didn't take anything. Even if material like prototype cellular telephone software isn't stolen, only copied, it remains intellectual property that could easily give an industry rival an important competitive market edge. In those cases in which real damage is done to software and even hardware when a cracker breaks in, companies are forced to spend tens of thousands of dollars cleaning up. In a particularly complex computer it often takes a great deal of effort just to figure out what has been damaged, or what has been taken. There isn't any way to justify Internet joyriding, and its most long-term and corrosive aspect is that it causes network users to put up stronger barriers, destroying the community spirit that has long been the hallmark of the Net.

The conversation shifted to computer hacker and cracker cultures, and how the potential for mischief was actually a great deal more significant than what we tended to see. I pointed out that among computer criminals, it is usually only the dumb ones who get caught. Katz didn't seem comfortable with this line of reasoning, for he really wanted to believe what we were seeing was a harmless prank. But to me, the Well's intruder didn't seem harmless. I explained to Katz how password-sniffing worked and how it had the potential of permitting an electronic trespasser to gain access not only to a single system, but to systems all over the Internet. I also tried to explain that the only real security lay in the extensive use of cryptography. The problem is that most current crypto systems make networks more difficult and expensive to use, and so people tend to avoid adopting them.

It was clear Katz wanted to do the right thing, and he was willing to learn about computer security. The problem was that because he didn't understand the technical details as he himself admitted, he wasn't sure what the right thing was. The Well runs some private conferences used by consulting groups and other private organizations. He wanted to know if it was possible at least to fence those conferences off, and guarantee their security.

Unfortunately it wasn't, I told him. I mentioned using digital tokens, credit card-sized devices that produce a new password every minute, but when I told him their price, he acknowledged they were out of the question.

"Couldn't we just shut the guy out?" Katz asked. He wanted to know if it might not be sufficient to simply have all eleven thousand Well users change their passwords.

"Probably not with any degree of confidence," I answered. At this point, since the interloper had been root for an unknown period of time, at least many months, before he was discovered, the Well had to assume that all of their operating system software had been thoroughly compromised. In addition, there was no way of knowing for certain that all of the accounts the cracker had created had been identified. Maybe he'd stashed a handful of accounts, and left them secretly sitting in reserve just in case he was detected and needed to use them later. Even worse, we were pretty sure he could make himself root from a normal account.

"If you try to shut your doors by changing passwords and closing his accounts, he's almost certain to have hidden a Trojaned program somewhere that would allow him to come right back in," I said. "Only this time you won't know where he is."

I summarized the list of stolen software that Andrew and the others had found, and admitted, "I still don't know exactly what's going on, but one thing I do know is that there is a huge amount of data of great commercial value that someone is hiding there."

I began to understand that the Well directors were looking for easy solutions and assurances that I couldn't give them, because I hadn't even visited the Well yet. This was something I might not be able to accomplish on my own, I warned. I would probably also require support from other Internet service providers, as well as law enforcement officials. Gathering data on the Well was a start, but it was possible I would eventually need trap-and-trace information from telephone companies to actually locate the intruder. I tried to convey my sense of urgency as I explained all this, and told them that in a situation like this you had to go full speed ahead, or you might as well forget about it. One hint leaked to our intruder that we were watching him, and any trail might instantly be obliterated. The main issue confronting us was whether the Well's directors were willing to keep their system open, and not do anything to tip off the intruder that he had been detected, so that we might have a chance to track him down.

The Well group listened carefully, but it was clear they were in a high state of anxiety about how their users might react both to the break-ins and to management's reponse. The Well has always been an unusual place in cyberspace. Besides attracting a coterie of Bay Area hackers and Deadheads, the Well had also become a favorite online watering hole for the computer media digerati— technology writers who engage in online gossip and who were likely to be among the most verbal critics of any missteps by Well management. From what I had heard, the Well as a community has its own strongly held sense of values, and anyone who trans- gresses the group's conventions does so at the risk of becoming a social pariah. As a recent arrival to this digital world, Bruce Katz could not afford to be shunned.

The Well's vice president of administration, Claudia Stroud, who had been Katz's top lieutenant before he purchased the Well, was nervous about the liability the company might face because of our surveillance operation. Besides the matter of an intruder who was reading other people's mail, she noted that there were privacy-rights activists among the Well's members who would freak out when they learned that investigators had been systematically filtering all of the system's data traffic on the network.

"How will keeping the doors open longer and not telling the users what's going on yield any better results?" she demanded to know.

Claudia, who related to Katz with the protective familiarity of a big sister, commingled with time-tested respect for a mentor, was probably only doing her job. But from my perspective, the only sure way for the Well to return to normal would be if we found the intruder, and it looked like Claudia might try to stand in our way.

"From what I can see," she said, "the Well has been in sus- pended animation for the past week and a half, and this investigation has little to show for it."

The Well had been planning to transfer its operations to a new Sun Microsystems SPARCcenter 1000 computer, and throughout dinner the discussion kept returning to the question of how quickly they could and should cut over to the new equipment. Replacing all of their hardware and software might temporarily improve their security situation, but it would complicate our monitoring operation.

By the end of the evening, Katz was sobered by the extent of the break-in and the sheer quantity of software, credit card information, and data files we'd found. He seemed to have decided that the only way to make the Well secure was to shut it down, and transfer its operation to a new computer with trusted software. And yet, we seemed to have made our point that the best way to ensure security would be to put this cracker out of business.

"I'll give you a little more time," Katz said at last.

After dinner we followed Pei and Andrew in the light mist that had replaced the day's rain to the Holiday Inn nearby in San Rafael, where Julia and I were going to stay. Andrew was driving the red Cherokee the Well had rented him, which he had taken to calling the +4 Jeep of Intimidation, a reference to the powerful imaginary weapons players are awarded in fantasy and role-playing games like Dungeons and Dragons.

As I followed the jeep, I thought to myself: *I wonder why the Well thought our investigation required a four-wheel drive vehicle?* My second thought was: *It's going to be a pain to park, but at least we can park on top of things.*

Levord Burns, the FBI agent, had asked Andrew to call him after the meeting to tell him what the Well had decided to do. So even though it was midnight when we reached the hotel, and 3 A.M. in Virginia where Burns lived, I telephoned. He sounded sleepy, but calls in the middle of the night are part of life for a Bureau field agent, and within a few moments he was speaking in the formal, somber demeanor that we were familiar with.

I reviewed what the monitoring had turned up so far, and told him that I was going to the Well's operation center the next day to look at the data. While we talked he told me that, despite having recently been made the Bureau's primary field agent for computer crimes, he had little in the way of a technology background or experience in cases that involved the theft of information.

"I usually deal with bank robberies, Tsutomu," he said.

I concluded by telling him the Well had agreed to let us continue monitoring for a while, and he said he would wait to see where it led.

Andrew and Pei left after the phone call. Before Julia and I fell asleep, she said that she no longer felt like she had a home, that in recent weeks home seemed to have become whatever hotel we were currently staying in. "And as hotels go," she said, "this one is a definite step down from the resorts we've been staying at lately."

We arrived at the Well around eleven-thirty Tuesday morning. The nondescript office building was nothing like the nearby quarters, backing up to a row of houseboats, in a funky section of Sausalito where the online service began in 1987.

The original site was the offices of the *Whole Earth Review*, and the Well—an acronym for Whole Earth 'Lectronic Link—was closely associated with Stewart Brand, one of Ken Kesey's Merry Pranksters and the creator of the Review, and of the *Whole Earth Catalog*. Originally a leading light of the back-to-the-land movement in the 1960s, Brand had written an article for *Rolling Stone* magazine in 1972 in which he described a crazy group of researchers at the Xerox Palo Alto Research Center who were trying to reinvent computing. Within a few years they had succeeded, coming up with the forerunner of the personal computer.

In the late 1970s, when the personal computer industry first emerged, it was still largely a collection of hobbyists with a strong countercultural flavor. In the late 1980s the Well mirrored this same eclectic mix of hackers and hippies. Well members began connecting first from around the Bay Area, and later from all over the country, to chat about things that were on their minds. When the Information Highway hype took off, dozens of reporters wrote stories about the Well, giving it influence far out of proportion to the size of its membership. And so it had a certain cachet in 1994 when Katz, already a Well investor, bought the remainder from the nonprofit group that controlled it and embarked on an ambitious plan to turn the Well into a significant national for-profit service.

One of his first moves was to shift the Well from its houseboat neighborhood to an office complex several blocks away where we arrived Tuesday morning. Pei led Julia and me through a large open space where the support crew and administrative staff worked on PCs and Macs, and showed us to the back, where her office and the computer systems and file servers were located. Down the hallway was a large open closet with a rack of modems so that users could dial in and connect to the Well.

I could tell that Pei, a woman roughly the same age as Julia, was competent, bright, and capable, but she seemed a little too hesitant. The job had been a one-person operation when she began at the Well in the middle of 1994, but it had quickly grown to the point where she oversaw four or five people, and she was clearly new and unsure of herself about the management side of her job. She complained to us about how hard it was to get the Well to listen to her, particularly about security matters. It had taken Andrew coming in as an outside expert to recommend things, and to get her the support she needed.

Julia and I had shown up in time for lunch, actually our breakfast, which was being brought in for the small group of systems people that ran the Well under Pei's guidance. In order not to tip off anyone at the Well who didn't have a need to know about our activities, we were to remain hidden in the small room at the back of the building where Andrew had been operating for the last week. When we walked in Andrew was faxing a page of information to Levord Burns that the trap and trace at UCSD had turned up about the voicemail messages that had been left for me. That same morning Andrew had learned that the voicemail messages had come in over Sprint's long distance lines; that probably meant our caller wasn't in San Diego. Andrew was sending the information to Burns in hopes that the FBI would be able to get precise location information from the phone company.

Andrew had also been following up on his suspicions that we were up against Kevin Mitnick. Earlier, Andrew had called the local FBI office, which referred him to Kathleen Carson, an agent in Los Angeles, who was apparently running the Mitnick investigation for the Bureau. She had been willing to tell him only a few things, and things that weren't very useful, including some of the names of a number of Mitnick's past and present associates, including Kevin Poulsen, Justin Petersen, Eric Heinz, Lenny DeCicco, Ron Austin, and Lewis Depayne. She said the FBI knew of one recent computer account Mitnick had used, named "marty," but she wouldn't reveal any of the specific Internet sites that were involved. When Andrew ran off the sites we knew were related to the Well's break-in, she merely grunted a few times.

As we ate the mild Chinese scallops, shrimp and snow peas, and kung pao chicken that had been brought in, I began to assess what we now knew. Since the previous night the Well had seen more traffic to and from Internex, so I called Bob Berger and left a message warning him that Internex had been broken into. Then I called Markoff and alerted him that somebody might be reading his electronic mail. He said that more than a year earlier a private message sent to him at the Well had shown up on a public newsgroup, so he had largely stopped using the Well for mail and instead had set his Well account to forward his messages to his *New York Times* account which was handled by Internex. Now Internex did not look very secure either.

Because the Internet had become an essential tool for most technology reporters, and every journalist dreads getting scooped, Markoff was naturally concerned about someone peering over his shoulder and reading his mail. But he agreed to do nothing to tip off any snoops and wait to see what my investigation turned up. He did, however, take one precaution. His computer at the *Times* bureau in downtown San Francisco automatically connected to Internex every hour to check for new mail. He decided he would increase the frequency to once every twenty minutes so that mail waiting at Internex would be vulnerable to snooping for a shorter period of time.

After I finished my calls I turned my attention to the Well's monitoring operation, which was obviously in disarray. Pei was collecting some information on a Sun workstation using a standard sniffer program called "snoop," while Andrew was collecting different data on an RDI laptop, which he had connected to the

Well's internal network. I was disturbed by this setup, because it provided no easy way to compare the findings from Pei's and Andrew's machines. Worse, nobody seemed to be doing much to analyze the data they were collecting.

Some intriguing information, however, had already shown up. In addition to the Computers, Freedom, and Privacy account, and the dono account that Andrew had been watching, there were at least four others being used by the intruder: "fool," "fairdemo," "nascom," and "marty"—yet another indication that it might be Mitnick. All of the accounts were demo accounts, so there were no billing records kept for them. This suggested that whoever was behind the break-ins had some detailed knowledge of the Well's accounting practices, and had set up or taken over accounts where a bill wouldn't tip off the account holder that someone was racking up unauthorized charges.

Pei and Andrew had also generated a list of other Internet sites which they now knew the intruder was either coming from or going to over the Internet. This included Internex; Colorado SuperNet, a commercial Internet service with headquarters in Boulder; Motorola Corporation; NandoNet, the online service of the *Raleigh News and Observer*; and Intermetrics. There were also connections from a New York City–based public access Unix system which seemed to have a suspicious name: escape.com.

Also, there was a list of comings and goings from Netcom whose customer credit card numbers had been stashed on the Well. The day before, Andrew had called Netcom and let them know that one or more intruders had been ransacking their system.

As Pei and Andrew spoke of their efforts, it seemed to me that they had prematurely narrowed their scope of inquiry. They seemed to be saying, "We're looking at these five stolen accounts, and we're looking at the usage of these accounts."

It was an attitude I had feared the night before, when I talked to Andrew from Truckee.

"How do you know this is all there is?" I asked him. It was obvious we needed to cast a broader net.

Andrew had many pieces of paper stapled together. Some had listings of log-in and file-access times, but it was really hard for me to tell what they were. Nothing had really been sorted into any rational order that I could see. If we were going to catch the intruder, we needed to systematically conduct what the intelligence community calls traffic analysis. Rather than looking at what was in each individual connection, I was more interested in seeing when the connections took place, where they came from or went to, and what else happened simultaneously. And before we could find our way to the bigger picture, I was going to need to understand how the Well's internal network was laid out, and find a single point where we could see all the information coming from and heading toward the Internet. Unfortunately, these steps would have to wait. The Well had scheduled a meeting at 2 P.M. with a Justice Department attorney and the FBI to discuss the break-ins and the stolen software. I was to serve as the designated technical expert.

The gathering took place at the offices of the Rosewood Stone Group, Katz's holding company located just a couple of blocks from the Well. Julia, Andrew, and I attended, along with Pei, Claudia, and the Well's lawyer, John Mendez. Representing the Government were Kent Walker, an assistant U.S. attorney in San Francisco, and two FBI agents from local field offices: Pat Murphy from San Francisco and Barry Hatfield from San Rafael. I'd heard of Walker, who had formerly been involved in Justice Department computer-crime policy and cryptography issues in Washington. He had a reputation for being tough on computer-crime issues but I didn't have any idea how technically savvy he was. Now that I was meeting him, an athletic six-footer in his early thirties, he struck me as having a quick mind and aggressive demeanor.

Andrew and Pei began describing some of the keystroke monitoring results captured in the past week, and talked about analyzing the intruder's behavior patterns, like trying to study a specimen. As I listened I became increasingly impatient. Like participants at academic computer security conferences focusing on theoretical results rather than real events, they were more concerned with classifications than direct action.

"That's fine and well, but it's all botany!" I interrupted, no longer able to contain myself. "We're searching for a carbon-based life form!"

The room was silent for a moment, but my outburst had the effect of refocusing discussion away from what we could do to secure the Well from the threat, toward my point of view, which was that the only way we could secure the Well against the threat was to go and apprehend it. Instead of a duck-and-cover posture, we needed to shift into attack mode.

I began outlining a plan to establish a base of operations at the Well, and then to quickly move in whatever direction our surveillance operations led us. In practice, my plan was for an organization like that of a mountain-climbing expedition. We would have an advance team and a base team. We would jump forward through the network until we'd pinned the intruder down to a specific location. And when we actually found him? I figured that was the FBI's problem.

In such situations, when I'm trying to guide the agenda, I tend to talk very fast. I later learned I'd overwhelmed the FBI agents, neither of whom had much technical expertise. "I didn't understand a word he said," one of the agents told Walker later. "He was speaking at 9600 baud, and I can only listen at 2400."

To drive home my point that we were combating a live opponent, a carbon-based life form at the end of the wire, I used the speaker phone to call my voice mail in San Diego. A new message had been left there, one that had been sent during the previous week and which I had listened to for the first time the day before. It seemed that my antagonist was unhappy that I had turned publicity's spotlight on him by putting his earlier messages up on the Net as tweedledum and tweedledee.

"Ah, Tsutomu, my learned disciple," he began in a bogus Asian accent, and then he started to sputter like someone who hadn't rehearsed his lines perfectly: "I see you . . . you put my voice for *Newsweek* . . . you put it on *Newsweek*. And you put it on the net. Don't you know that my Kung Fu is the best? My Kung Fu is Great! Why you put my voice on the net?

"This is not good. Have I not taught you, grasshopper? You must learn from the master. I know . . . I know all the techniques and styles. I know tiger-claw style. I know train . . . I know crane technique. I know crazy monkey technique.

"And I also know rdist and Sendmail. And you put it on the net. I'm very disappointed, my son."

It was apparent that I had gotten my intruder's attention. Which was what I'd wanted. He had risen to the bait, and with the trap-and-trace data from the call, we might be able to begin homing in on his location. Playing the message also reminded everyone that we were after a real criminal, not just some captured lines of Unix commands.

A short time later, we were interrupted by a conference call from Netcom, the company that had managed to let a thief carry off its customers' credit card information. There were three vice presidents from the company on the other end of our speaker phone, and they seemed very anxious to be cooperative, giving us a number of contact names. I suspected from their tone they were worried that somehow they might be held responsible for the attacks on the Well, and they wanted to make it plain to the law enforcement types gathered in the room that they were willing to cooperate in the investigation. Walker and the FBI agents said they would be back in touch.

Earlier in the day when I had looked at the sheet showing logins to one of the Well's hijacked accounts, I had immediately recognized one of them—art.net, Lile's machine at Mark Lottor's house. It was the same machine that Kevin Mitnick had taken over the previous fall. More and more clues were pointing to Mitnick, both at the Well and in my break-in, and the FBI agents, Murphy and Hatfield, began to go through their files on him.

Murphy said the Bureau had a lot of information but couldn't share very much with us, only what was in the public record. Trying to figure out what they could release, the agent excused himself to call the Los Angeles FBI office. L.A. was reluctant to release anything but allowed Murphy to go through the material he had in his folder and read "sanitized" portions to us.

While he looked through the file I wandered over and peeked over his shoulder and saw a document stamped "Confidential" and a Kevin Mitnick "Wanted" poster.

He read aloud the list of sites suspected of break-in since Mitnick had gone into hiding in late 1992: the Los Angeles office of SunSoft, Sun Microsystem's software subsidiary; the University of Southern California; Colorado SuperNet; Novatel, a cellular telephone manufacturer; Motorola; Pan American Cellular; Netcom; Fujitsu; Qualcomm; Oki; US West; and L.A. Cellular.

If they were right, Mitnick was certainly obsessed with cellular phones.

The FBI documents also described a raid in Seattle the previous fall in which the target had narrowly avoided being captured. Without knowing who their suspect was at the time, McCaw Cellular security officials, a private security investigator, and the Seattle police had conducted a surveillance operation to track someone who was making fraudulent cellular phone calls and using a computer and a modem. After following their suspect for a number of days they went to his apartment near the University of Washington, and when no one answered they broke down his apartment door. The team confiscated his equipment, which included a portable Toshiba T4400 computer and a lot of cellular telephone gear, and left him a John Doe warrant. The Seattle police staked out the apartment after the search for several hours and then left. The suspect, who they later determined was indeed Mitnick from the data on his computer, came back to his apartment, spoke briefly with his landlord, and vanished.

Oops, I thought.

Another item in the FBI documents concerned Mitnick's possible whereabouts. The Los Angeles FBI office had information that, besides Seattle, he had been in Las Vegas, and more recently, in Boulder, where the Los Angeles agents believed he might still be residing. In fact, the agents now told us, the Los Angeles office apparently was working with the operators of Colorado SuperNet in an attempt to monitor the intruder's activities and was confident it was closing in on its quarry.

Murphy asked me if it sounded plausible that Mitnick might be running his computer modem through a cellular phone. It didn't sound very likely, I replied. I had tried it, and the transmission reliability was quite poor, for calls tended to be dropped repeatedly. Data transmission might have been plausible with a powerful three-watt phone, but with the 0.6-watt hand-held units the FBI believed that Mitnick favored, it didn't seem very practical. It would take an enormous amount of patience, because modems tend to deal poorly with the automatic hand-offs that happen in the cellular telephone network as the phones move from cell to cell.

"If he is going over cellular he'll have an easily identifiable signature, because he'll have to constantly reconnect," I told them. I made a mental note to look for any telltale signs of repeatedly dropped connections that we might have collected in our network traffic data.

Finally the FBI agreed to share with us the accounts and passwords Mitnick had been using on other systems, including the "marty" account. A password for one of these accounts was pw4nl. It occurred to us the most obvious translation of that shorthand was "password for the Netherlands"—a country where the computer underground was still extremely active, despite the fact that the Dutch had finally enacted computer-crime laws. From Andrew's monitoring we had already learned that the Well intruder had an account on a Dutch machine called hacktic.nl, frequented by crackers. It was operated by a Dutch anarchist computer group known as Hacktic.

I wasn't sure how much credence to give any of the FBI data, since a lot of it was from the computer confiscated in Seattle, which Mitnick knew was in their possession.

Some discussion followed about whether Mitnick might be violent and whether the Well was in any physical danger.

"You know John Markoff wrote the book about Mitnick," I said. "Why don't we call and ask him?"

The FBI agents didn't think very much of the idea of patching a newspaper reporter into the meeting, but Walker overruled them. When we reached him on the speaker phone, Markoff explained that everything he knew about Mitnick was already in *Cyberpunk*, or in his front-page *Times* article the previous July. He also said that he, too, was skeptical about whether Mitnick was the culprit. He said he had heard the break-in was actually the work of a shadowy group of people acting in concert, none of them Mitnick. But if it was Mitnick, Markoff said, there was no reason to think Mitnick had the capacity for violence. A story recounted in *Cyberpunk* described how, in one of Mitnick's first arrests in the early 1980s, a Los Angeles detective pulled him over on the freeway, and he began crying.

After everyone was satisfied on that score I pressed Walker about the legal limits of the surveillance operation we were planning. One of the biggest privacy issues on the Internet concerns the rights and responsibilities of commercial systems operators. As data packets flow through their networks, system operators potentially can record every keystroke and every piece of data, effectively monitoring every action and every conversation. Packet sniffers, like the ones we had set up at the Well, can be employed both responsibly and irresponsibly. In setting up our filters at the Well we were attempting to capture packets for only the sessions we were trying to monitor. Often, it was difficult to draw clear boundaries. There was no way of knowing if there was one or several intruders, and it appeared that he or they were using a half-dozen or more separate accounts. There was a good chance that some innocent data was being caught in our wide nets. We had a brief run-through of the provisions of the Computer Fraud and Abuse Act and the Electronic Communications Privacy Act for guidelines as to what we could and couldn't do in our investigation. The laws allow the use of monitoring where fraud or crime is suspected. Walker and the FBI agents said that what we were doing should be covered by these laws.

"This is a situation in which you're not going to be acting as technical support for us," Walker said. "We're going to be serving as legal and administrative backup for you." His attitude impressed me. Up to this point I really hadn't held out much hope we had a chance of finding the attacker, for I'd seen many of these investigations botched before by the FBI.

I told them I would need several STU-IIIs, special scrambled government telephones for secure communications. Kent said he didn't know about the STU-IIIs, but he had access to lots of Clipper phones. They were based on the data scrambling chip with the eavesdropping back door that the National Security Agency had been trying to convince the government and public to adopt—without notable success. I said I'd rather have the STU-IIIs.

Finally Claudia and Mendez raised the Well's concern about potential liability if they kept their system open while we conducted surveillance. They asked if the Justice Department could give them a letter endorsing their decision to continue operating business as usual, and Walker agreed to provide them with such a document.

The meeting concluded at nearly four o'clock, and Julia and I stayed behind in the conference room to return various calls I had received on my cell phone during the meeting. One was from Mark Seiden, a Unix hacker and a computer security expert who had agreed to help Internex deal with their security problems. When I'd come to the Well that morning Andrew had told me that the monitoring team had seen the intruder move a 140-megabyte file containing the contents of my home directory on Ariel to Internex the night before, and I began to feel as if we were dealing with a squirrel burying his nuts, scurrying around and hiding them in various holes all over the Internet. When I returned Seiden's call, I told him about the file and said I wanted it deleted. Since we didn't want to tip off the intruder, however, we agreed that Seiden would erase the file and then send the real user of the account a message that said something like, "We've deleted your file because you've exceeded your disk space allocation. We've told you time and time again not to leave huge files lying around."

After all the calls were dealt with, Julia and I walked back down the street to Pei's office at the Well. Claudia had been hovering around waiting to present me with the same document she had forced Andrew to sign, a nondisclosure agreement intended to keep me from mentioning anything I learned about the situation to anyone outside the Well. It had already created a huge problem for Andrew, who had been trying to warn other companies that their systems had been broken into, and software had been stolen.

Because of the agreement he'd been reduced to calling people and saying, "I can't tell you who I am, and I can't tell you the details of what happened, but I want to let you know you have a security problem." It was an impossible constraint to work with, and earlier in the day I'd suggested he ignore that part of the restriction.

Claudia was also trying to enforce her understanding that all the stolen software found stashed on the Well was the Well's property. This was creating another tremendous headache for Andrew in attempting to talk to the victims of the theft and to get their assistance. I explained to her that another company's intellectual property did not automatically become the Well's property just because someone had stolen it and hidden it there. She was worried that if it was disclosed that the Well was the staging area for break-ins around the Internet it would be liable for any damages. I pointed out to her that the Well might have equally serious liability problems if it became known that the service was aware of break-ins at other sites and failed to notify the victims, as her constraints on Andrew had already made happen in some cases.

Finally, I tried unsuccessfully to convince her that what should matter most to the Well was lowering the roadblocks and letting us go full speed ahead if we were going to have any chance of solving their problem.

"Tsutomu, I have to ask you to sign this to protect the Well's potential liability in the investigation," she repeated.

I stared at her trying to silently communicate, *I have no intention of signing anything so ridiculous*, but finally tact got the better of me. "I don't think I can agree to this now, but I'll review it and get back to you." What I actually meant was, *Which part of "no" don't you understand?* The fact I'd agreed to take a look at the document appeared to mollify Claudia, and as I went back to work I couldn't help thinking about what a friend had once told me: diplomacy is the art of saying "nice doggy" until you can find a stick.

Having spent the better part of a day dealing with bureaucrats I was at last able to turn my attention toward trying to understand the topology of the Well's network. Andrew had attached an RDI PowerLite to the network in the right place, so that all of the Well's packets would flow past his computer, but odd things were happening. It was soon apparent the Well's routing was totally scrambled, so that more than a quarter of the packets in its internal network were moving in an extremely inefficient and round-about fashion. One of the router computers was throwing up its hands and sending packets to another router to make decisions on how to send each bundle of data to its correct address. I felt a little like a plumber who shows up at a customer's house and has to tell the owner that someone has routed the bathroom pipes through the bedroom.

The screwed-up routing wasn't my problem. What was important was that we begin logging the right packets as quickly as possible. We wrote a variety of filters to capture packets both coming into and going out of the Well. By putting together a watch-list of all the known compromised sites and then logging other suspect places data might come from, we had a good chance of creating a complete record of the intruder's activities.

What I had in mind was to start by putting a broad set of filters in place on two separate computers to make certain we had redundancy. I wanted to search a lot of sessions for a little while to watch for our intruder's telltale signature and then narrow the focus again. That way we would be able to see if any covert activity was being missed. As we set the system up, however, I realized the Well was the busiest system I'd ever dealt with, and there was far too much data if we monitored both directions, so I confined our monitoring to inbound data. By ten o'clock, I thought I understood what it would take to get the packet logging and filtering systems set up, so Julia, Andrew, and I took off for dinner.

The three of us drove in the +4 Jeep of Intimidation to the Cantina, a Mill Valley Mexican restaurant Julia knew. According to house legend, Carlos Santana's father once played there in a mariachi band.

Over dinner we talked about the trouble Andrew had gotten in for being up in northern California helping me. My deal with Sid Karin had been that SDSC would contribute his salary for a few weeks, but somehow word hadn't reached Andrew's managers. I told Andrew that I'd placed a call to Sid about it earlier in the day, and it looked like it would get straightened out. We also spent a little time chatting about Andrew's academic career and his hunt for a new Ph.D. thesis adviser. I told him that I would be glad to provide advice and direction, but he was going to need to find someone else to be his formal adviser and handle administrative issues.

Sometime after 11 P.M. we drew up a list of things we needed to do to get our monitoring systems completely in place, and drove back to the Well. Pei had gone home at a sane hour, but several people were still monitoring in the cramped back room that was the Well's network operations center. We were capturing tens of megabytes of data each hour, far more than we could hold on our disks, even overnight, so we tightened our filters.

After midnight I began looking through the log file data we had gathered during the previous day and immediately found something: the keystrokes of the intruder looking through Markoff's directory and mailbox. As I studied the data I could easily see how he'd found his way to Internex: he had simply looked at a file called forward in Markoff's Well directory that automatically routed his electronic mail to Internex. I also saw that he was looking through a number of mailboxes on the Well besides Markoff's and Littman's. He had gone through the mailboxes of Emmuel Goldstein, the editor of the phone phreak magazine *2600*, and who in real life was Eric Corley; Ron Austin, a Southern California programmer who had been in trouble for a number of computer crimes; and Chris Goggans, a reformed member of the computer underground who published an online computer underground magazine called *Phrack*.

By 2 A.M. we'd done everything we could within reason. Julia and I did not want to spend another night at the Holiday Inn, so we drove across the Golden Gate Bridge into the city. We ended up in the guest room at Dan Farmer's near the park. Earlier in the day I'd called Dan and told him we'd found the source code to his SATAN program and his electronic mail on the Well. I'd been hoping to talk to him about the break-ins, but by the time we arrived, he'd already headed out for the San Francisco club scene.

I could brief him later. For now, I knew we had cast our nets as widely as feasible. It was a question of waiting and seeing what we were able to haul in. We had already seen suspicious traffic from Colorado SuperNet, Intermetrics, and Netcom, and it looked like we would soon have to make a decision about which way to head upstream in the InterNet. Somebody had already established the rules we were playing by, and now that I was joining the game, I had decided to dive in and not look back.

CHAPTER 10

We returned to the Well late the following morning. Any doubt over whether I was committed to the hunt had been erased the day before. I've always felt strongly that the way you do something matters as much as what you do, and if I was going to hunt this thief I felt it was unacceptable to approach the challenge with any less than all of the intensity and focus I could muster.

There seemed to be a slowly accumulating body of evidence that it was Kevin Mitnick who was sitting with a portable computer systematically launching attacks throughout the Internet, but there was still no conclusive proof. Was he directly responsible for stealing my software in December? The evidence was still sketchy. What I did know from the data Andrew had collected earlier was that even if Kevin himself hadn't been the one who had attacked my machine, the Well intruder had in his possession a copy of my software within twelve hours of the original break-in.

Now the chase was on, and the challenge was to move forward faster than any leaks might get back to our intruder. Security had become a real concern, because I realized people were talking about me, and that my days of comfortable anonymity were ending. Walking back to Pei's crowded office that morning, one of the Well system-support people stopped me and said, "Didn't I see your picture in the papers?" The publicity about the break-in was obviously starting to complicate our activities, and it would be a disaster if somebody mentioned something about my presence on the system and it was picked up by the intruder.

Pei went to the Well employee a little later, and asked if he could please keep it quiet. I had the impression that both Claudia and Pei thought they could keep things under wraps, although I feared that was already proving to be impossible. In fact, the situation almost immediately became worse when Kevin Kelly, the editor of *Wired* and one of the founders of the Well, showed up and asked if he could take my picture for an article in his magazine.

"It would be better if we did it tomorrow," I mumbled and tried to disappear quickly.

Slipping into the back room, I began to look over the progress we had made in setting up our monitoring station. One of the RDI machines was now logging data along with Pei's SPARCstation, and we'd apparently done pretty well at tuning our filters the night before, as the amount of data we were saving for later analysis had become a little less overwhelming. However, our software tools wouldn't read the data that was being filtered on Pei's SPARCstation and it was being used for other tasks as well, so we kept working with the second RDI trying to attach a disk Pei had lent us.

Tuesday had been a fairly quiet evening. Our intruder had only made scattered appearances, giving Andrew the time to return phone calls. He learned that the security people at Colorado SuperNet had been detected by the intruder, who quickly deleted all the files he'd stored there and then left them a cocky message: "You lamers!"

I took note of the times at which the intruder was active. He'd logged in to the Well at around 8 A.M. on Wednesday. If he was keeping normal hacker hours, working till the wee hours and sleeping late, it seemed obvious he wasn't in our time zone: the Midwest or the East Coast would be more likely. The data also seemed to suggest that our attacker was a single individual and not a group, for there was never more than a single log-in session using the stolen accounts at any one time. Furthermore, just as Andrew had described on Sunday night, his pattern seemed to be remarkably repetitive. The Well was clearly a staging ground or jumping-off base from which, over and over again, he would come and fetch his tools and then take them to the site of a new attack.

My growing suspicion that Kevin Mitnick was the Well's intruder explained some things that had puzzled me earlier. I had one of those strange flashes of insight that I occasionally get as I was scanning through text on the workstation display and I saw the letters VMS scroll by. VMS is DEC's operating system, and I recalled that several years earlier I had read in *Cyberpunk* that Neill Clift was the British computer researcher who specialized in finding security loopholes in VMS. Neill Clift might have the right middle initial to match the password "fucknmc." Might Mitnick have some score to settle with him?

I called Markoff to ask him to check on Neill Clift's middle initial and then invited him to come over and see our monitoring operation in action. Markoff arrived about an hour later, and we looked through some of the keystroke information we'd captured, showing what the Well's intruder had been up to.

Claudia also paid a visit and asked me what the status of our operations was. The Well board was meeting the next day, she said, and it would be making a decision about whether to take the Well computers off-line or not.

"We are feeling very exposed," she announced, "and I think we should consider taking steps to resecure the system, like removing the back doors we know about, and asking users to change their passwords."

I explained that I had convinced Katz at dinner the night before that to take these steps now would be a disaster for us, and would probably end any chance we had of catching the intruder.

"Tsutomu," Claudia snapped, "you've been here a week now, and I don't see anything in the way of progress."

"Excuse me," I shot back. "Get this straight—I've been here about twenty-four hours and it is obvious that you guys were just thrashing before I got here. I'm busy and I don't have time to deal with you right now," I said, and abruptly turned back to the conversation I'd been having with Andrew.

Julia thankfully was more diplomatic, and took Claudia aside to explain the real progress we'd made so far, and what our plan of action was for the next couple of days. She also learned that Claudia was upset in part because Pei had her employees on-site around the clock looking at the snoop data, and it was costing the Well a fair amount of money.

A while later Julia came back and said it didn't look as if Claudia was going to recommend that the board throw us out immediately. The crisis had been averted for the moment, but it was becoming increasingly obvious that we were going to have to move forward as quickly as possible or the investigation would be terminated.

Most of our time on Wednesday was spent waiting for a program I'd written called Crunch to run. It was designed to take the filtered packet data we'd accumulated from the night before, sort through it, and organize it into distinct sessions, which should make it possible to reconstruct exactly what the attacker was up to. But Crunch was running slowly, taking twice as long to sort data as it had taken to collect it. We had managed to speed it up a bit by playing around with some things in the Well's network that were broken, but it was a larger filtering net than I'd ever cast—and it was on a busier computer than I'd ever dealt with before.

While I waited, I sat down at Pei's computer console and began my own hunt through the data we'd collected. Among the hundreds of stolen files hidden in the purloined accounts we'd found so far was the credit card database file from Netcom. Among the names were those of a few people I knew, including a friend of mine who was a housemate of Castor Fu. Castor was out when I called, but I left him a message asking him to read the credit card number to my friend. It would probably leave him with a queasy feeling.

I next phoned Mark Lottor, and together we tried to figure out where his stolen code we had found at the Well had come from, and when it had been taken. As I described the file he realized it was a very old version of his Oki code, which meant that it had probably come from my computer, as Mark had the latest copies. I went back to poking around the stolen software when Andrew walked up and saw what I was doing.

"Hey, wait. How come when I go look at this data, it's botany, but if you look through it it's okay—it's science?"

I just grinned.

As I continued to look back through the earlier data, I noticed that on that morning we had captured packet data showing that a break-in from the Well to Internex had been dropped in mid-word. In a session from Netcom that began at 7:29 A.M., the intruder had apparently begun to type the command "uude-code," but the connection was dropped at 7:31 after he had typed only uudeco, the first six letters. Minutes later he came back and picked up exactly where he left off, using the command to decode and then run a program called 1.Z that made him root on Internex. But the broken session suggested that the FBI may have been right in their belief he was running over an unreliable cellular telephone connection. In either case, we had a precious clue, a signpost that would appear simultaneously in each of the connection logs of the computer network operators and the telephone companies' phone call records stretching all the way to our intruder's actual physical location.

I had been hoping that Julia and I would be able to go out for a skate sometime during the afternoon, but it was dusk by the time we took off gliding north along a bike path down Bridgeway, a road that stretches from Sausalito to Mill Valley. It was nice to be on skates, but as we started out I felt awkward as I tried to make the transition from the cross-country skis I had become used to. It didn't take long, however, to find my rhythm, and on a long downhill section I looped back and forth waiting for Julia who doesn't particularly like to go fast downhill. At the bottom my pager buzzed and although the number was one I didn't recognize, I punched it into my cell phone and returned the call anyway. It was David Bank, the *San Jose Mercury* reporter. I was busy, I told him, and I couldn't talk to him. I hung up and thought to myself: *Now that I know his number, I'll know how to ignore his pages.*

We skated out for thirty minutes or so and then turned around. By now darkness had fallen so we stopped and phoned Andrew, and asked him to come pick us up. We skated in circles, until he arrived and drove us to the Samurai, a Japanese restaurant in Sausalito. Over dinner the three of us talked about where to go next. It was clear that we needed to move our base of operations, but I was still skeptical about the value of going to Netcom or Intermetrics, and it occurred to me that if the FBI thought our intruder was actually in Colorado then maybe we should head that way next.

Julia argued against this plan, however, because she wasn't convinced the FBI had adequate evidence to support their belief that the intruder was actually in Colorado. I pointed out that since we were seeing the most activity coming from there, it was worth a visit; if he wasn't there, however, we could figure it out quickly and move on. Andrew was worried that the Colorado SuperNet (CSN) systems administrators seemed a bit slow to catch on, and reminded us of the incident we had learned about that morning in which the CSN staff had managed to let themselves be counter-detected. I decided that I'd call them and see if they were willing to cooperate with us. We left the restaurant, realizing there was still a tremendous amount of work to do, including setting up our second monitoring station at the Well to give us a backup.

After we returned to the Well, Andrew called CSN. He talked for a while to one of their people who was working with the FBI and then passed the phone to me. I wanted to know whether the intruder was using the local Colorado dial-in telephone lines or whether he was coming over the Internet.

"We've been watching attacks on the Well coming from your computers and I thought we could find some way to share information," I explained to the CSN systems manager.

"We're working very closely with the FBI," he replied. "Thanks for your offer, but we have this under control. I've been instructed not to give you any information, but to ask you to contact the Los Angeles office of the FBI, and they will pass relevant information on to you in a timely fashion."

"Timely?" I couldn't believe what I was hearing. "But you were counter-detected this morning!"

"I know we made a mistake," he replied brusquely, "and we'll make sure it doesn't happen again."

I asked him whether CSN now had trap-and-trace in place and whether they were in touch with their local cellular telephone company. He said, yes, they had that covered.

He didn't seem very sincere, though, so as a benchmark test I asked, "Are you asking the cellular telephone company to watch for all data calls to see whether he's in the area?" This was something that was clearly impossible, because there was no way that a cellular phone company could conduct surveillance on all of its phone calls. "Oh, yes," he said blankly. Talking to these people obviously was a complete waste of time, so I hung up. If we went to Colorado, we were going to have to start from the ground up. It didn't look like a viable option.

After the phone call I turned my attention to figuring out why we couldn't get the new disk working for the second monitoring station we were trying to set up. Most workstations and an increasing number of personal computers use a standard hardware connection known as Small Computer Standard Interface—the acronym is pronounced "scuzzy"—to connect things like hard disks and CD-ROM drives. Our second RDI refused to recognize the disk that Pei had lent us, and though Andrew had tried another cable to connect it, we still had no luck. Now I took a stab at the problem. Ordinarily, a SCSI bus needs to be properly terminated—a damping function that makes sure the signals on the cable don't reflect and interfere with each other, but after playing around with a variety of different things we realized that when I left the external termination off the drive it suddenly started working. Odd, but hardware can be like that.

With all of our monitoring stations running I returned to the filter data. Around eight that evening our intruder had been prowling the Well, following his normal routine of making himself root and then hiding his presence with a cloaking program. He checked briefly to see if Jon Littman had received any new mail, found none, and so turned his attention to Markoff. As he opened the mail file he used a standard Unix text search command:

```
# grep -i itni mbox
```

Wait, I thought to myself, *this is something we haven't seen before.* He was looking for the four letter string "itni" in Markoff's electronic mail file. The intruder was trying to be discreet, but to me, it was a dead giveaway: it looked as if Kevin Mitnick was on the run; he had apparently taken a keen interest in knowing what people might be telling Markoff about him. In this case he was out of luck, for there was no Mitnick material to be found.

While Andrew and I had been methodically tracking our intruder during the week through the Net, we were now getting indications from Mark Seiden at Internex that a similar break-in pattern was beginning to emerge there as well.

I knew Seiden a little because we'd spent some time together at the annual Hackers' Conferences at Lake Tahoe and other computer conferences over the years. He was also a friend of Markoff's and Lottor's. With curly black hair, a graying beard, and wire-rim glasses, Seiden tended to affect what some people see as the same anti-fashion statement typical of Andrew and me. You can usually find him dressed in a T-shirt emblazoned with some technology theme, shorts, a fannypack, and sandals, and he is seldom without his pager, cell phone, and RadioMail terminal. A graduate of Bronx Science High School, where he was in the same class as Bruce Koball, and a one-time researcher at IBM's Thomas Watson Research Center in Yorktown Heights, New York, he is another member of the first generation to have grown up with computers. A skilled Unix hacker, Seiden has had a range of consulting jobs with some of the nation's biggest online companies. He also has had a good business installing firewalls for all kinds of companies ranging from Internet providers and software companies to prestigious New York law firms.

Seiden took a special interest in the Internex break-in because his consulting group, MSB Associates, was located in the same building as Internex in downtown Menlo Park, and MSB also had its Internet connection provided by Internex. When we first talked by phone when I returned his call on Tuesday, I sketched the scenario out briefly, telling him we had seen a large file being transferred to gaia.internex.net and asking for his help. I also explained that we were doing everything possible to avoid tipping off the intruder, that we had growing evidence that our interloper was Kevin Mitnick, and I wanted the file which contained my personal data removed from Internex quickly, because I didn't want it propagated all over the Internet. Mark agreed to do his own surveillance and later on Tuesday talked to Andrew to coordinate the details. After Andrew described the agreement he had made with the Well not to copy materials, Mark decided he didn't want to limit his own freedom according to those terms, and said he would prefer to continue to work independently from us.

Once he had begun examining the Internex system, he soon found that an account named brian had been commandeered on the company's computers which were located on the second floor of a downtown office building above a barbershop. The account actually belonged to Brian Behlendorf, a former Internex consultant who was now working at *Wired*, doing Internet and World Wide Web development. When Mark peeked to see what was stored in the brian directory, he found a copy of tsu.tgz, the same bundled and compressed file of my directory that we had found at the Well. Working from his own computer down the hallway, which was connected to the larger Internex network by a local Ethernet network, Mark set up his own sniffer programs to monitor all external connections to Internex. Since his computer was not obviously a part of the Internex network, and was being closely monitored, he had told me he was fairly certain the intruder hadn't broken in to his machine. He was confident he could use it as an observation post from where it was unlikely that the invader could know that someone was dogging his every step.

As Mark began exploring the Internex computers for Trojan Horse and back door programs left behind by the intruder, it took only a few minutes to spot an innocuous-looking program running on Gaia, their mail-handling computer, called in.pmd. Pmd would normally be the name of a program known as the Portmaster daemon, a tiny piece of software that communicates with hardware devices that would normally connect users dialing in from the outside world to the computer. In this case, however, it was immediately noticeable because Internex was not running any Portmasters. The intruder hadn't bothered to check to see if his ruse made any sense in the context, or maybe he didn't care.

Mark took the tiny program apart and discovered it was minimally camouflaged. Its operation was simple: If someone connected to port 5553 on the Internex computer and typed "wank," they would automatically become root, with all the power that entails. Interestingly, in.pmd existed only in the computer's memory; there was no corresponding version of the program to be found on the hard disk. This meant that the cracker had copied it over to Gaia's hard disk, started it running in the computer's memory, and then erased it from the disk, which made its presence harder to detect. The program had been left running for the intruder to use whenever it was needed with the assumption that no one would notice it.

Andrew had tipped Mark off to some of the cracker's tricks, and as Mark continued to investigate he found that someone had tampered with a standard, but now rarely used Unix system program called newgrp, a utility program that assigns a user to a particular group for organizational or access purposes. The intruder had replaced the original newgrp with another program that has the same name, but which secretly had other functions as well. We were familiar with it, as it is a fairly common Trojan Horse program that floats around in the computer underground. The Trojaned version of newgrp allowed the intruder to make himself root or to pose as any other user on the system. The more Mark investigated, the more he realized Internex had been thoroughly penetrated. He discovered a handful of other Trojaned programs and innocuous accounts with names like "sue," set up and left lying unused, apparently as a backup in case the intruder found himself shut out.

Shortly before midnight on Tuesday Mark rebooted Internex's computer to flush out any hidden backdoors or secret daemons he hadn't been able to find, and also erased the Trojaned version of newgrp.

By Wednesday, just after 7 A.M., the intruder was back, this time connecting from escape.com, trying to use his now missing back door. Failing to get in, he logged-in seconds later to the brian account. He had changed the password to fucknmc, which had clearly become a mantra to him. Once inside he checked to see who was currently logged-in and who had been on the system recently. He then fetched a copy of the daemon program Mark had deleted the day before and installed it in Internex computer's memory, once again deleting it from the disk after he was finished.

Thirty minutes later he was back from the Well, laboriously reinstalling and hiding his Trojan newgrp program that Mark had erased the night before. As Mark monitored from his computer, he watched the intruder check through all of the Internex mail aliases for "mark," presumably to find out where Markoff's mail was being sent. Not only did Markoff show up, but so did the name Mark Seiden—but the intruder didn't seem interested. Shortly afterward the invader checked to see if Markoff's *New York Times* Internet address was connected to the Net. He might have been interested in breaking in to that computer but it didn't answer, so he instead altered Markoff's mail alias so that a copy of all of his inbound electronic mail would automatically be sent to a mysterious account at Denver University. The attempt to redirect the reporter's mail failed, however, because it was set up incorrectly. Almost twelve hours later the cracker was back making himself root and browsing through all the subject lines in Markoff's mailbox. Although there was a lot of junk mail, one subject line did say "Intel stuff," but the intruder didn't seem to be interested in that topic.

Since the illicit programs had been immediately reinstalled, that evening Mark decided not to erase them again, but instead to write his own small program that would not only send him an alert each time someone connected through the covert back door, but also included a surveillance countermeasure. Since he received information on where the intruder was coming from each time, he wrote the program so that it could check who was currently logged in at the offending site, by running finger against the attacking computer. As he observed the intruder's comings and goings over the following days he would see that although in some cases the intruder would connect to Internex from the Well, he would most frequently enter via escape.com, which he learned was a New York City Internet service provider run by an enterprising high school kid. The listings of current users that came back frequently included names of people who were currently connected to the system including Phiber Optic, and Emmanuel Goldstein. I wouldn't call it a slum, but it was probably one of the Internet's more seedy neighborhoods.

Everywhere we looked there were more signs pointing to Kevin Mitnick, but my immediate challenge was making sure that the filters provided clues about his location, and on Wednesday after midnight at the Well as I ran through the elements of our monitoring setup in my head, it occurred to me to ask Andrew whether he had time synchronization running. Time synch is a computer network utility that ensures that each computer's clock matches the others in the network. It is a useful tool for all kinds of computer-related activities, and it's essential for computer security work. In big computer networks you may have hundreds of people logging on and off every minute and thousands of events taking place. The only way to ensure accurate reconstruction of this activity is to be absolutely certain that the clocks match across the network.

"I assume it's in place," was Andrew's response.

Assume? We checked and of course the Well wasn't running time synch, neither were we.

What that slip meant was that all the data we'd collected from the night before would be difficult to use, at least for traffic analysis. If the clocks weren't synchronized, it would be far more difficult to match events taking place on different machines, a necessary step to tracing someone who is connected through a string of computers on the Internet.

"I don't ever want to hear the A-word again," I told Andrew.

He seemed miffed. It had been a long, rough week of twenty-hour days for him, and he was bearing the brunt of everything that was going wrong. But it was wrong to *assume* that because we ran time synch back at SDSC that everyone else did. From my point of view running time synch is an absolute, non-negotiable requirement, for the essence of everything I do is related to time.

I spent some more time that night working on tools I could use to look at the data we were collecting. Earlier in the evening John Gilmore had called my cell phone looking for Julia, and she had disappeared into another room to talk to him and was gone for several hours. She had been working on a tool for searching through the data that we needed as soon as possible, and when it didn't get done I picked up the project and finished it. When she came back she was distraught, and the two of us went outside and took a walk along the Sausalito waterfront.

"John wants me to go to Wylbur Hot Springs this weekend," she said. It was to be the weekend together that Julia had agreed to before she had come to the Vanguard conference in Palm Springs. Wylbur Hot Springs was a funky, sixties-style retreat north of San Francisco. We talked about it as we walked along the waterfront near the pilings and the houseboats. In my mind it seemed that there would be much more to the weekend than what appeared at face value.

"It's a place we used to visit, when things were better between us," Julia said as we walked a little farther.

Even though the idea was supposed to be to say goodbye, we both realized John had something else in mind, and Julia found this disturbing.

We strolled on in silence. I didn't have an answer.

"We have to go back to work and finish up," I finally said.

It was after 3 A.M. when we drove back to Dan Farmer's house. I felt a growing urgency to do something to find the intruder quickly, but I still wasn't sure which direction to move in. One thing I could see clearly, though, was that we didn't gain anything by remaining at the Well.

Our room at the back of Dan's house contained a bed, a Sun workstation, and many shelves full of science fiction books. It also had a water fountain with an artificial stone basin, several tiers of dark stonelike material with pebbles strewn about. I was exhausted, and I barely heard the water cascading over the sides, making a soft burbling sound, a white noise masking the whining of the workstation sitting in the opposite corner of the room, before I fell into a deep sleep.

CHAPTER 11

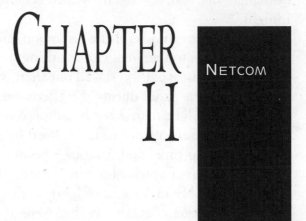

NETCOM

I awoke on Thursday to the sound of falling water and although the bedroom was still dark, I saw that it was late morning. Several of the household cats were careening about, and in the dim light I could make out Dan's housemate's collection of single malt scotches dotted around the room. I knew the time had come to choose the direction for our next move.

Andrew had been at the Well for a week, and now we had some real data, and a few potentially solid leads. But our intruder was still running amuck, and we needed to get moving. With Colorado SuperNet an increasingly unfeasible option, I had to face the idea of doing our observing from Netcom. As one of the nation's largest InterNet service providers, it was going to make our search like looking for someone in Grand Central Terminal. Being blocked at CSN was frustrating to me and I spent several fruitless hours in the early afternoon trying to see if there was a way to circumvent the L.A. FBI's roadblock in Colorado.

Afterward, because Julia was feeling agitated, we talked for a while. It was clear to both of us that John was counting on the pleasant memories of Wylbur Hot Springs to weaken Julia's resolve to leave him.

"I'm afraid I won't be able to maintain my sense of perspective when I'm with him," she said. Julia was uncertain about her ability to stay independent from John and she was worried about being sucked back in to their relationship. "This is going to be difficult," she added. "I want to make sure I get enough rest tonight."

It was now the middle of the afternoon, and I decided I didn't want to go back to the Well. For one thing the *Wired* photographer I was trying to avoid was staked out there, waiting. Andrew had paged me several times during the afternoon, and I kept putting him off with "I'll be there," but it had become clear that we ought to accept Netcom's offer of support. We'd been seeing traffic from there for a long time, and a vantage point at their headquarters would give us a nationwide listening post on their nationwide network, and possibly an "upstream" location that would place us closer to our attacker. Besides, we had several telltale events—the abruptly interrupted sessions—that we might be able to use to pin down the intruder's identity on the Netcom system.

I contacted Rick Francis, the Netcom VP of software development who had been involved in the telephone conference call at the Well on Tuesday, told him my plan, and asked if his offer still held. I apologized for calling him at the end of the business day, but he didn't seemed to mind, and he told me that his staff would still be around for a while to talk to us.

Before leaving I called Andrew and had him read me the precise times of several events corrected with his best estimates of our times-synch error, so that we would have something to correlate with Netcom's records. It was almost four in the afternoon when Julia and I picked up burritos at Zona Rosa on Haight Street and drove down I-280 to San Jose in her Mazda. I figured one way or another we'd be able to get my computer from the Well later on.

Tracking a stretch of the San Andreas fault, 280 is considered by many to be the world's most beautiful freeway. It's a nice description, although I've always found it to be an oxymoron. Tucked up against the Santa Cruz mountains, 280 runs down the center of the Peninsula, and is actually Silicon Valley's Mulholland Drive. On the way south the highway winds through Woodside, Portola Valley, and Los Altos Hills, where the Valley's new and old money commingle. As you drive by the thousands of acres that were once Leland Stanford's farm, you can still see dairy cows grazing not far from 3000 Sand Hill Road, the brain center of the Valley's venture capitalist community, which is the principal beneficiaries of what has been described as the largest legal accumulation of wealth in history.

As we drove I ate my burrito and phoned Kent Walker to let him know about our next step. I told him about being stymied in Colorado and asked about the limits of the Electronic Communications Privacy Act, which made it illegal to intercept cellular telephone calls. Even if it was illegal to listen to voice calls, I wondered, would it be a violation of the law simply to look for the presence or absence of a data carrier being sent by modem over a cellular telephone call? He replied that as long as we weren't deciphering the content of the data, such an interception would probably be legal. At this point my question was only hypothetical, but at some point it had occurred to me that that course of action might be our only option.

Twenty-five kilometers farther south in Cupertino, I-280 passes Apple Computer's new research and development campus. Here in 1993 former Apple chairman John Sculley planned to install himself as the company's chief technical officer only to be deposed in a boardroom coup much like the one in which he ousted Apple's original visionary, Steve Jobs, eight years earlier. From Cupertino the highway arcs through the heart of Silicon Valley, offering endless vistas of low-slung semiconductor fabrication and computer design and assembly plants.

Netcom itself is located in a twelve-story steel and glass tower across the street from the Winchester Mystery House just off 280 in San Jose. Now a tourist attraction, the Winchester home was designed by the paranoid widow of the inventor of the Winchester repeating rifle and is full of hidden rooms and secret passages that lead nowhere. The Winchester name was later borrowed by IBM's disk drive manufacturing division, located at the very south end of the Valley, for the first modern hard drive.

After we stepped through the front doors and began our search for the Netcom offices, it felt as if we had made a wrong turn and had found ourselves instead across the street at the Mystery House. We ended up going down one flight of stairs, reversing directions after sticking our heads into a lobby, and then heading up several flights before we finally found Rick Francis's office.

Sociologically speaking, Silicon Valley can be divided into "techies" and "suits." The difference between the two is often only that the suits know how to dress and have managed to work their way out of the engineering ranks and into management. Francis was clearly a suit, dapper in a buttondown shirt, tasseled loafers, and a patterned sweater, the typical uniform of product marketing managers and engineering vice presidents throughout the Valley. Dealing with an outsider on a computer security issue was obviously new territory for him, and though he wanted to be helpful he wasn't quite sure what to expect from me and so was a bit guarded.

After I quickly filled Francis in on what we knew from our time at the Well, we went upstairs and rounded up two members of his technical staff. One of them, John Hoffman, a systems administrator, was a quiet engineering type who configured and maintained Netcom's computer systems. The other, Robert Hood, was a network administrator who appeared to be a genuine hacker who really knew his stuff. He was calm, knowledgeable, and didn't seem arrogant about his abilities. He was also the stylistic counterpoint to Francis. Plump and clean-shaven, Hood had masses of curly dark hair that fell twenty centimeters below his shoulders. He was wearing a faded black Metallica T-shirt adorned with a grinning skull, blue jeans, running shoes, and had an alphanumeric pager hanging from his belt. I liked him immediately. Robert was the classic Silicon Valley hacker who genuinely liked his work. He'd grown up with Netcom from its first days as a local Internet provider.

After Francis told Hood and Hoffman, "Give them any of your time and any equipment they need," we found a conference room and got to work. I made it clear that our goal was to locate our quarry as quickly as possible and keep moving upstream until we pinned him down. Once again, I reviewed the data from the Well, and pointed out that the connections we were interested in were coming repeatedly from Netcom and CSN. I also explained that we had a growing suspicion that we were dealing with Kevin Mitnick. The Netcom crew already knew who he was; it seemed that he had caused a lot of trouble for them in the past.

I showed Robert the list of events that Andrew had read to me and asked him if it provided enough information to help figure out what account the intruder might be using at Netcom.

"No problem," he answered.

During the meeting Robert and I did most of the talking as we assessed the obstacles in doing packet filtering at Netcom. I asked about their internal network, details of recent break-in incidents and what kinds of precautions they were taking. I also asked about the stolen credit card numbers we had found in the dono account on the Well, and it turned out that these had initially been stolen almost a year earlier and had been floating around in the computer underground for some time; their existence had been mentioned the previous year in *2600* magazine. Francis said that initially, Netcom had no firewall protection, and customer data had been kept on computers that were relatively unprotected. The oversight had been a costly error, and they knew it. He wanted to know if we had a copy that was taken after mid-January of this year. If the credit card data had been stolen again, it meant they had a huge problem.

It ended up being a short meeting, which impressed me, as we had been able to circumvent most of the social niceties and got down to business immediately. Afterward Francis said that he wanted me to listen to a tape, and he took us into a room near his office and played a recording made from a conversation between one of the system crackers who had been plaguing Netcom and a technical support person. Francis was obviously curious to see if the voice sounded similar to one in the messages on my voice mail system in San Diego. The taped call involved the Netcom person talking to the cracker about his motivation for breaking into their computers and asking about some of his methods, but Julia and I agreed that the voice on the other end of the line sounded nothing like the one on my voicemail.

It was almost 6:30 P.M., and Francis apologized for having to leave early. He would have loved to stay around and observe, he explained, but he'd scheduled an essential business trip for the next morning. Before he left, though, he gave a final authorization to our pursuit.

"Remember, anything you need, we'll pick up the tab," he said. "And if you have to travel somewhere to track this guy down, Netcom will pay."

After locking horns with Claudia, and being second-guessed by everyone at the Well, Netcom's unconditional support was a welcome relief. For the first time I began to feel we had a reasonable chance of finding our data thief.

Julia and I and the two Netcom systems guys went upstairs and squeezed into Robert's tiny office, which barely had room for a Sun workstation and was crammed full of technical manuals.

The list I had taken from Andrew over the phone gave us precise start and end times of sessions coming from Netcom to the illicit accounts on the Well, so our challenge was to find out if there was a single user who had been logged on to Netcom at all of the times on my list. We had one critical clue: the time of the dropped connection on the Well should correspond to a similar log-out on Netcom, an event that should stand out in the mountains of accounting data. Moreover, finding that our attacker turned out to be a single person, rather than several people or a gang sharing one account, would greatly simplify our task—there would be only one location to hunt for. I was counting on Occam's Razor, the principle in science and philosophy that when competing theories exist to explain some unknown phenomenon, the simplest explanation is preferable.

Robert took a seat at his workstation and the three of us crowded around him and watched as he searched through his files for log-ins and log-outs that had occurred at particular times. I could immediately tell that he qualified as a genuine Unix wizard. He never hesitated at the keyboard, and commands just flowed from his fingers. When I asked questions he wouldn't pause to remember how to find a particular piece of information, but the results would just appear almost instantly. Robert was also committed to catching our intruder. "This guy has been really plaguing us," he said. "I've begun to take this personally. If you find him, I'll be there with you. Rick Francis and Bob Rieger, our chairman, will be there, too. They're totally pissed off about this."

He was clearly jazzed by our arrival. With Netcom's continuing expansion in different cities his plate had already been quite full. Now he was looking forward to an adventure in which he wouldn't have to balance his official system administration work against the hunt for the intruder.

To look for a match between the Netcom and the Well data, he needed to hunt for information on the 23 Sun SPARCstations that made up Netcom's online service. Robert had a script that would search through system accounting records on all the machines going back to January 1, but it would take a while.

While his script ran, Robert started to tell me about Netcom's internal network. He explained that the 23 SPARCstations were all connected to a Fiber Distributed Data Interface, or FDDI, local network ring. Also connected to this ring were the routing computers that provided connectivity to the Internet, as well as their own transcontinental T-3 network, capable of moving almost 45 million bits of information per second. This backbone, in turn, was connected to a nationwide web of T-1 data lines, linking both their high-speed data customers and their local Points of Presence, or POPs, back to their San Jose network hub.

Instead of having a single 800 or long distance phone number, most national Internet service providers place POPs with small pools of dial-up modems in dozens or even hundreds of cities around the country. It was this ability to establish a private data network—one that bypassed the standard public telephone long distance network—that created the economies of scale that made it possible for Netcom to do business as a nationwide Internet service provider with local dial-ups in even fairly small cities around the country.

Perhaps Netcom's efforts to make their network easy to access would work in our favor. While we had never seen the intruder using the Well's telephone dial-up lines to come directly to the Sausalito online system—he had always connected over the Internet—Netcom had local dial-up lines in 51 cities around the country—if the intruder was sloppy, it was possible he would tip his hand as to his actual location with a phone call to a local Netcom number. Trap-and-trace information from the phone company might then allow us to pin him down even if he was using a cellular phone.

We talked about what would be involved in setting up monitoring on a network of computers that was larger than any I'd ever faced before. What I needed was a single point from which we could get access to all of the packets that were percolating through Netcom. Dealing with the Well had been like standing at a street corner on Main Street in a small midwestern town and intercepting all the red Fords or all the cars with California license plates as they went by and photographing the driver of each one. Netcom, in contrast, would be like coming to Los Angeles and doing the same thing on the Santa Monica freeway.

It turned out that there was a single choke point in their network.

That was the good news. The bad news was that it was on their main FDDI ring. FDDI is a very high-speed computer network standard which transmits data at 100 million bits per second, ten times faster than the Ethernet network we'd been dealing with at the Well. Monitoring this network would require additional hardware and special software, as the Ethernet monitoring tools we'd employed at the Well were useless here.

By now the data had been collected on user log-ins and Robert began plowing through them, looking for a match. After a while it became increasingly obvious that there was a single account that matched with the log-ins of the trespasser at the Well in each case.

A user of an account named gkremen appeared to be our culprit. There were several local log-ins this month from San Francisco, but every remote direct dial-up access to gkremen came exclusively through their remote POP in Raleigh-Durham, North Carolina.

"I'm sure it's him," Robert said, though I was hesitant about jumping to a conclusion prematurely, particularly because we had only four data points, three log-ins to the Well and one ftp session, to work from. We looked more closely at gkremen. Who was this guy? We found Netcom account information that indicated that gkremen was a legitimate user, not a made-up account like many of those we'd found on the Well and Internex. Gkremen was leasing a high-speed network connection from Netcom directly from his computer's location, but he also had a secondary account on Netcom's systems, known as a "shell" account. It looked like the real gkremen used the account on rare occasions, and as we examined the connection records it became increasingly apparent that his account had been taken over.

Robert scanned through gkremen's home directory, and it was pretty boring except for one thing that caught his attention: a small program called test1. He explained that it was a version of the telnet program which didn't log its usage. Normally when anyone uses the standard Netcom telnet program to connect to another computer, the user's name and remote computer name are recorded. Robert had already begun working on a modification for Netcom's operating system so that the record-keeping function couldn't be circumvented. Obviously, someone had commandeered gkremen's account and was using it secretly.

It was looking more and more as if we'd struck gold. Scanning through the log-in records for gkremen, we could also see connections from familiar sites like escape.com and csn.org. Raleigh seemed to be his favorite, though; in the past five days he'd come through there 26 times. He'd been on almost every day, including a few sessions that morning.

I thought I remembered some of my friends who live in Raleigh complaining about the quality of their phone service.

"Robert, do you know who the phone company is near Raleigh?" I asked.

"Yeah," he replied, "It's GTE."

Groan. "Oh no, I was afraid of that."

GTE had a reputation for having lax security. Their central office switches were notorious for being commandeered by phone phreaks who would secretly reprogram them to get free phone calls and often play esoteric and nasty tricks. Our task would be made much more difficult if our intruder had also managed to tamper with the telephone company's equipment, but that was a hurdle we wouldn't have to face for a while.

Potentially the Raleigh discovery was a significant break. If the intruder was simply connecting to Netcom from the Raleigh POP, our monitoring operations might be greatly simplified. At each of their POPs Netcom used an Ethernet network to connect equipment ranging from Portmasters to routers. If we could find a single local site on the periphery of Netcom's national data network we would avoid having to build an FCCI-monitoring system, and sort through the vast quantities of data that ran along the FDDI network backbone here in San Jose. We began checking airline schedules to see how quickly we could get someone to Raleigh, and at the same time I called Kent to ask him to get a trap-and-trace order for the Raleigh POP.

"I can't do it tonight, because it's too late," he answered. "But I'll get it set up first thing in the morning. Who is the phone company?" I told him, but he didn't seem to have the same reaction to GTE that I did.

While I was talking to Kent, Robert wrote a simple script so that every time the gkremen account was used, an alert would be sent to his pager telling him which Netcom POP the call was coming from.

It was almost 8:30 P.M., and Robert's pager went off almost immediately after he'd finished installing the alert, but this time it was with bad news. Gkremen had logged in, but he was not coming into the Netcom system through their Raleigh POP, this time he was coming through Denver!

Damn, I thought to myself, *he's been incredibly consistent for the past five days and now we show up and he shifts his location.* It meant that we couldn't be sure he would go through Raleigh, and we would therefore have to look at all the data from across the country in the Netcom network to trace him. I wondered briefly if he'd been spooked or was actually somewhere else. Although it was possible that he was dialing in to different POPs in an attempt to be covert and hide his real location, Robert mentioned that they were having technical problems in Raleigh and it was also possible that the intruder was just phoning to a different POP to get a working modem line.

As we watched, Robert used a diagnostic utility at the POP to peek at gkremen's keyboard session. Although the software wasn't meant for monitoring a live session, it worked in that capacity—sort of. As the person who was using gkremen's account typed, Robert would click on his mouse, and the contents of a small memory buffer from a Portmaster at the Denver site would be displayed on his screen showing us what the intruder was typing. Unfortunately the buffer could only display sixty character snippets of the activity going in each direction, which meant that we could see most of what the intruder was typing at his keyboard, but only an occasional glimpse of what he was actually seeing on his screen. We also encountered another problem that made it even harder to see what was happening clearly. At the time Netcom was grappling with a software bug in its largest Cisco routers. These are the computers that are responsible for directing the billions of packets of data per day that were circulating around the FDDI network ring and sending them to the right destinations in the Internet. Every thirty seconds or so, the entire network would have a miniseizure, meaning that we lost more keystrokes. It was a little like wiretapping someone while playing the 1812 Overture loudly in the background.

Despite the dropped packets, however, we were still able to form a rough idea of what he was doing. We watched as he tried to break in to a computer at CSN, apparently without success, and then he turned to another computer at the Colorado facility and tried to edit one of its system configuration files, but found that it was a read-only file, and could therefore not be tampered with.

We watched as the trespasser next used the file transfer command to connect to the public archive computer of CERT, the government security information center.

I started laughing. "Looks like I was right, the anklebiters are reading technical manuals," I said.

He was searching through CERT's files for the word "monitor," and his intentions were obvious: he was trying to figure out how to insert a small network-monitoring program back inside the operating system of one of the CSN computers. The program, known as NIT, or Network Interface Tap, is a standard part of the computer's basic operating software, but it is usually removed for security reasons. If he could reinstall it in the operating system he would be able to secretly capture passwords and other useful information. He found what he was looking for in a file named 94:01.ongoing.network.monitoring.attacks. The file gave instructions on how to turn off the monitoring software, and now he was trying to figure out how to turn it back on. Ironically, the CERT file wasn't even a recent advisory, but was actually more than a year old. But he nevertheless attended to it as diligently as someone following a recipe in a cookbook, working right under the noses of the CSN system administrators.

After seeing that our intruder was now coming from Denver, I placed another call to Kent to tell him we'd now need trap-and-trace there as well as in Raleigh. While Robert and Julia stayed entranced with the snippets of the intruder's sessions, I began thinking about how we were going to put a monitoring operation together to allow us to actually trace him. Each of Netcom's POPs had banks of modems plugged into devices called Portmaster communications servers, manufactured by Livingston Enterprises, a Pleasanton, California company. The Portmasters let dial-up users access Netcom's computers over its own network. Our problem was that the Portmasters, unlike other models, combined the separate sessions to each computer into a single stream of data and we were unable to break them out individually.

Robert knew Livingston's founder, and said he would make an emergency call to ask him if he could help us in unravelling the sessions.

Figuring out how to monitor the FDDI ring was our next problem. This would require a fast computer, interface card and a concentrator to hook the machine onto Netcom's ring. Unfortunately Netcom didn't have any spares of this hardware. Assuming we could find the hardware, we would still need source code to the software driver for the card so that we could modify it to let us monitor the ring. I remembered I had FDDI software on a backup tape in my house in San Diego, but since nobody there had a spare key, it wasn't going to do us much good.

I paced around Robert's crowded office trying to think about where we could get a FDDI concentrator to hook a monitoring computer onto the Netcom ring.

I was racking my brain trying to think of someplace where I might get the necessary equipment late at night in Silicon Valley. I couldn't just walk in the door somewhere and help myself, and they wouldn't have what we needed at Fry's, the Valley's techie supply store famous for selling everything from computers to potato chips—FDDI concentrators typically cost many thousands of dollars.

I suddenly realized I knew just the person.

I called my friend Soeren Christensen, an ATM network wizard at Sun and someone whom I had worked with. He was still at the office when I phoned and, after explaining our predicament, I told him it was vital we have a working monitoring station in place by 7 A.M. the following morning, the time our intruder usually reappeared each day.

"Soeren, do you remember that FDDI concentrator that used to be in the ceiling of your lab in Mountain View before you moved to Menlo Park?" I asked him. "You didn't hang on to it and have it lying around somewhere now, do you?"

"I think I can find what you need, Tsutomu. I think I remember where it is," he answered. "I can probably dig up some extra hardware too. I'll look around."

"That would be great," I said. "Where can we meet you?"

It turned out Soeren was planning to have dinner with his wife at a microbrewery in Sunnyvale called the Fault Line, not far from Netcom's offices. "We'll get organized here and meet you there in a little while," I told Soeren.

When I got off the phone Robert and Julia were still watching the attacker's antics and it took me a while to pull them away to make sure we got to the restaurant in time. It was now almost 9:40 P.M., and the brewery was scheduled to close in twenty minutes. We decided to take one car to dinner, since we were all planning to return and spend the rest of the night setting up our monitoring operations. Julia's Mazda was stuffed with my ski gear, and so we piled into John Hoffman's shiny blue-green Mustang. Both Robert and Hoffman had what looked like brand-new American muscle cars. While the standard issue Silicon Valley engineer's car is usually a BMW or a Saab, both of Netcom's technical engineers must have had a little of San Jose's remaining native culture in them. It felt a little bit like *American Graffiti*, George Lucas's 1973 account of the early sixties in a California Central Valley town where life still revolved around cars instead of computers.

The Fault Line is one of dozens of microbreweries that have sprung up in the Bay Area during the last decade. An upscale replacement for the beer-and-burgers taverns of an earlier era, the microbreweries have a more sophisticated California cuisine as well as a selection of exotic beers, which are brewed in large vats usually set off beyond glass partitions at the back of the building.

Both Julia and I were intrigued by the beer list, but conceded that after a couple of glasses there would have been no way we could function through the night, which looked like what was in store for us.

Soeren and his wife Mette had already arrived by the time the four of us showed up. I noticed the waitress brought Mette an order of horseradish mashed potatoes. *Only in California*, I thought. While I told Soeren what we were up to, we all tried to relax, because we knew this might be the last break we would have for a while. Over dinner we talked about the monitoring system we needed to set up and our problem in getting a computer fast enough to keep up with the Netcom's FDDI ring. Soeren, who was one of Sun's best designers of networking gear, said that he'd been able to find enough random hardware parts for us to custom-build a computer. He also thought he had the

FDDI driver source code on a backup tape at his apartment, which was close to the restaurant. So we arranged for Julia to go back with him later and pick it up.

After dinner we all stood in the parking lot as Hoffman backed his car up to the trunk of Soeren's car.

"This is like a Silicon Valley drug deal," Julia said. Everyone laughed nervously.

Of course, in reality it was unlikely anyone was even giving us a second glance. Half the companies in the Valley probably began with the salesguys working out of the trunks of their cars. Soeren handed me two carrying bags full of random gear, including connectors, memory, a processor module, and various interface cards. I looked at it and said, "Gosh, you shouldn't have gone to the trouble of tearing it apart, you should have just brought the whole computer."

As soon as we drove back to Netcom, Hoffman began assembling the new monitoring computer, placing little green stick-on dots on all the Sun equipment so we could identify it easily. It was after 11 P.M. when I paged Andrew. He was over in Berkeley having dinner with Mark Seiden at the Siam Cuisine, the first, and some say still the best, of the East Bay's Thai restaurants. We had agreed to give Mark some of our monitoring functioning to make it easier for him to track the intruder at Internex.

"Andrew, I need you to go back to the Well and get my RDI computer and bring all of our software monitoring tools down here to Netcom," I told him. "It's going to be a long night, because we need to have monitoring in place by the time he's active again tomorrow."

Our interloper would usually begin his day at about 7 Pacific time and then log-on intermittently throughout the day. He would usually vanish for a few hours at around three in the afternoon and then come back with a vengeance and frequently remain active until well past midnight. It was increasingly clear that whoever was on the other side of our computer screens wasn't a casual anklebiter, but an adversary who had a deep obsession with whatever he was doing.

Julia returned around midnight with Soeren's FDDI tape, and it took some time to find a proper tape drive to read it. When I finally looked at his software my heart sank. It was FDDI driver software source code all right, but it was written for Sun's Solaris 2 operating system. Netcom was running Solaris 1. It was hopeless.

I had hoped to be able to insert Soeren's software easily into our monitoring computer. If we'd actually had the source code this would have been fairly straightforward. I had wanted to use my modified Berkeley Packet Filter software because it was written efficiently enough to keep up with the torrent of data packets that were flowing through the Netcom fiber-optic ring. Now we were going to have to use another strategy.

As we pursued our various tasks the intruder came back on-line at 12:40 A.M. He was still logging in from Denver, and he was still messing around with the CSN computers. A short while later Robert saw him break into fish.com, Dan Farmer's computer. He watched as the intruder looked through Dan's mail for any occurrence of two different text strings, itni and tsu. The first one meant he was certainly still looking for the word Mitnick, and the second was probably for me. If my opponent was indeed Mitnick, he had now taken an even more consuming interest in me. After a while he was back on the Netcom computers, this time trying to find out where Rick Francis's mail was being routed.

Andrew showed up about two in the morning with our hardware and software, and he immediately set to work trying to figure out how to install the Berkeley Packet software into the FDDI driver software from scratch. Without the source code I was pretty sure it wasn't going to work, but Andrew was optimistic and he set to work seeing if he could make it work by trial and error.

Most of the Netcom staff had departed hours earlier, leaving us alone among the partitioned cubicles in windowless rooms. The only other people who were around were some telephone installers at the other end of the floor, putting in a new PBX in the Netcom machine room. The company looked like a typical Silicon Valley business in the midst of hypergrowth. As quickly as these organizations move into new quarters they tend to outgrow them. Everything seems to be in flux. Unfortunately, another trademark of the Valley is things tend to collapse as quickly as they expand.

By 3 A.M. all of us were already fairly sleep deprived, and Robert, Hoffman, and Julia kept making runs for the soft drink machine that was set in an open space across from Robert's office.

Caffeine has never had much of a positive effect on me. After a while "Make another selection" lights began showing up next to the different drink buttons.

"We're going to run out of everything with caffeine pretty soon," Andrew said.

I paced back and forth between Andrew, who was hacking the FDDI software; Robert, who was monitoring network operations; and John Hoffman, who was working in the Netcom machine room still bringing up our new monitoring station.

Despite the complaints about Netcom, I was actually quite impressed by their organization. I walked into their machine room and saw rows and rows of SPARCstation server computers. Everything was remarkably neat and professionally set up. It appeared that the engineering of the system was well thought out.

It was almost three-thirty in the morning when we finally turned on the new computer which had been set up behind the locked door of Netcom's machine room. Hoffman named it Looper, a reference to the FDDI network which was set up as a ring that the packets flowed around.

Andrew hadn't been able to insert BPF without the source code, and we were rapidly running out of time for further experiments.

I thought about our other options. We had two different FDDI cards from Soeren: one built by Sun, and another from a company called Crescendo. I was pretty sure that the Sun card with its standard driver software, even running on a fast SPARCstation, wouldn't let us filter packets quickly enough to keep up with Netcom's FDDI ring under full load. The Crescendo card and driver had a better reputation for performance than the Sun card, but I didn't know by how much.

I tried the Crescendo card first. I was hoping that it would function well enough so that even though we weren't able to get the BPF software to work, NIT would do the job. NIT is slow, but maybe the speed of the card and SPARCstation 10 could make up for the inefficiency. If this didn't solve the problem, the only other option was going to be to think of something else clever, which I hadn't figured out yet.

Once it was in place, it took only a couple of minutes to realize that it wasn't anywhere near fast enough, and that we would be fighting a losing battle as the East coast came on line. Around five or six every morning, the number of packets flowing through their FDDI network would start to soar as people on the East coast first logged in to check their mail and get their net fix. From his computer Robert watched the display that monitored the number of packets coursing over the FDDI network backbone. It read about 4,000 packets per second.

"That's about as low as it ever gets," he said.

Andrew, meanwhile, was watching looper's performance.

"Tsutomu, this isn't cutting it," he said. Netcom's network was barely ticking along, and we were already losing one percent of the packets that were flowing past our monitoring station.

"This isn't acceptable," I complained to no one in particular.

We decided to try the Sun FDDI card, but it turned out to be even slower than the one from Crescendo—and buggier. The Crescendo card was reinstalled, and we resumed our attempt to monitor the network.

It wasn't. As we watched the display on the SPARC station we saw that it was running at about 70 percent of capacity. Shortly it got worse. While we were sitting watching, the the number of data packets being dropped started to spiral upwards as the network load began rising. I had a vision of people all along the East Coast, still in their bathrobes, holding mugs of coffee, going into their dens and logging in to Netcom. I wondered to myself, *Do they have any more of a life than we do? Well, at least they got a good night's sleep.*

"Tsutomu, in a little while we're going to be up to twenty thousand packets per second," Robert said.

It seemed obvious that we needed to do something that would take only a couple of minutes and would work, even if it was a kludge—computer jargon for a Rube Goldberg device.

"It might work if we put something in front of NIT," I said to Andrew. "I could write a quick and dirty prefilter that will sort packets before they even get into NIT."

Andrew nodded in agreement, but at this point I'm not sure he really cared. He was stretched out in an office chair across from where I was sitting, and seemed already to be half asleep.

I thought about the problem a little further and read through the source files for the operating systems I had in order to try to understand what was happening between the system software and NIT a little better. It seemed like a tiny prefilter would be fairly fast—not blazingly fast, certainly, but I hoped it would be fast enough to be able to deal with the number of packets flowing past our monitor machine even at Netcom's peak loads. My program would be the crudest of solutions, a little piece of very low-level software that would sit in front of NIT and discard most of the packets before they ever got to the cumbersome, inefficient program. I called it snit____foo and wrote it without even bothering to use an editor. I simply copied each line I wrote into a file and then compiled it so that it could be run by the computer.

I sat down in front of the RDI and wrote as quickly as I could while Andrew watched over my shoulder. After I finished I turned to him and said, "Did I do anything obviously wrong here?"

He took a cursory look over my code to see if any of it had the potential to crash. My program was designed to filter for up to eight separate network addresses and reject all the other packets. If it worked correctly NIT would have to deal with no more than a few percent of the packets that were flowing around the FDDI ring.

After Andrew inspected the code I compiled it on the RDI and it seemed to work. We copied the program onto a floppy disk and carried it into the machine room where we put it on looper. It was an ugly kludge, but at this point there was nothing to lose.

I was exhausted, but still managing to function under the pressure of knowing that we might see our opponent at 7 A.M. I fumbled around for a while, trying to correctly patch my program into the operating system kernel. It took several attempts until I figured out what I was doing wrong. It was almost 6 A.M. when packets began trickling into files for us to reconstruct later in the day. By now Netcom's network was coming alive. I ran a few test cases and everything appeared to be functioning properly and the load on the machine was manageable. Then Andrew and I spent some time configuring the filter. With everything in hand for the moment, I left the machine room and went to see what had become of Julia. She was still planning on going away for the weekend with John and about an hour earlier she had bailed out and gone and curled up under one of the desks in the office outside of Robert's cubbyhole. She was still tucked in the corner, using my parka as a pillow.

Robert was concerned that Netcom workers coming to work in the morning might be startled to find a strange woman sleeping under a desk. I noticed that Andrew had dealt with *that* problem by hanging a piece of paper above her head which read: "Do Not Disturb!"

CHAPTER 12

In the first morning light Julia and I stood on a balcony of the Netcom building opposite Robert's office. Through a cold mist I could see the early morning commuter traffic was already flowing on Winchester Boulevard. I'd put my parka on, but the morning fog still chilled me.

"Tsutomu, everybody has something to do here but me," she said. "I feel like a fifth wheel. I shouldn't be here."

It was true. Through most of the long night Robert had managed the network, Andrew and I had hacked the filtering code together, and John Hoffman had set up the monitoring station. After Julia returned from Soeren's with the driver tape, she had been left on the sidelines, while the rest of us had been focused on making this work. She resented being the gofer on our team.

I pointed out to her that at the Well she'd been our diplomat, acting as a liaison with Claudia, whom I was basically ignoring. I thought back to the previous weekend when Julia decided to come along on the trip to the Well.

"When we started this you told me you wanted to be here because this would be an opportunity to watch and learn," I reminded her. I could see that she was exhausted and feeling bad about herself and that something else was troubling her. But I didn't want to have that conversation now. We had both been awake for almost twenty hours and we were approaching the time the intruder usually became active. We needed to be back inside because our monitoring gear would require careful attention, as in the past twelve hours his patterns had changed and he was no longer coming exclusively through the Raleigh POP. We had tracked him this far and now we needed to quickly figure out what the next step would be. My sense of urgency was growing, and I didn't want this opportunity to slip away. The longer we waited, the greater the possibility something would go wrong. I had been hoping he was a creature of habit, and now I was concerned about losing any more of our advantage.

We stood there for a while longer staring west out toward the hills, which were barely visible through the fog. It was cold and I was feeling nauseous, the way I feel sometimes when I've gone without sleep for too long.

Finally, to break the silence, I said, "He comes online as early as 7 A.M., I have to go back inside. I need to make sure we're ready."

I walked into Robert's office and sat for a while. Having spent the night with us, he was now back at work doing his regular job. We watched as the performance monitoring software on his workstation showed the FDDI network load begin to rise steadily. There was still a great deal of work to be done, for the information that we were now seeing from each POP was being saved as an undifferentiated glob of data. Without the software that Robert had asked Livingston to supply us, we still couldn't break it out into individual user sessions. It was as if we had been handed a box containing pieces to several different jigsaw puzzles. We first needed to sort the separate puzzles from one another, which is precisely what the Livingston software would help us do. Only then could we piece together what was actually happening in an individual session.

After about an hour Robert suggested we all go downstairs and get some breakfast at a deli located on the ground floor of Netcom's building. Andrew had spent all his money, and was going to only have a cup of tea, but when I looked through my wallet and found six dollars, I gave him most of it so he could buy something to eat. Julia had coffee and I bought an Earl

Grey tea in a styrofoam cup, and since Andrew and Robert had already settled deep into a technical discussion, we walked outside to sit in a patio in the courtyard of the building. On the way outside we laughed about how it was impossible to talk technology all of the time, the way Robert and Andrew seemed to. We both agreed a little balance was necessary in life.

I picked at my empty cup and listened to her. I could hear the stress in Julia's voice. This was a familiar feeling, every time she had to go back and deal with John she would become tense and nervous. But this time she didn't see it.

"I'm going to have to get some rest if I'm going to deal with John this weekend," she said. "If I go up there totally exhausted, it's just going to be another disaster."

We spent an hour and a half trying to talk about what was bothering her, but we weren't getting anywhere and I was feeling increasingly frustrated. We went back upstairs and I continued to work on our monitoring tools. The software for untangling the data from the Portmasters had now arrived, but to be able to use it, I still needed to do a lot of work with my own tools first.

Our filter was losing packets and I spent some time fiddling with the Livingston program to be certain that it would faithfully capture any of gkremen's sessions on Netcom's computers.

The intruder had returned a little after 10 A.M. and about an hour later Andrew and Julia went into Robert's office to see what the intruder was doing. Robert told us that so far today he had seen gkremen logged in through the Raleigh and Denver POPs. While they watched over Robert's shoulder, I continued to work on the software while listening to their comments through the door to his office.

The cracker had connected from Netcom to hacktic.nl, the computer in the Netherlands that is an electronic gathering place for the computer underground. He was using the account name martin. Later we would be able to extract a precise videotape of his activities, but for the moment we had to rely on Robert's cruder tool that captured characters in a small temporary memory buffer and displayed them on the screen.

"My mouse finger is wearing out," Robert said. Every time

there was a break-in during the last day Robert had been tracking it by repeatedly clicking his mouse button and picking up
snippets of the intruder's keystrokes.

They watched on the screen as the intruder attempted to set up
a talk session with somebody whose user name was jsz. A network
information center database revealed he was located in Israel. The
database also indicated that he was typing from a Silicon
Graphics workstation. The Israeli connection was an interesting
one, for Kevin Mitnick had been rumored to have fled to Israel
while he was a fugitive in California in the mid-1980s. It was
another tantalizing clue.

The intruder started a program called talk, which divided his
screen in half and allowed him to see what he was typing in the top
half of his screen and what jsz responded in the bottom half.

```
[No connection yet]
[Waiting for your party to respond]
[Ringing your party again]
[Waiting for your party to respond]
[Connection established]


martin:   fuck this is lagged


jsz:      hey. OK, just a sec. Iím in another window as
          well.


martin:   hello


jsz:      hello


martin:   yes , i am lagged to hacktic.


jsz:      AHhh. OK. whats up?
```

```
martin:    can you send me sol & mail stuff?
```

After complaining about their very slow connection Martin was
apparently asking his contact in Israel for information. "Sol" probably referred to Solaris, the version of Unix distributed by Sun
Microsystems, and "mail" might have meant sendmail. Security
weaknesses in mail systems have traditionally been a way to break in
to computers.

```
jsz:       ok. i sent you sol already.

martin:    i need you to send it again it was corrupted.
           laso can you send me the mail thing now too?

jsz:       ok. yup. let me send it, then,

martin:    ok pls send both again your last pgp msg was
           fucked up.

jsz:       ok. will do let u/l again :0

martin:    ok do you want to try the mail thing with me
           now?
```

There was a long pause at this point. Martin was obviously persistent.

```
jsz:       now? no; later i will try myself, perhaps... you
           want to try it @oki?

martin:    ok can you send me now so I can try it :-)

jsz:       OK. I sent you sol stuff. check it out now,
           ok?

martin:    yup

jsz:       will dig up and send 8.6.9 thing later.

martin:    hmm... i was hoping you would send me the
```

```
mail thing right away so I can get to certain
things.
```

Another long pause. They were indeed discussing sendmail; the current version was 8.6.9.


```
jsz:      OK. sendmail is sent.

martin:   hold on

jsz:      check your mail

martin:   i am on the phone too.... ok so you sent me both
          sendmail & sol?
jsz:      yes

martin:   thanks you dont want to try oki now?

jsz:      no
```

At this point it seemed that Martin was trying unsuccessfully to persuade his acquaintance to use his special cracking tools to attack an Internet gateway computer belonging to Oki Telecom, the cellular telephone manufacturer.

```
martin:   ok, are the complete details there in sendmail
          so I can do it w/o your help?

jsz:      take a look, and you'll see yourself. if you
          know how to set up identd, i guess.

martin:   ok, hey are you at labs?

jsz:      not the CS one.

martin:   ohh ok well wanna meet online later?

jsz:      yup. dont make this bug useless though :-)

martin:   gimme a break. CERT will do that ina few days :-(

jsz:      Hehheheh.
```

Jsz was telling Martin not to share this information about a particular system vulnerability he had just given him. They both knew as soon as they exploited this weakness the computer security community would be alerted, and the back door would vanish.

```
martin:    thanks for the trust. I'll protect it too i want
           to use it just as bad as you!

jsz:       no worries B-)

jsz:       "Give me a place to stand," said Archimedes,
           "and I will move the earth" :-)
           (just reading through someone's mail, as we
           speak :-)

martin: :-)
```

These guys were using other people's electronic mail the way most people use the library.

The session ended, and Robert told everyone to get out of his crowded office. From the session data, I reviewed what I knew about our intruder's technique. He obviously believed he was immune from surveillance. As had been the case at many of the other computer sites he'd broken in to, he had probably tried to set up a sniffer at Netcom and found he was unable to monitor the high-speed FDDI backbone. When he failed, he would have assumed that because he couldn't install a sniffer, nobody else could, either. He would have concluded that he had a great security advantage by going through Netcom on his first hop into his pillaging forays on the Internet, where he could not be detected. He was wrong, for we had accomplished something he had probably believed wasn't technically possible. In this game we were playing he had made an incorrect assumption, and he might have to pay for it.

I was still sitting in the open space just outside of Robert's office, mesmerized by the LED scrolling advertising sign on top of the candy machine when, moments later, he yelled out, "There's a gkremen session coming from Atlanta."

Atlanta! We hadn't seen sessions originating from Atlanta before. Was the intruder trying to mask his location by entering Netcom's network from even more locations? I logged back into looper and patched the Atlanta address into our filter, and immediately the information we were saving turned into a cascade. Atlanta alone was generating more than nine megabytes of data a minute.

Worse, I was spooked.

Until the evening before we had arrived at Netcom's offices, their records had shown that the intruder had been connecting exclusively from their Raleigh dial-up, except when he entered Netcom via the Internet from escape.com or CSN. By Thursday night, he'd come several times from Denver, and now from Atlanta; from the logs we saw a brief connection from Chicago, as well. Worst of all, the new pattern had started almost immediately after I'd asked Kent, the assistant United States attorney, for a trap-and-trace order.

Did he know about the traces? Did he have the ability to tap the telephone company? Or was he able to eavesdrop on us? If we were right and our adversary was Kevin Mitnick, he had been known to illicitly wiretap law enforcement officials to stay one step ahead of them. It was possible he was just thumbing his nose at us. If that was the case our task was going to be much harder. I told myself to wait patiently and not panic, hoping the new pattern was just an anomaly.

Andrew and Julia returned to watch as the intruder connected again from Netcom to hacktic.nl, logging in as Martin, with the password "oki,900."

He first checked his mail, which had three messages from jsz. The first was a reply to a query, "Hey, where are you, dude?" It contained only one line, "okay, back."

The second and third messages were the text files encrypted with PGP, or Pretty Good Privacy, the free data encryption program. Martin saved them with the file names solsni.asc and sendmail.asc. Although the file names were intriguing, their contents were beyond our reach. With a long enough encryption key, PGP files would even be beyond the decoding powers of the world's intelligence agencies.

Next the intruder typed "w jsz," a command that checked to see if jsz was still connected to the Hacktic computer, but jsz had vanished. Martin now backtracked, disconnecting from Hacktic and returning to Netcom. He typed, "ftp hacktic.nl" and then again logged into the Dutch system as Martin. This time he transferred to gkremen's account the two files jsz had left him from the Netherlands computer. Finally, he completed the process by downloading the files from the gkremen account on the Netcom computer in San Jose to his own personal computer—wherever he was hidden. After finishing the transfer he immediately deleted the two files from his account.

There was a long pause. Was our trespasser thinking? Was he decrypting and reading his files? Suddenly he connected again to hacktic.nl and ran a program called Internet Relay Chat, or IRC, which permits thousands of people all over the world to participate in hundreds of simultaneous keyboard "chats." It's the CB radio of the Internet. When IRC requested, "Please enter your nickname," he typed "marty."

Marty! Andrew and I had seen "marty" before—it was the name of the account on the Well where we'd found a stash of stolen cellular telephone software. With IRC he joined a public channel called #hack, an open gathering spot for some of the world's computer underground types. Instantly his screen was filled with the scurrilous chatter of dozens of anklebiters, much of it obscene.

Ignoring the babbling, he sent a private message to jsz. "helo jsz?"—and then corrected his spelling, "hello jsz?"

No luck. A message came back, "jsz's away, email me."

As he was contemplating his next move he was interrupted— jsz had answered. Acknowledging each other's presence the two conspirators made secret contact again using the ntalk program.

```
[No connection yet]
[Connection established]


martin:    hi read that stuff VERY interesting I KNEW
           mastodon would be GOLD!


jsz:       :-) i knew so too.
```

```
martin:   Hey we need to setup a bd so I can use it too.
          so far I havent FUCKED up one site you let me on
          so history shows. :-) you like history, right?

jsz:      I am history major :)
```

They were apparently talking about a computer named Mastadon where they had apparently found useful information about a back door ("bd").

```
jsz:      hehehe. you mean, you want to be on the alias
          too? :-) meanie :0

martin:   hey, thats pretty slick so: when someone con-
          nects to 25 it actually connects back to inetd
          on the remote?

jsz:      back. yes, exactly — that's how it actually
          works (ie identd..)it might be a nasty bd in
          there :-)

martin:   Heheheh. Why didnt I THNK of it. question: it
          seems you can dump anything into the que, can it
          execute portd as root or just mail stuff?

jsz:      I am thinking of it. i dont think you can get it
          execute anything as root, but you might trick it
          into running something for you, i will work on
          it later today.

martin:   hmm.. like finger :-)
```

As Andrew, Julia, and Robert watched they realized to their alarm that Martin's Israeli friend had learned about a new security hole in sendmail.

"Hey, they have a new sendmail bug," Andrew said to me through the doorway. "It has something to do with identd."

"I'll turn off the feature right now," I replied. I dropped everything and dialed-in to my computers in San Diego, making sure that if our intruder tried the new trick on our machines he would run into a stone wall. At the same time Robert was on the phone to John Hoffman, instructing him to do the same thing on all of Netcom's computers.

Julia and Andrew began reading what was being typed on Robert's screen aloud so I could hear it while I worked on closing the sendmail hole.

```
jsz:      eric allman is my hero ;)

martin:   my hero is japboy!

jsz:      finger into markoff's butthole :)

martin:   see markoff is not acting right. a reporter
          doesnt HELP catch someone its not ethical. he is
          the reason why my picture was the front page of
          the new york times
```

We had proof! Martin could only be Kevin Mitnick and he was calling me "Japboy." This was getting personal, but it felt remote and a little surreal. "That's not very nice," I said.

```
jsz:      yeah, I think markoff is nigger, he's tired of
          his blaklife, and needs some adventure. He
          should be killed :-) I will send him a package
          from Saddam Hussein, or Collonel Kadaffi, what
          sounds scaries, hussein, or kaddafi?

martin:   nah someone :-) needs to get to nytimes.com and
          create a story about japboy that he is a con-
          victed child molester and get it printed with
          markoff's by line.

jsz:      AHAHAHA., that'd be funny as hell. :-)

martin:   can you imagine the results.

jsz:      tsu will be pissed as hell

martin:   yes, or add to a real markoff story that men-
          tions tsutomu is real dan farmers gay lover. and
          that they secretly meet on queernet.org
```

```
jsz:        for netsex :-) AHAHAHA. That'd be even funnier.

martin:     that would be the hack of the century!

jsz:        hahaha. really :-) markoff will *die* too, tsu
            will find it a matter of honor to buttfuq him :)
```

The running commentary continued, but none of us could believe how childish and inane it all sounded. Rather than sounding like murderers, the pair sounded juvenile.

```
martin:     hey does 8.6.9 by default connect back to the
            src inetd dor identd?
jsz:        yeah, it ddoes (by default..) so does the send-
            mail that casper dick runs :-) dik, even.

martin:     :-) hmmm... well obviously we can have it mail
            out shit (example in memo) but to execute code
            is the best technique. :-)

jsz:        you know sendmail techniq  :)

martin:     see I do KNOWtsendmail technique! the trick is
            to do it soon so we get to our targets before
            cert announces the bug.
```

At this point I thought back to the first voice mail I'd received when my caller boasted, "I know sendmail technique." I'd put the recording on the net, but they obviously knew all about the break-in to my machines.

```
jsz:        OK, I will work on it, i think it'd not be hard
            to do it. there aaint many, me thinks, okidoki,
            and some other folks :-)

martin:     well mot, oki, dsys.
```

Martin was referring to Motorola, Oki Telecom, and a computer system in Colorado, possible targets to attack.

```
jsz:        telnet to 'em and see :-0

martin:     i dont have windows here like you. i would have
            to disconnect from talk then you wanna hold on.
            hold on brb
```

At this point Martin exited from the talk program and briefly checked to see what version of Sendmail the Motorola gateway computer was running.

```
Stopped
xs1% telnet motgate.mot.com 25
Trying 129.188.136.100 ...
Connected to motgate.mot.com
Escape character is '^]'.
220 motgate.mot.com. 5.67b/10a - 1.4.4/mot-3.1.1 Sendmail is
ready at Fri, 10 Feb 1995 15:01:15 -0600


500 Command unrecognized
quit
221 motgate.mot.com closing connection
Connection closed by foreign host.


xs1% fg

martin:     no go 5.67b sendmail i just checked

jsz:        hang on ahh... thatís IDA sendmail.

martin:     I suppose it doesnít do the same identd trick.

jsz:        not sure, i run the same sendmail on netsys

martin:     hey is netsys.com a service which sells shell
            accounts like escape?
```

Netsys was a computer system that belonged to a computer programmer named Len Rose who had been convicted of stealing software from AT&T while serving as a consultant for the telephone company. He had served a year in jail.

```
jsz:       nope

martin:    how do you connect?

jsz:       you wont be able to connect to netsys from out-
           side even :-)
           try it. nasty firewall by moi :-)

martin:    lets see: we can run tap on ramon NOT!
```

"Tap," we recognized—it was the program that had been used to hijack my connection between Osiris and Ariel.

```
jsz:       ramon is SGI, it doesn't support loadable mod-
           ules :) :) :)

martin:    just kidding if I could I wouldnt violate our
           trust.

jsz:       I know! Weee, beavis & butthead on MTV (we have
           tv at labs at EE)

martin:    hey they just showed sneakers on t.v. this weel
           old marty whata guy.

jsz:       hmm, we have european channels here, only
           CNN is from the US. [I saw sne]akers a while ago
martin:    hey do we have playnyboy.com yet?

jsz:       no time yet :) will take care of 'em later
           today, i suppose, or tommorow.

martin:    ahh do you have a bd on the sunos.queer box i'll
           do some sniffing if you want.

jsz:       not yet. maddog.queernet.org is the sun, last
           time i checked : what a name, eh  ddog.

martin:    normal bd like access1
```

When Andrew mentioned access1 my ears pricked up. That was the name of a firewall computer that Sun used to protect its internal corporate network from the unruly Internet. So it had a back door, too!

```
jsz:        ^F-your-lastname :-)
            or ^F-your-initials :)

martin:     HAHAHAHHAHAHAHAHok ^fbishop

jsz:        ^F^B^I :-) rsh ard.fbi.gov -l marty csh -fbi
            :-)

martin:     we have to NEVER let that bd out , so do oyu
            have it installed on maddog?

jsz:        nope, as i said: no time ;-(

martin:     ahhh i thought you would always do a bd for
            later access oh well...

jsz:        yes will do it sometime this weekend. anyways, i
            am back to coding :-)

martin:     hey we have to go over the procedure again so I
            can start doing it as well. I have some nortes
            but its been a while. too bad your so far away.

jsz:        some nortes?

martin:     notes - sorry.

jsz:        i sent you getpass once :-0
martin:     ahh you did i'll check my other encrypted disk.
            hey you have been REALLY a great help with unix
            stuff. I am going to send you a hole that works
            on EVERY VMS box up to 6.0 by mty friend nmc.

jsz:        wow. that'll be impressive. I wish I knew VMS
            better ;-)

martin:     but NO ONE else has it so its like giving you
            fr. PLEASE NEVER share it, ok

jsz:        nmc does, no? fr /:0) I have none to share it
            with, and I really have no desire to spoil your
            VMS fun :-)
```

Nmc was obviously Neill Clift—one more piece of evidence confirming that Martin was actually Kevin Mitnick.

```
martin:    great ill pgp it later tonight i am going out
           now. it will work on bguvms :-)

jsz:       Thanks.. I will appreciate it.. Ok, I will be
           coding tonight..talk to you on tommorow or so.

martin:    I dont even let anyone else know I have it but
           you trust me and I trust you so maybe you can
           use it too in your explorations :-)

jsz:       email me, ok? thanks!

martin:    ok no problem its actuully the BEST VMS bug I
           have in my toolkit.

jsz:       thanks :-) from remote? : )

martin:    no, not[remote. I dont have a remote bug on VMS
           5.0 and greater.
           but I do for vms 4.7 and lower.

jsz:       cool.. I think bguvms is 6.0, (not sure, will
           have to check..still)
           Thanks anyways :-)
```

The conversation ended abruptly, apparently because the connection had been dropped, but in Robert's cramped quarters a mild pandemonium set in. Now there was little doubt about who the trespasser was. As far as I was aware there was only one computer criminal whose picture had been on the front page of the *New York Times*.

On July 4, 1994, Markoff had written an article in which he called Mitnick "cyberspace's most wanted." It had described some of his escapades and noted that he had managed to evade the FBI and other federal and state law enforcement officials for more than a year and a half. At the time, I thought that the piece had made the FBI look inept.

I called Markoff and told him about the conversation Robert had just seen, and asked him if there was anyone else's picture that had appeared on the front page of the *Times* with one of his articles.

"The only other person I can think of is Robert Tappan Morris, and this obviously isn't him," he said.

We finally had a face and a set of motives to attach to the ghostly electronic footprints we'd been following for more than a month, but there was still a great deal left to be explained.

Who was jsz? I made some calls, and people I spoke to said they'd heard of him before. One person said he thought jsz was working as a subcontractor for a United States semiconductor company which had a design laboratory in the Middle East.

It was clear that Mitnick was relying on jsz as a source of Unix cracking expertise, in exchange for his own knowledge of DEC's VMS operating system. Talk about honor among thieves! I also had a hunch that jsz was involved in some way in the attack on Ariel in San Diego—possibly he'd provided the tools, or maybe he'd been the one who had actually led the raid.

We'd also learned another important fact, for while we had seen that Eric Allman's mail files had been stolen and stored at the Well, neither Andrew nor I had looked inside them to see what kind of information they contained. Allman was the author and maintainer of the sendmail program, and now we knew that it was likely that jsz had found a detailed discussion of a new security flaw while reading through Allman's mail after breaking into mastodon.cs.berkeley.edu, the computer where it was stored.

Mitnick and jsz were systematically trawling the Internet, and it appeared they were specifically targeting the computers of security experts to rifle through their mail. With the techniques they had pilfered, they subsequently attacked the computers of corporations like Apple, Motorola, Oki, and Qualcomm.

At 2:11 P.M. Mitnick connected from Denver through Netcom to escape.com. From my post next to the soft drink machine I could hear the other members of our team laughing as they watched him copy a file called girls.gif into a directory belonging to jsz on Escape. He then looked through Markoff's mail file and scanned the subject headings, stopping only to read one personal note that had been sent to Markoff by a friend.

Several minutes later he found his friend jsz again for an impromptu chat:

```
Message from Talk_Daemon@escape.com at 17:20 ...
connection requested by jsz@ramon.bgu.ac.il
```

```
respond with: ntalk jsz@ramon.bgu.ac.il
```

martin: hi there

jsz: hi
            ...
martin: what bd are you plotting :-(
            :-) i mean
jsz: :-)
            we'll see after it's done!
            it'll execute portd itself.

martin: I can hardly wait; is it sexy?

jsz: yah, dan farmer would fall for it :)

In their dreams maybe. Don't these guys have a life?

martin: hehehh. ok ill let you get back to it i am going
            out now to at lunch and work on finding a real
            job.

jsz: send me pizza :)
            (kosher tho) :) ok.
martin: with ham?
jsz: good luck with your searches.

martin: Can you sugest any good reading books on sysadm
            on unix boxes?

jsz: sure: read cyberpunk :)

martin: ya yay ya

It looked like Mitnick was using *Cyberpunk* as his resume.

martin: i moved some file into escape:~jsz/marty ok

jsz: hey, you can use ~jsz/.elm/.4_m dir for your-
            self.. if you want.. I will make it world-write-
            able, but not readable, so you'd have to know
            the EXACT path to it.

martin: ok will move them later, ya since posse fucks
            with you maybe I should.

```
jsz:       hehehe. ok.

martin:    they will fuck with me by mistake and they dont
           want to piss me off :-)

jsz:       AHAHAHAHAHAa. B-)

martin:    or their phones wont have dialtone!

jsz:       go for it :) naah.

martin:    ok i will talk withn you later.

jsz:       Ok, talk you later today..

martin:    bye

jsz:       bye!
```

Nice guys, I thought. *Is this how they spend every waking moment?* I began to recall what I knew about the Posse, the gang that Jim Settle, the former FBI agent, believed was responsible for breaking-in to my computers. What did we have here, internecine war in the cyber underground? My reverie was interrupted by Robert, who had pushed back from his desk and stood up.

"I have to get some sleep, and you have to go, because I can't leave you here," he said determinedly. Robert had now been up for more than thirty hours, and three in the afternoon was the customary time the trespasser would generally take time out. He assured me that his pager was working and that if Mitnick returned, we would be alerted. I realized he was right, and in any case, for the first time in days I felt comfortable with our position. The monitoring system was now working, we were fairly confident that we knew who our target was, and we needed to get some food and rest, for we were going to have to be prepared to deal with Mitnick later in the evening. From here on it would be necessary to work with the FBI and the telephone companies to pinpoint precisely where he was physically located. We agreed to meet again at 8 P.M.

Out on the street Julia, Andrew, and I were in that zombie-like state that comes when you go beyond lack of sleep, but I couldn't take time to rest, for there was much to be organized if we were going to see any progress that night.

I needed to make phone calls, and so we drove to a Hobie's restaurant located a couple of blocks away in a shopping center. Hobie's is a distinctly California-style health food chain specializing in serving breakfast all day—it's the kind of place where sprouts seem to come on everything you order. Inside we spread our gear out on our table. We were trying to be circumspect, but with a cell phone, beepers, and a RadioMail terminal, we were probably pretty noticeable, which gave us all a tinge of paranoia. Julia thought people around us were listening to our conversation while trying to appear as if they weren't.

Finally the waitress walked over, took a look at the table littered with electronics, and said, "You guys look like you've been working."

"Still working," I answered.

I asked her about the difference between two of their veggie burgers and she launched in to a detailed and entertaining technical dissertation about the distinction between their Soy Burger and their Garden Burger. One of them, it turned out, came with mozzarella cheese. It tasted better, but it was higher in fat.

The other house speciality was fruit smoothies, and we each ordered one. When they came the waitress offered to spray whipped cream on them from a can. In my mind, that basically expresses the true nature of the California approach to health food restaurants. They're healthy, at least ostensibly, but actually they tend to be places you can go and not feel guilty about eating junk food.

After we finished ordering I walked outside to the pay phone and called Kent Walker. I'd already talked to him several times during the day to check the status of the trap-and-trace orders. I told him we were almost certain it was Mitnick we were after, and asked again if he had had any luck in getting the Denver trap-and-trace.

"Tsutomu, would you like the good news or the bad news first?" he said, sounding clearly unhappy.

"I'll take the bad news," I replied.

"The Denver assistant United States attorney called the Los Angeles FBI and they told him not to do anything on this," he said.

"Can I infer that I've stumbled into a turf war?" I asked him.

Kent didn't respond to that, but he didn't need to. "The good news," he said, "is that we have a trap-and-trace in Raleigh that should have been active as of 5 P.M. East Coast time."

Getting a warrant for Raleigh meant that the next time Mitnick connected to Netcom from their Raleigh POP, the phone company would be able to determine where the call was coming from.

Still I wasn't ready to give up on the Denver order.

"Can they actually do this? Isn't this obstructing justice or something like that?" I asked him. "The most recent activity has been from Denver, and it would be really good if we could get trap-and-trace there as well for the weekend."

"Hey look, Tsutomu, it's four-thirty now in Denver," he said. "it's almost the end of the day."

"Well, you still have a half an hour," I pressed, still hoping.

After a long pause he said, "I'll try, but don't count on anything."

Kent gave me Levord Burns' SkyPager number and told me that the next time we had a Raleigh connection, Burns would help us get the trace for it from the phone company. When I groaned and asked why I couldn't go to the phone company directly, he gave me some telephone numbers of phone company people, but told me I should try to reach the FBI contact first.

I thanked him and hung up. Just because the L. A. FBI had been chasing Mitnick for more than two years, that wasn't a reason why we shouldn't be able to conduct our own investigation as well. It was frustrating, but I was glad that Kent was with us.

We left Hobie's, and Andrew drove off to pick up some supplies, including fresh clothes, for he hadn't had time to go back to Pei's the night before to gather his belongings. Julia and I walked across the Hobie's parking lot to a field which was full of wet green grass and flowering yellow mustard. The ground was wet with rain, but it was as close as we could get to nature in the midst of San Jose's suburban concrete sprawl.

It was still several hours before Robert was returning, so we climbed into Julia's car and dragged the sleeping bags over us in the front seats. A while later Andrew drove up and parked near us. He left the +4 Jeep's engine running to stay warm and reclined the front seat and and fell asleep.

It was almost dark, and we looked over at Andrew's car and saw that a good samaritan was peering in his window wondering if the person who appeared comatose with the engine of his car running was in need of assistance. We assured her he was okay, he just been up all night and was resting.

Having had lunch, Julia seemed a little more energized, but was still very tense. It was almost time for her to leave for the weekend, and she didn't feel she was prepared to deal with John. It would have been difficult enough even under ideal circumstances, but now she was exhausted and fearful that she wouldn't be able to hold her own.

Given her current state I was also nervous about her being with John for the weekend. At this point in the investigation the last thing I wanted to have to deal with were Julia's conflicts. I was feeling badly overloaded and I was juggling a series of balls trying to keep this operation going forward: technical, legal, and political. I was feeling that I couldn't deal with any more stress.

We talked for a while about whether she really should go away for the weekend. After a while I found myself growing frustrated because it seemed to me that Julia was trying to put me at ease rather than facing her own internal turmoil and disquiet.

"Look," I said. "Whether I'm concerned about your going is my problem, but whether you should go or not is something you need to decide for yourself."

She considered this for a moment.

"Tsutomu, having come this far I'd like to see the investigation all the way through," she said.

"I can't tell you that nothing is going to happen while you're away," I replied. I don't know what's next, only that if we don't move quickly, we stand a good chance of losing him."

"If I leave now am I going to miss the end game?" she asked.

"I'm hoping to have trap-and-trace information from Raleigh tonight," I said, "and as soon as we have a solid lead, I'm moving our base of operations. If he's coming from Denver, I'm heading in that direction; if it's Raleigh, then that's where I'm going."

I told her that she could try to catch up, but we couldn't wait for her.

She was feeling uncertain about what she should do because she had made a promise to John and felt she had to keep it.

I found myself getting even more frustrated.

"You want to have the best of both worlds and you can't do that," I told her. "At some point you're going to have to make a decision."

It got later and later while she wrestled with whether she was going to stay or go. Several times she called John on the cell phone to tell him she was going to be late. It was 7:30 P.M. when she finally decided to leave. I got out of the Mazda and we transferred my ski gear into the +4 Jeep. Julia said that she would come and join me when she got back and I told her she could get in touch with Andrew to track me down.

I had now been up for almost thirty-two hours. Andrew and I drove back to Netcom and waited for a while, dozing, and then we went back upstairs to continue our watch.

Back inside, under the unrelenting soft hum of the fluorescent lights, we looked over the logs and saw that Mitnick had been gone for more than an hour. His last session, which had ended at 6:58 P.M., had come through Denver.

I was worried. We had the ability to trace him in only one city out of dozens of possibilities, and he now seemed to be avoiding it. I was hoping that it was only the technical problems that Netcom was having in Raleigh that was causing him to reroute his calls, but I couldn't be sure that he wasn't already tracking us as well.

I was also bleary with exhaustion, and though it would have been an incredible luxury to go off and find a hotel to crash in, I knew that tonight might be our best and only opportunity to get a trace on him. Since I was very young I've always had the ability to stay awake for long stretches by putting myself in a zone and just focusing on the problem. But as I sat in front of my computer that Friday and tried to make sense of the data we had collected during the day I could see that this was a capacity that was deserting me with age.

As I sat with Andrew getting our software tools in order and

waiting for Mitnick to return I realized that Julia's disappearance
had left me with a sense of relief. I was surprised, but I hadn't
realized how distracted I'd been. Now I felt I could finally focus
on the hunt. Although it was Friday evening, there was more
than the usual activity at Netcom as a handful of telephone
installers moved through the offices, replacing telephones on
each desk. I got up and walked into Robert's office at one point
and realized there was a large, fresh pyramid of Coke cans sitting
on his desk. We had been here a long time.

I went back to looking over the information we'd logged, when
at 10:44 Mitnick logged on. And he was calling from Raleigh!

"Andrew, why don't you see if you can wake up Levord?"
Now it was time to see if the FBI could make its own contribution. Levord was asleep at his home in Fairfax, Virginia, a
Washington suburb, but he said he would work on it. Fifteen
minutes later he called back. Andrew spoke to him briefly and
then leaned his head out the office door and said, "He says that
the GTE guys told him the phone number we gave them does-
n't exist."

I looked at my notes and dialed the number myself. Through
the earpiece I heard the familiar mating call of a high-speed
modem. I walked into Robert's office and took the phone from
Andrew.

"Hey, it works for me, would you like to hear the modem carrier tone?" I said angrily. "What is going on with those bozos?"

This squared with everything I'd heard about GTE. *Just our
luck*, I thought to myself. Levord sounded as if he was still
more asleep than awake, but promised to ask them to check
again.

Unlike some of Mitnick's sessions, this one was a long one, last-
ing nearly thirty-five minutes.

Shortly after Mitnick logged off, Levord called back and said,
"He's gone, they didn't get a trace."

"Yeah, well, your guys had a half an hour."

Levord didn't sound that upset. "If you see him on again, call
me back," he answered. "They have the tracing equipment in
place now."

"My understanding was that they were supposed to have it
working eight hours ago!" I told him.

"They didn't seem to have heard anything about it," he replied.
Great.

It was now 11:20, but fortunately we had to wait for only a few minutes. Robert's pager buzzed again, and sure enough, Mitnick was back as gkremen, once again from Raleigh.

"Call Levord back again and tell him to get these guys going, and get them to trace where the call is coming from this time," I said to Andrew.

He made the call and we waited again.

Thirty minutes later the phone rang.

Special agent Burns reported that they had a successful trace. They had a phone number, which was assigned to Centel, a local cellular phone company recently acquired by Sprint Cellular. Beyond that he wouldn't tell us anything. But we had a phone number, and that might lead us to a physical address! It looked as if the FBI had been right: Mitnick was making his data calls via cellular phone. Levord and I agreed that in the morning he would contact Sprint and arrange to trace the call through their switch.

Mitnick was still electronically prowling around the Netcom computers. As Robert watched he connected to one of the company's server computers called Netcomsv. This was a machine that ran special services available for all users such as the Usenet computer conferencing system, and we discovered that he had installed a back door. He logged in as root and used a password ".neill."—he was still obsessing about Neill Clift—and looked around for a while and then left. Robert was furious. He got on the phone to John Hoffman and made sure that the backdoor was closed immediately

We continued to follow the sessions from the evening and watched a remarkable attack unfold. From Netcom Mitnick had connected to CSN and made himself root at a little after 11:30 P.M. He was still fiddling around with the operating system files of one of their main computers, attempting to install and conceal the system we had seen him build the night before. After about a half an hour he managed to reinstall NIT successfully and then he rebooted—restarted—the computer to make it run his program. He had done it right under the noses of the CSN administrators!

As we watched the session with our own monitoring software Andrew turned to me and said, "A lot of gall!"

As a system administrator, Robert couldn't believe what he was seeing. "I want a videotape of that," he told me.

We watched for a few minutes more, but it had become obvious that none of us were going to be able to fight off sleep any longer. It had been thirty-nine hours since I'd woken up in San Francisco on Thursday morning, and exhaustion had taken its toll.

I hunted through the phone book and found a nearby Residence Inn. I reserved two rooms, and Andrew and I drove about five kilometers through San Jose's deserted streets. It was three in the morning by the time we'd checked in and fallen asleep.

CHAPTER 13

I had certainly been aware of Kevin Mitnick long before the traces of oki.tar.Z on Ariel made him a suspect in my break-in. He had achieved legendary status in the computer underground over a fifteen-year period stretching back as far as 1980, and he'd had numerous run-ins with local, state, and federal law enforcement officials and been sent to jail several times.

My first run-in with him took place during the summer of 1991, when he attempted to "social engineer" a piece of computer security information from me over the telephone. "Social engineering" is a tactic used by people in the computer underground to access a computer by talking unsuspecting computer system administrators and telephone company employees out of valuable information. They rely on people wanting to be helpful. When someone calls and says that they are a new employee in the company, or somebody in another division who has misplaced a password, or someone with a legitimate need for temporary network access to a computer, a person's natural inclination is to give him the information.

Kevin's call came a few months after I discovered a fairly glaring security loophole in Digital Equipment Corporation's ULTRIX operating system. You could get root on a DEC workstation by sending the computer an electronic mail message to a magic address and then typing a few commands. This bug was what software designers call a "buffer overflow condition," and

Robert Tappan Morris's worm program exploited a similar flaw in a network service supplied with the Unix operating system. The software was expecting a character string of no more than a certain length, and when it got a longer one, rather than handling it gracefully, the program could be made to alter its behavior in a particularly nasty and odd way that had the consequence of granting the user all system privileges.

I described the bug in a message to CERT. In principle, CERT is supposed to serve as a clearinghouse for information on computer vulnerabilities so that the people responsible for administering computer networks can learn about and patch them before the computer underground can exploit them. The reality is that rather than make such information freely available so that security loopholes will be attended to, CERT has instead attempted to control its spread as much as possible. It will never publicize the names of organizations that have suffered a break-in, arguing that is the only way it can obtain cooperation. It also tends to produce advisories so general they are not very helpful.

A few months after I reported the ULTRIX bug, CERT produced an advisory that described it in so sanitized a fashion that the report didn't provide enough information to enable someone to reproduce the error. Brosl and I had moved from Los Alamos to San Diego by this time, but I had flown back to Los Alamos to spend a week at the Center for Nonlinear Studies. One morning I heard from my secretary in San Diego that she was getting repeated phone calls from someone at Sun Microsystems who said it was urgent that he reach me. Several hours later I was sitting in a borrowed office when the phone rang.

"Hello, this is Brian Reid. I'm a field specialist for Sun Microsystems in Las Vegas." The caller was speaking smoothly and rapidly. He told me that he had seen the CERT advisory and that he was now at a customer site and needed more information. "I'm not able to recreate the flaw," he explained.

I was immediately on guard. I knew of one Brian Reid, but he worked at DEC, not Sun. This made no sense. First of all, why would someone from Sun Microsystems, at a customer site, be so anxious to get technical information about a security flaw in one of his competitor's computers?

"How can I verify who you are?" I asked.

"That's not a problem," he replied. "Just call this directory number at Sun and they will confirm that I work for them."

He gave me the Sun number, as well as a number in the 702 area code where I could reach him, and then hung up. I called my friend Jimmy McClary, a Computer Systems Security officer for Los Alamos National Laboratory, and told him about the call. He came downstairs and sat with me while I dialed the Sun number the caller had given me. I asked the operator for an employee named Brian Reid, and was told there was no such person working for Sun. I hung up and was chatting with Jimmy about what to do about the caller, when my phone rang again.

This time a much less professional-sounding voice identified itself as a co-worker of Brian Reid at Sun, and said he was also attempting to obtain the information that Mr. Reid had requested.

"Why don't you give me your address, and I'll drop it in the mail on a floppy disk?" I suggested. This seemed to startle my second caller, who began to "um" and "ah." Finally he came up with an address that sounded as if it had been made up on the fly, and hung up abruptly.

I tried the 702 number the first caller had left, and I got the whistle of a computer modem. The 702 area code covers all of Nevada, so I gave the number and the address to Jimmy, who went off to phone the Department of Energy security officials about it. Later I learned that the security people had traced the number I had been given to a pay phone on the University of Nevada at Las Vegas campus. Some of these phones cannot receive phone calls, but instead have a modem to communicate billing information and diagnostics.

Several weeks later I was speaking with Markoff and when I began describing the call from someone claiming to be Brian Reid, Markoff started laughing.

"What did I say?" I asked him.

"There is only one person who would use the name Brian Reid while he was trying to social-engineer you," he replied.

Markoff, who had been researching Kevin Mitnick for his book called *Cyberpunk*, explained that in 1987 and 1988, Kevin and a friend, Lenny DiCicco, had fought a pitched electronic battle against the real Brian Reid, a scientist at DEC's Palo Alto research laboratory. Mitnick had become obsessed with obtaining a copy of the source code to DEC's VMS minicomputer operating system, and was trying to do so by gaining entry to the company's corporate computer network, known as Easynet. The computers at DEC's Palo Alto laboratory looked the most vulnerable, so every night with remarkable persistence Mitnick and DiCicco would launch their modem attacks from a small Calabasas, California, company where DiCicco had a computer support job. Although Reid discovered the attacks almost immediately, he didn't know where they were coming from, nor did the local police or FBI, because Mitnick was manipulating the telephone network's switches to disguise the source of the modem calls.

The FBI can easily serve warrants and get trap-and-trace information from telephone companies, but few of its agents know how to interpret the data they provide. If the bad guy is actually holed up at the address that corresponds to the telephone number, they're set. But if the criminal has electronically broken-in to the telephone company's local switch and scrambled the routing tables, they're lost. Kevin had easily frustrated their best attempts at tracking him through the telephone network using wiretaps and traces. He would routinely use two computer terminals each night—one for his forays into DEC's computers, the other as a lookout to scan the telephone company computers to see if his trackers were getting close. At one point, a team of law enforcement and telephone security agents thought they had tracked him down, only to find that Mitnick had diverted the telephone lines so as to lead his pursuers not to his hideout in Calabasas, but to an apartment in Malibu.

Mitnick, it seemed, was a tough accomplice, for even as they had been working together he had been harassing DiCicco by making fake calls to DiCicco's employer, claiming to be a government agent and saying that DiCicco was in trouble with the Internal Revenue Service. The frustrated DiCicco confessed to his boss, who notified DEC and the FBI, and Mitnick soon wound up in federal court in Los Angeles. Although DEC claimed that he had stolen software worth several million dollars, and had cost DEC almost $200,000 in time spent trying to keep him out of their computers, Kevin pleaded guilty to one count of computer fraud and one count of possessing illegal long-distance access codes.

It was the fifth time that Mitnick had been apprehended for a computer crime, and the case attracted nationwide attention because, in an unusual plea bargain, he agreed to spend one year in prison and six months in a counseling program for his computer addiction. It was a strange defense tactic, but a federal judge, after initially balking, bought the idea that there was some sort of psychological parallel between the obsession Mitnick had for breaking-in to computer systems and an addict's craving for drugs.

Kevin David Mitnick reached adolescence in suburban Los Angeles in the late 1970s, the same time the personal computer industry was exploding beyond its hobbyist roots. His parents were divorced, and in a lower-middle-class environment in which he was largely a loner and an underachiever, he was seduced by the power he could gain over the telephone network. The underground culture of phone phreaks had already flourished for more than a decade, but was now in the middle of a transition from the analog to the digital world. Using a personal computer and modem it became possible to commandeer a phone company's digital central office switch by dialing in remotely, and Mitnick became adept at doing so. Mastery of a local telephone company switch offered more than just free calls: it opened a window into the lives of other people; to eavesdrop on the rich and powerful, or on his own enemies.

Mitnick soon fell in with an informal phone phreak gang that met irregularly in a pizza parlor in Hollywood. Much of what they did fell into the category of pranks, like taking over directory assistance and answering operator calls by saying, "Yes, that number is eight-seven-five-zero and a half. Do you know how to dial the half, ma'am?" or changing the class of service on someone's home phone to that of payphone, so that whenever they picked up the receiver a recorded voice asked them to deposit twenty cents. But the group seemed to have a mean streak as well. One of its members destroyed files of a San Francisco–based computer time-sharing company, a crime that went unsolved for more than a year until a break-in at a Los Angeles telephone company switching center led police to the gang.

That break-in occurred over Memorial Day weekend in 1981, when Mitnick and two friends decided to physically enter Pacific Bell's COSMOS phone center in downtown Los Angeles. COSMOS, or Computer System for Mainframe Operations, was a database used by many of the nation's phone companies for controlling the phone system's basic recordkeeping functions. The group talked their way past a security guard and ultimately found the room where the COSMOS system was located. Once inside they took lists of computer passwords, including the combinations to the door locks at nine Pacific Bell central offices, and a series of operating manuals for the COSMOS system. To facilitate later social engineering they planted their pseudonyms and phone numbers in a rolodex sitting on one of the desks in the room. As a flourish one of the fake names they used was "John Draper," who was an actual computer programmer also known as the legendary phone phreak, Captain Crunch. The phone numbers were actually misrouted numbers that would ring at a coffee shop pay phone in Van Nuys.

The crime was far from perfect, however. A telephone company manager soon discovered the phony numbers and reported them to the local police, who started an investigation. The case was actually solved when a jilted girlfriend of one of the gang went to the police, and Mitnick and his friends were soon arrested. The group was charged with destroying data over a computer network and with stealing operator's manuals from the telephone company. Mitnick, seventeen years old at the time, was relatively lucky, and was sentenced to spend only three months in the Los Angeles Juvenile Detention Center, followed by a year's probation.

A run-in with the police might have persuaded most bright kids to explore the many legal ways to have computer adventures, but Mitnick appeared to be obsessed by some twisted vision. Rather than developing his computer skills in creative and productive ways, he seemed interested only in learning enough short-cuts for computer break-ins and dirty tricks to continue to play out a fantasy that led to collision after collision with the police throughout the 1980s. He obviously loved the attention and the mystique his growing notoriety was bringing. Early on, after seeing the 1975 Robert Redford movie *Three Days of the Condor*, he had adopted Condor as his nom de guerre. In the film Redford plays the role of a hunted CIA researcher who uses his experience as an Army signal corpsman to manipulate the phone system and avoid capture. Mitnick seemed to view himself as the same kind of daring man on the run from the law.

His next arrest was in 1983 by campus police at the University of Southern California, where he had gotten into minor trouble a few years earlier when he was caught using a university computer to gain illegal access to the ARPAnet. This time he was discovered sitting at a computer in a campus terminal room, breaking into a Pentagon computer over the ARPAnet, and was sentenced to six months at the California Youth Authority's Karl Holton Training School, a juvenile prison in Stockton, California. After he was released, he obtained the license plate X HACKER for his Nissan but he was still very much in the computer break-in business. Several years later he went underground for more than a year after being accused of tampering with a TRW credit reference computer; an arrest warrant was issued, but it later vanished from police records without explanation.

By 1987, Mitnick seemed to be making an effort to pull his life together, and he began living with a woman who was taking a computer class with him at a local vocational school. After a while, however, his obsession drew him back, and this time his use of illegal telephone credit card numbers led police investigators to the apartment he was sharing with his girlfriend in Thousand Oaks, California. He was convicted of stealing software from the Santa Cruz Operation, a California software company, and in December 1987, he was sentenced to thirty-six months probation. That brush with the law, and the resulting wrist slap, seemed to only increase his sense of omnipotence.

In the summer of 1988 Markoff obtained a copy of a confidential Pacific Bell memorandum from a teenage computer hacker. The phone company had no idea how it had been leaked, but confirmed that it was authentic. The memo, written the year before, concluded that "the number of individuals capable of entering Pacific Bell operating systems is growing" and that "computer hackers are becoming more sophisticated in their attacks." As a result, the document acknowledged, personal computer users could illegally connect their machines to the phone network and with the proper commands could eavesdrop, add calls to someone's bill, alter or destroy data, intercept facsimile documents being transmitted, have all calls to a particular number automatically forwarded to another number, or make someone's line appear permanently busy. In one of the cases cited, a group of teenage computer hobbyists was able to pull such stunts as "monitor each other's lines for fun" and "seize another person's dial tone and make calls appear on their bill." One of the crackers used his knowledge to disconnect and tie up the telephone services of people he didn't like. In addition, "he would add several custom-calling features to their lines to create larger bills."

The leaked memo was described in a July 1988 front-page article in the *New York Times* written by Markoff and Andrew Pollack. Although he did not know it at the time, Markoff later learned that Mitnick had been the source of the document. Mitnick, whose technical tools included amateur radio, had heard about the memo from a fellow radio operator. Placing a call to the secretary of the author, a security executive at the telephone company, he masqueraded as another Pacific Bell executive and asked her to fax him a copy of the memo. What the secretary didn't know was that Mitnick had rerouted the telephone number so that the memo, instead of being received by a Pacific Bell fax machine, was soon scrolling off a fax machine in the office of a friend. The friend had even programmed the machine so that the secretary received confirmation that the document had reached the correct fax number.

While the Southern California press would soon be referring to Mitnick as the "Dark Side Hacker" and "the John Dillinger of the computer underground," he was really more of a con man or a grifter than a hacker in the true sense of the word. Before the 1983 movie *War Games*, in which Matthew Broderick portrayed a young man with some of Kevin Mitnick's traits, the word "hacker" had been used to refer to a computer culture that had emerged at MIT in the late 1950s. The culture was made up of mostly young men who were obsessed with complex systems as an end in their own right, a culture that was based on the principles of the open sharing of software and hardware designs with friends and of the creation of clever "hacks"—ingenious programs that pushed the state of the computing art.

The true hackers were people like Richard Stallman, who as an MIT student during the 1970s wrote EMACS, a programmer's editing tool. EMACS gave programmers a way to repeatedly revise programs to approach a perfect state, and versions of it are still in wide use by many, if not most, of the nation's best programmers today. But after *War Games* became a blockbuster in 1983, the popular definition of "hacker" became a teenager with a modem who was brazen enough to dial into a Pentagon computer. The true hacker community has been attempting to reclaim the original spirit and meaning of the word ever since, but to little avail. A particularly discouraging incident occurred in 1987 when a small annual gathering known as the Hacker's Conference invited a CBS news crew to attend its meeting in the hills above Silicon Valley. The Hacker's Conference is a low-key event, and perhaps the only professional conference that offers attendees a second full dinner, at midnight, to take account of the nocturnal habits of the hackers. Unfortunately the CBS reporter wasn't about to let the mundane truth get in the way of a good story. He began his broadcast with the alarmist warning that he had visited the encampment of a guerrilla army set to undermine the country's security in a new kind of information warfare.

The world he was describing had little to do with true hackers, but was home to a growing number of people like Kevin Mitnick.

After he finished his prison time and his halfway-house counseling sentence for the 1989 DEC conviction, Mitnick moved to Las Vegas and took a low-level computer programming position for a mailing list company. His mother had moved there, as had a woman who called herself Susan Thunder who had been part of Mitnick's phone phreak gang in the early 1980s, and with whom he now became reaquainted. It was during this period that he tried to "social engineer" me over the phone.

In early 1992 Mitnick moved back to the San Fernando Valley after his half-brother died of an apparent heroin overdose. He briefly worked for his father in construction, but then took a job he found through a friend of his father's at the Tel Tec Detective Agency. Soon after he began, someone was discovered illegally using a commercial database system on the agency's behalf, and Kevin was once again the subject of an FBI investigation. In September the Bureau searched his apartment, as well as the home and workplace of another member of the original phone phreak gang. Two months later a federal judge issued a warrant for Mitnick's arrest for having violated the terms of his 1989 probation. There were two charges: illegally accessing a phone company computer, and associating with one of the people with whom he'd originally been arrested in 1981. His friends claimed Mitnick had been set up by the detective firm; whatever the truth, when the FBI came to arrest him, Kevin Mitnick had vanished.

In late 1992 someone called the California Department of Motor Vehicles office in Sacramento, and using a valid law enforcement requester code, attempted to have driver's license photographs of a police informer faxed to a number in Studio City, near Los Angeles. Smelling fraud, DMV security officers checked the number and discovered that it was located at a Kinko's copy shop, which they staked out before faxing the photographs. Somehow, the spotters didn't see their quarry until he was going out the door of the store. They started after him, but he outran them across the parking lot and disappeared around the corner, dropping the documents as he fled. The agents later determined that the papers were covered with Kevin Mitnick's fingerprints. His escape, subsequently reported in the newspapers, made the authorities look like bumblers who were no match for a brilliant and elusive cyberthief.

Mitnick's disappearance sent agents of the Los Angeles FBI down a series of blind alleys. During his time on the lam Mitnick used his social engineering skills to resume harassing Neill Clift, a British computer researcher from whom he had stolen information while he was battling DEC several years earlier. In 1987 one of the richest treasure troves for Mitnick had been in reading the electronic mail of DEC's security experts. There he had found private messages detailing security flaws that had been discovered in the company's VMS operating system. Clift, who explored the weaknesses in the system as something of a hobby, informed DEC of his findings so the company could fix the problems.

Now Mitnick once again began breaking into computers that

Clift used. In a series of long international telephone calls, Mitnick, who has an actor's talent for altering his voice, also convinced Clift that he was an employee of DEC, interested in obtaining details of new security flaws that Clift had found in the latest release of the VMS system. At Clift's request, Mitnick supplied him with DEC technical manuals that he believed could only have come directly from the company. The two men then agreed to set up an exchange of data, encrypting it with PGP. Clift sent Mitnick a detailed accounting of the latest security flaws he had found, but in a later phone conversation he became suspicious and realized that he had been tricked. Without letting on to Mitnick, Clift contacted the FBI, which attempted for weeks to trace the calls without success. Around the same time Clift was contacted by the Finnish Bureau of Economic Crimes, which suspected that Mitnick had stolen software source code from Nokia, a Finnish cell phone maker with a factory in California.

After receiving a mysterious phone call requesting a Nokia technical manual, the company mailed it to the specified address, a California motel, but alerted the FBI. Agents staked out the motel, only to find that someone had called the front desk and had the package forwarded to a second motel, and the trap failed. Several weeks later, Mitnick somehow discovered the FBI's telephone-tracing attempts and outraged, phoned Clift, called him a "stool pigeon," and again disappeared.

In March 1994 the FBI was publicly embarrassed after they showed up at a gathering of the civil liberties and computers crowd at an annual event known as the Computers, Freedom, and Privacy Conference, and arrested an unfortunate attendee whose only crime was the mistake of registering at the conference under one of Mitnick's aliases. He was nabbed in his hotel room in his underwear, and although he and his roommates protested that he was not Mitnick, the man was handcuffed, and taken to the local FBI office. His fingerprints were checked, and about thirty minutes later word came back that the arrested man was not the fugitive. The FBI had to take him back to his hotel, apologizing profusely.

At about the same time Markoff received a call from Qualcomm, a San Diego firm developing a new digital cellular telephone technology known as code division multiple access, or

CDMA. This technology is particularly valuable because it will allow cellular telephone service providers to pack many times the number of calls into the same amount of radio frequency spectrum. Qualcomm was in the process of setting up a joint manufacturing plant in San Diego with the Sony Corporation to build the new hand-held digital telephones that will employ the CDMA technology.

The Qualcomm executives had read *Cyberpunk*, the first third of which detailed Mitnick's exploits up through his arrest in 1988, and wanted to know if Markoff had any information that would help them confirm what they believed—that Mitnick was behind a recent, well-executed computer break-in during which someone had stolen copies of the software that controlled Qualcomm's cellular telephones.

The theft had begun with a series of phone calls to new engineering employees from someone who claimed to be a Qualcomm engineer from another group. He was traveling, he said, and needed access to a particular server but had forgotten his passwords. Trying to be helpful, the new workers were only too happy to oblige. With passwords in hand, it was only a matter of the caller's logging onto Qualcomm computers, which were connected to the Internet, and downloading the source code for the new phones. When they discovered that their security had been compromised, the Qualcomm executives notified the FBI and were eventually put in touch with the Bureau's Los Angeles office. A group of its agents was already on a case involving the theft of cellular telephone software from more than a half-dozen companies, including Motorola and Nokia. The FBI agents showed up at Qualcomm, took down the evidence in their notebooks, and left. Weeks went by, and nothing happened. The Qualcomm executives called repeatedly asking if any progress was being made in the case, but they found the FBI was unwilling to tell them anything about the investigation or their suspect. All they would say was, "Read *Cyberpunk*."

The increasingly frustrated Qualcomm group tried to figure out more about their break-in on their own. How had the caller been able to systematically identify new employees, who would be the most likely to unwittingly give away company secrets? They finally concluded that someone had snuck into their building and taken a copy of their monthly in-house newsletter, which routinely contained names, photos, and short biographies of new employees. Qualcomm had long been dominated by an engineer's culture, based on mutual trust and a shared team spirit, but the theft made the executives feel that the company was under siege, and created an atmosphere of paranoia within it. At one point, perhaps hoping to find an employee to "chat" with, someone called sequentially through an engineering work area, and several anxious Qualcomm engineers stood and listened as the phones rang one after another.

It wasn't clear to the Qualcomm engineers what the thief intended to do with the software. Simply possessing it, even the source code, would not permit someone who wanted to tamper with the new digital cellular network to get free calls or clone existing phone numbers, as would have been possible with older, analog technology. Conceivably, the Qualcomm executives told Markoff, it would be possible to sell the software, perhaps in Asia, to some black-market counterfeiter who wanted to make cheap knock-offs of their phone, but this seemed hardly worth the effort. Still, according to the FBI, someone was going to a great deal of trouble to steal software from all of the major cellular-telephone makers. Why, they wondered.

Except for the brief 1991 incident, none of this affected me directly until October 1994, when Mark Lottor had some of his Oki cell phone software siphoned from his computer. He warned me to be on guard, and sure enough, several days later Andrew began seeing probes on Ariel. At one point someone started electronically scouting the network portals to our systems. Andrew could see that the interloper was testing widely known network security loopholes in an effort to enter our machines. To repel the invader, he began closing off various potential access routes in response to the attacks. The probes continued until nearly midnight one night. Somebody was clearly interested in our computers, and because of what Mark had told us we later guessed it might be Kevin Mitnick. Piece by piece the puzzle had slowly fallen into place. From the transcripts we had seen at Netcom, I could see Mitnick was aware of me and although he didn't know it yet, now I was on his trail.

CHAPTER 14

"TACTICAL NUCLEAR RANGE"

I was awakened by the beeping of my pager sometime on Saturday morning. In the darkened hotel room I reached over, and peering at its display I saw it was John Markoff's home number.

"What happened last night?" he asked after I groped for the phone and returned his page.

"We got a trace. We have a phone number. I think you should come down and see some of this. We have transcripts of a conversation he was having with someone in Israel and they were talking about you. I want you to look at them."

"Where is he?"

"The evidence suggests that he's in Raleigh, North Carolina."

"Where are you?"

It was a good question. I told him I was in a Residence Inn somewhere in San Jose. I switched on the light and read him the hotel's address. He said he would drive down and meet me in an hour.

I hung up and rolled over and went back to sleep. Forty-five minutes later I got out of bed and stood in the shower trying to wake up and preparing my strategy for the day. A phone number was a good clue, and it would give us something to follow. But it was also no more than that—a single clue. Knowing our adversary was Kevin Mitnick, I realized any given phone number in itself was likely to be of limited value. I suspected that Mitnick may have been trying to mask his location electronically by tampering with telephone company switching equipment, so that tracing attempts would give false information. In 1988, when FBI and state law enforcement officials had tried to track him down in California, their own telephone tracing efforts had led them badly astray. One number supposedly belonging to Mitnick ended in a raid on a Southern California apartment where police and telephone security investigators found an immigrant cook watching television in his under-clothes.

In the movies you get a phone trace and from it an address and then you're done. But in real life tracing through a telephone net-work is a much more subtle and less predictable process. Placing a call is similar to giving someone directions to find a given address: go down this street three blocks, and then turn right, and so on. Tracing, in contrast, is like following directions backwards, and it can be a frustrating exercise. As I stood in the shower, I knew that I couldn't be certain Kevin was in Raleigh: the trace could be wrong, or the phone call might be simply passing through the cellular phone company switch en route from some-where else.

Mitnick's last arrest, in 1988, came only after his partner DiCicco confessed to a DEC investigator. I'd heard people in the computer underground say that the lesson he claimed he'd learned from that incident was that in the future he would oper-ate solo, minimizing the chance of betrayal.

From the past week's surveillance I could tell he was still pret-ty cocky, a bit sloppy, and a creature of habit. And from what I'd seen so far he didn't seem to be as brilliant a hacker as legend claimed.

Without knowing it he had made the same mistake as Mr. Slippery, the protagonist of Vernor Vinge's wonderful 1987 cyberspace classic, *True Names*: he'd accidentally revealed his identity. In his novel Vinge describes a virtual world of powerful computers and fast networks much like the one through which I was chasing Mitnick. And the first rule of that world was to keep your *True Name* in the physical world a secret.

Although he was making an effort to remain elusive by enter-ing Netcom's network from different cities, he had grown lazy, and his repeated use of the Raleigh POP was an indication that he was coming to believe he could operate with impunity. Of course, I realized that I might be the one who was too cocky. It was possible that he had done something sufficiently arcane to protect himself so that he didn't have to worry. My hunch was that he was betting that the cellular telephone companies were more concerned about toll fraud—stealing long-distance time—than about making fraudulent local cellular calls. He was gambling that if he laid low and made only infrequent long-distance calls, he would avoid their attention.

I sat on the bed in front of my RadioMail terminal and read my e-mail from the day before. One message immediately caught my eye—another request from David Bank, the San Jose *Mercury News* reporter. In recent days I'd received numerous pages from him, which I'd ignored. He clearly wouldn't give up on the story.

```
From: Dbank@aol.com
Received: by mail02.mail.aol.com
(1.38.193.5/16.2) id AA22563; Fri, 10 Feb 1995 21:35:42 -
0500
Date: Fri, 10 Feb 1995 21:35:42 -0500
Message-Id: {950210213540_18424375@aol.com}
To: tsutomu@ariel.sdsc.edu
Subject: SJ Merc News questions
Status: RO


     Greetings. I'm sorry we didn't get to connect on
  Thursday or Friday. I'm still interested in meeting
  with you in person and am able to come to San Diego
  if that's easier.
     The gist of the story is that there are a number of
  people who had clear motives for breaking into your
  computer. As it happens, one of them is you. I don't
  mean any disrespect but we need to talk.
     Please call me at home on Saturday or leave a mes-
  sage at work so we can make an arrangement.


                    Thanks.
                    David.
```

Well, he might need to talk to me, but I didn't need to talk to him. The idea I'd broken-in to my own computers and then detected the break-in in order to attract attention was off the deep end. I would have to be certifiable to have presented a technical paper at a conference sponsored by the NSA less than three weeks later.

In any case if he wanted to write his story and jump off that particular cliff I was quite prepared to let him. I had no intention of calling him back or meeting with him anytime soon, no matter how aggressive he was in pursuing me.

I was still drying my hair when Markoff arrived. While I was getting my things together I described what had happened on Thursday and Friday. We talked about the Israeli connection with the student, jsz.

"I think the Israeli connection is significant," he said. "If I were a foreign intelligence agency or anyone for that matter who wanted to steal technology from United States companies, what better cover than to have a fugitive computer felon as a cut-out?"

Markoff was sitting on my bed fiddling with the RadioMail terminal. A single light was on in the tiny convenience kitchen, but the room was still quite dark. Although it was gray outside I hadn't bothered to open the curtains.

"Maybe this is actually a Mossad operation," he continued. "Say this guy befriended Kevin on Internet Relay Chat, or through Hacktic in the Netherlands. Now he's goading him into attacking various American computers. Afterwards they share the spoils."

I didn't particularly see it. It would be easy for jsz to disguise his identity in the Internet, and he could easily be connecting to the school's computers from anywhere in the world. And in any case, why would an Israeli intelligence agency have such a great interest in cellular telephone software and development tools? It seemed more plausible to me that Mitnick believed that by hacking the cellular telephone code he could in effect make himself invisible, for he had a huge stake in not being captured. Another possibility may have been that he was involved in industrial espionage in some way—perhaps he was stealing the software for someone who had a real use for it.

It was 1 P.M. by the time we left the hotel. Robert wasn't due back at Netcom until later in the day, and we had arranged to meet Mark Seiden for lunch somewhere between his San Mateo home and San Jose. We settled on Buck's, an informal Woodside restaurant and bar frequented by the venture capitalists and Silicon Valley CEOs who live in the exclusive bedroom community.

While we waited for Seiden at Buck's, I paged Kent Walker. When he returned my call, I said I would find a landline and ring him back. I walked across the street to a phone booth, told him about the Israeli connection, and gave him a quick summary of where we stood in our efforts to get a trace. We agreed to meet in Menlo Park at Seiden's office, since Walker was on his way to Stanford for a meeting and could come by and talk to us afterwards. He was planning on leaving the Justice Department in only three weeks, and I realized that he was hoping to see this case solved before he left government service.

I next called Levord Burns, who had been in contact with Sprint Cellular, one of the two cellular phone providers in Raleigh. The GTE technicians had told him the call had come from Sprint. He'd spoken to a technician at Sprint, who had told him the phone number didn't belong to Sprint, that it actually belonged to GTE.

"The number's funny," he said. "It doesn't go anywhere."

This didn't make any sense to me, because a telephone number has to go somewhere. My first thought was, *Who's being inept here?* "Is the call from Sprint or isn't it?" I asked him impatiently.

I listened as Levord tried to repeat what he had heard from the Sprint technician.

"I'm sorry, but I don't think you completely understood what he told you." I said, as politely as I could. "I want to talk to the people at Sprint directly."

He said he would prefer to pass my message back to the cellular technician himself.

"Levord, that isn't going to work," I responded. "I'm sorry, but I need to talk to him directly."

Although initially he balked at giving me their phone number, after further cajoling he agreed to try to find the Sprint engineer and set up a conference call for the three of us.

Seiden showed up and we all sat down in a booth and ordered lunch. He told us about his own run-in with the Colorado SuperNet administrators. While he was monitoring, Mark was also able to see attacks against CSN, because some were being launched through Internex. He had called and wound up speaking to a different person than I had spoken with, and Mark warned him that an intruder was messing around with the CSN computers. He described how he'd been able to see their operating system kernel modified and then watched while the intruder restarted the computer. Mark had several suggestions for them and several questions as well, but the technical support staffer at CSN was not about to accept this story blindly, and told Mark, "I'd like your middle initial, your date of birth, and your social security number."

"What!" said Mark, "Why do you want that kind of information?"

"I want to do a full NCIC scan on you before I call you back," came the response. NCIC is the National Crime Information Center database which is supposed to be accessible only to law enforcement people.

"NCIC?" Mark was stunned. "Why would *you* be able to use NCIC?"

"I have my contacts," the technical support person responded.

Obviously, his contacts were the L.A. FBI agents who believed they were closing in on Kevin Mitnick in Colorado.

"I couldn't believe what I was hearing," Mark said, but he gave the staffer the information and then hung up. Hours later, when there was still no reply from CSN, he called him again.

"What the hell is going on here anyway?" he asked. "Don't you realize this guy just rebooted your machine?"

It was futile. As Andrew and I had already concluded, Mark decided he was wasting his time dealing with the people at CSN.

Mark had spent some time carefully examining the files of stolen material that had been stashed at the Well. After watching the intruder attack Internex repeatedly, each time bringing over a range of system-cracking tools from the dono account on the Well, Mark had decided to go into the account himself, and download the entire directory so that he would be prepared for whatever tools he was going to be attacked with. In one of the stashes he found sniffing sessions from CSN that indicated their administrative computer had been sniffed; as the files contained both user and administrator passwords. One of the other things he learned, which was an obvious privacy issue, was that Colorado SuperNet kept their customers' social security numbers. If you have somebody's name, address, telephone number, social security number, and a credit card number you have everything you need to make a royal mess out of his life.

While we were waiting for lunch I paged Kathleen Cunningham, the United States marshal, and a short while later she called me back. This time I walked to the pay phone at the back of the restaurant. I needed more information on Mitnick's m.o., and I was hoping the marshal would be more forthcoming than the paranoid FBI agents we'd been dealing with.

I was in luck, for Cunningham was quite willing to give me information about her efforts to capture Mitnick on an outstanding federal probation violation dating back to late 1992. She told me the FBI had sent a surveillance team with a Triggerfish radio direction-finding unit to Colorado to track him.

"Kevin is misguided, but he's not particularly dangerous," she said.

She seemed to feel sorry for the fugitive and to regard him as a poor screwed-up kid, whom it was her job to find. She suspected that he was still in contact with his family, and she said she had talked to them recently in an effort to get a plea to Mitnick to turn himself in. We talked about the time in Seattle, where he'd narrowly escaped local police and telephone security investigators, largely because they hadn't known who they were watching. She had learned that a McCaw Cellular investigator and a telephone company security consultant had tracked Mitnick for several weeks as recently as last October. They had followed him on foot as he walked around his neighborhood carrying a hand-held cellular phone and athletic bag, and trailed him into a Safeway store and to the local Taco Bell. On several nights they'd gone as far as walking up to his apartment door (the name on the mailbox was Brian Merrill) and listened to his phone conversations where they overheard him talking about cracking passwords.

On another occasion they listened in on his cellular phone conversations and heard portions of a conversation about getting even with somebody's manager.

"We'll really fuck them up," Kevin told his friend.

He also mentioned Denver, indicating that he had been there recently.

After Mitnick fled, the police made an inventory of what they found in his apartment. The evidence they collected included gear for making illegal clones of cellular telephones. They also found a portable computer, as well as a $1,600 medical bill for treatment of a stomach ulcer and a prescription for Zantac, an ulcer drug. On his kitchen table they found a radio scanner and Aerosmith and Red Hot Chili Pepper CDs.

Cunningham said that the FBI apparently believed that Mitnick had recently been in San Francisco, at least briefly. An FBI agent had been listening to a telephone conversation of an associate of Mitnick who lived in the Bay Area, in which the man had turned away from the phone to talk to somebody in the room, whom the agent had clearly heard him address as, "Hey Kevin."

After I had been on the phone for about twenty minutes Markoff came back and told me my soup was getting cold. I thanked Cunningham for her help, and we agreed to stay in touch as things developed.

When I came back to the table Mark described another intriguing clue: the Paul Kocher connection. Mark had looked up Kocher after finding mail from between February and March of 1994 taken from his computer. Paul Kocher, a senior biology major at Stanford University, had been interested in code-breaking since junior high school. He had become an ace cryptographer as a hobby and then turned it into a business on the side. He was consulting for both RSA Data Security, Inc., a Silicon Valley company that is a dominant force in public key cryptography, and Microsoft.

He'd also written a paper with the Israeli cryptographer Eli Biham sketching out a way to break PK Zip, a widely used compression and archiving software program that has a built-in encryption feature. Biham is in the computer science department at the Technion, a prestigious science and engineering school in Israel, and is known as one of the world's best cryptographers. In December 1991 he had also published a paper with Adi Shamir, another Israeli cryptographer, that had laid out one of the first partially successful research efforts demonstrating potential weaknesses in the U.S. Data Encryption Standard, the nation's coding standard used by the government, industry, and by banks, and other financial institutions.

After Kocher and Biham had published their report, Kocher had also posted on the net a portion of it describing the method for breaking passwords beginning with the letter *z*. His intention had been to prove that the Kocher/Biham technique was a successful way to break the code, without making it available for all passwords. It appeared that Mitnick had seen the posted material and had decided to target Kocher's files in order to get the complete version of the program.

Mark called Kocher, and the Stanford student drove up to his home in Belmont to look at the files. He had a remarkable story to tell. About the same time that my computers had been attacked in December, Paul Kocher had gotten an electronic mail message from Eli Biham, "Paul, can you send me a copy of the PK Zip decryption program? I really need a copy of it for my research."

Kocher didn't respond to it, because the request seemed out of character. Biham surely knew it was a violation of United States export control laws to transmit cryptographic software out of the country without an export license.

A week later a more strident note arrived from Biham saying, "Paul, where is that source code I asked for?"

This time Kocher responded with a note back to Biham saying, "Eli, you know about the cryptography laws much better than I do. Why are you asking me for this?"

A few days later he received a reply from Biham addressed to a long list of people saying, "Anyone who received mail from me during the last month should distrust it. I have reason to believe my account was broken-in to and taken over."

Just as we were getting up to leave, Laura Sardina, one of Sun Microsystems' first employees and a longtime friend, walked by. She is a person who really knows how to get things done in the company, and I asked her if I could borrow some SPARCstations, thinking that if this turned out to be a protracted hunt, we were going to need more hardware to set up monitoring in different locations. She wanted to help and told me to come by her office on Monday.

After we left Buck's we followed Seiden to Menlo Park to meet with Kent Walker, driving down Woodside Road, which stretches down to the Bay from the hills, and where the Valley's most successful computer moguls have their mansions and horse ranches.

Dressed in jeans, Walker looked even younger than he did in his weekday business suit attire. I recounted what we'd learned in the past two nights and continued to press him for more help in getting warrants from the phone companies in Denver, as well as a trace order with Sprint Cellular in Raleigh.

"I can't help you in Denver," he said, "but if you want a trace in Raleigh you've got it."

It was now past five in the afternoon and was already starting to get dark. At Netcom, Robert and Andrew had resumed their watch, and we got back on the freeway and drove down to San Jose to join them. When we arrived I found that we had what might become a more pressing problem. Andrew had called Pei at the Well, who told him that, on the previous night at about ten-thirty, their monitoring had revealed the password Mitnick was using to log-in to his account at escape.com. After he had left, Pei had decided on her own that she would log-in as Mitnick and look around for herself.

The problem was that in doing so, she might have given away our element of surprise. Most computer operating systems alert the user each time he connects as to the exact time he logged-on previously. It's a simple security precaution that can tip a computer user off if someone else is using his account.

"Why did Pei do this?" I was irate. "What was she hoping to learn?"

"I have no idea," Andrew said.

"Did she clean up after herself?" I asked.

"No," he replied.

I couldn't believe that anyone would do anything so foolish, particularly someone who supposedly understood computers and computer security issues. Our problem now was that unless Mitnick was totally careless, he would discover that someone was aware of his presence the very next time he used his account on escape.com.

Even worse, if we were unlucky and he was running his own sniffers on escape.com or the Well, he would know exactly who was following him. There was nothing we could do to correct

Pei's mistake, and our only option was to watch and wait. Maybe we'd be lucky.

"Call her back and explain to her what she did wrong," I said to Andrew. "Ask her to please give us just a few more days before they go waving a red flag in Kevin Mitnick's face."

At our portable computer set up outside of Robert's office, I played back for Markoff the keyboard conversation between Mitnick and jsz from Friday, and when he saw that the fugitive thought it would be possible to falsify a *New York Times* story by breaking in to nytimes.com he laughed. "If they only knew," he said. "*Times* management is so paranoid about something like this happening, that the Atex editorial system has no interactive connection to the Net."

From reading the conversation between Martin and jsz again we gained another clue. Martin had mentioned seeing the movie *Sneakers*, and Markoff recognized the significance of the marty user name and *control-f bishop*. Kevin Mitnick, it seemed, had a continuing obsession with the actor Robert Redford. First there was Condor, and now it appeared that Mitnick had adopted another one of Redford's guises. In *Sneakers* Redford had played Marty Bryce, an antiwar activist and a computer hacker who'd gone on the run in the 1960s and years later had taken the name Marty Bishop. In the film, Bishop has created his own computer hacker's "dirty dozen," a group that ends up doing contract work for the National Security Agency.

The Marty connection was one more confirmation that it was Mitnick we were tracking, and I hoped that it might also be an important clue about his location. I called a friend in Boulder and asked him to check the television schedule to see if the movie had shown recently, for it might indicate what region Mitnick was in. Unfortunately, it turned out that *Sneakers* had played on network television throughout the country.

The log-in records indicated that Mitnick had last been on Netcom in the middle of the afternoon. We looked back through our filter data and found that he had connected to a computer called mdc.org, the Internet domain for Lexis-Nexis, the online database company. He used a stolen password to access their current news database and then typed the following search command: MITNICK W/30 KEVIN. He was looking for any occurrences of his name in recent news stories! Our transcript showed that he had looked at the complete text of one story after scanning the headlines of the most recent additions to the database.

LEVEL 1 - 46 STORIES
1. Newsweek, February 6, 1995 , UNITED STATES EDITION, BUSINESS; Pg. 38, 270 words, THE GREATEST HIT OF HACKING

2. Deutsche Presse-Agentur, January 24, 1995, Tuesday, International News, 614words, U.S. hunts master computer "cracker", Washington

3. United Press International, January 24, 1995, Tuesday, BC cycle, Washington News, California, 605 words, U.S. hunts master computer 'cracker', BY MICHAEL KIRKLAND, WASHINGTON, Jan. 24

4. United Press International, January 24, 1995, Tuesday, BC cycle, WashingtonNews, 606 words, U.S. hunts master computer 'cracker', BY MICHAEL KIRK-LAND, WASHINGTON, Jan. 24

5. U.S. News & World Report, January 23, 1995, SCIENCE & SOCIETY; COVER STORY;Vol. 118, No. 3; Pg. 54, 3666 words, Policing cyberspace, By Vic Sussman

6. Pittsburgh Post-Gazette, December 20, 1994, Tuesday, SOONER EDITION, Pg. B1380 words, Six inmates sue, charging jail beatings, Marylynne Pitz, Post-GazetteStaff Writer

LEVEL 1 - 2 OF 46 STORIES
Copyright 1995 Deutsche Presse-Agentur
Deutsche Presse-Agentur

January 24, 1995, Tuesday, BC Cycle
23:04 Central European Time

SECTION: International News

LENGTH: 614 words
HEADLINE: U.S. hunts master computer "cracker"

DATELINE: Washington
BODY:
U.S. law enforcement authorities asked the public for help Tuesday in their effort to track down a legendary master manipulator of the information super-highway.

Officials said **Kevin** David **Mitnick**, 31, origi-nally of Sepulveda, California, is using his hacker skills to stay one step ahead of the law . . .

By about 7 P.M. everyone was hungry. Robert, who had been so enthusiastic about the chance to track his nemesis on Thursday, was now sleepy and taciturn. It looked as if we were facing another long night, so Markoff and I decided we would go out and find dinner for the four of us. We drove for several blocks past movie theaters and shopping centers until we finally located a Round Table pizza parlor. We ordered two pizzas, and while we waited we took seats at a long table in the mostly vacant dining room. We talked about Julia's weekend trip and I told him I'd felt a sense of relief when Julia had left Friday evening, but I also missed her.

Levord finally called back shortly after we returned to Netcom and said he would set up a conference call in a couple of minutes. When he rang back I could barely hear the Sprint technician on the other end of our call.

"Tsutomu, this is Jim Murphy, I'm a communications engineer with Sprint Cellular in Raleigh."

His voice was faint because it was a conference call and I asked if he was using a cellular phone. He was.

"Excuse me, but I really don't want to have this conversation while you're on a cell phone," I said. Levord had set up the call, but I was amazed that he hadn't considered the potential security problem. A radio scanner had been found in Mitnick's apartment in Seattle; hadn't anyone realized that he might easily be able to intercept this conversation?

Murphy explained that he was out in the field and that it would take him about ten minutes to drive back to the cellular company's main switching office. When we resumed the conversation Murphy was still so faintly audible on the other end of the line that we were shouting back and forth at each other. Neither of us had a good explanation of why both the Sprint and GTE switches were showing the call should have come from the other one, but we both realized it wasn't possible. I explained to him whom we thought we were dealing with, and that Kevin Mitnick had a fifteen-year history of tampering with telephone company switches. He was incensed at the idea of someone messing with *his* switch, and as we talked it turned out that Murph, as he preferred to be called, was in fact very sharp, so that we immediately dropped into technical detail.

I began by asking him questions about the telephone switch the Sprint system was using. Telephone company switches are actually just computers with their own specialized operating systems. Often they have dial-up ports for remote diagnostics and maintenance. Frequently phone phreaks and members of the computer underground have used these ports as back doors to tamper with the switches. They can get free phone calls or create chat lines which anyone can dial in to. The Sprint machine was a Motorola EMX 2500, in tandem with a DSC 630 switch, a device about which I knew nothing. I've had some experience with small telephone company and PBX switches, but not much with large central office switches like this. Murph gave me a tutorial on how his switch worked and what kind of data he had available. He had to be careful, because while we had a warrant for GTE information, Kent had not yet prepared one for Sprint, so Murph was limited in what kind of actual caller data he could offer me.

I asked him about the GTE number. It turned out the number that had been captured by the GTE trap-and-trace warrant was 919-555-2774. "Is this a cellular number, or is something in the Originating Number Identification information getting scrambled?" ONI is also used to provide Caller ID, the feature that passes the caller's telephone number over the network to the called telephone and identifies the caller.

"It's not one of our numbers," he answered. "That prefix isn't even a cellular phone prefix."

At this point I knew something was amiss. Normally, technicians can get call-tracing information by looking a number up in a database that is maintained at the telephone switching center. If the number is a local number controlled by the switch, the database will show the exact set of phone wires the call is coming in on.

In this case the GTE calling records were showing the call came from a permanent digital T-1 connection between the GTE switch and the Sprint cellular switch across town, used for routing calls between the two switches. A call coming in to a switch from another switch comes in on what is referred to as a trunk line—in this case the T-1. It can carry twenty-four telephone calls simultaneously. The switch looks in its database of translation tables and routes each individual call according to the information it finds. If it is a call being delivered locally, the translation tables will direct the call either to a particular telephone line, or in the cellular world to the equivalent, known as a Mobile Identification Number (MIN).

As we talked, Murph kept checking his switch to see if he could find anything obviously amiss or something that had been tampered with. While I waited on the other end of the line he explored the innards of the computer, examining its translation tables while he gave me a running commentary of what he was looking at. He said he had a theory that Mitnick might somehow have created a special number that would route his calls through the cellular switch, and then on to a Netcom local dial-up number. Every phone number has a direct route as well as an alternate route, and he wondered if one of the alternates had been messed with. He spent a long time probing his database to see if he could find any evidence of such a hidden route.

Nothing obvious showed up, however, and we began looking for alternative explanations. Murph had records in a database that could be searched and sorted with many different parameters. However, each of these operations took up to half an hour.

We talked about useful ways to sort through the data, and then it occurred to me to ask, "What happens when I dial the GTE trace number?" I did so and heard this eerie "click-click," "click-click," "click-click," which continued to repeat, getting fainter and fainter until it disappeared, and the call disconnected.

I came back on the phone and described to Murph what I had heard.

"My guess is what you're hearing is the call endlessly looping between the GTE switch and ours," he said. "Eventually the power falls below a certain level, and the call is dropped."

I tried it again, and this time Murph monitored it from his switch. Again I could hear the "click-click" sound, but at the same time I could hear the printer in his office register each time his cellular switch tried to set up a call. "Kerchunk," "Kerchunk," "Kerchunk."

"I'll be very surprised if he's tampered with our switch," Murph said. "We do have remote capabilities, but all remote accesses are logged. When Motorola, for example, connects to our switch, we first give them a password, monitor their activities, and then immediately change the password after the session ends."

"Let me try something else," I said. I dialed the phone number that was one number higher than our mysterious phone number. On the other end of the line I heard the familiar warble of a fax machine. Murph didn't see the call go through his switch this time. It made me even more suspicious of GTE. It told us that only one phone number in an entire block of phone lines had been routed to Sprint. Something was funny about that particular phone number.

"My guess is that the GTE switch has been hacked," I said.

We continued to puzzle. He said he could start three simultaneous searches to try to find a match to the Netcom log-in information I had, because he had three terminals.

"Let's try a different strategy," I suggested. "How far back does your database go and what kinds of things can you search for?" He said he could go back as far as 3 P.M. on Thursday, February 9, and he gave me a long list of sortable categories, including call start and end time, call duration, called number, and so on. Looking down my list of gkremen's log-ins from the Netcom POPs, I saw that there were several long sessions.

"Can you search for calls of a duration of more than thirty-five minutes on Friday?" I asked. I had decided that while it might have been possible for Mitnick to conceal where he was calling from, it would be much more difficult to conceal the fact that a call was taking place at all. This was the beauty of traffic analysis.

The second request I had for Murph was to search for all cellular telephone calls made to the range of numbers that were routed to Netcom Raleigh dial-in telephone numbers. Finally, I asked him to search for all cell phone calls to Netcom's Denver number.

Few people use cellular modems to transmit data, so any cellular call to a Netcom POP would be unusual. And in any case, given that Netcom was a local call, a long distance call to a dial-up number would be even more suspicious. In any case, if Mitnick had been making calls using the Sprint cellular system we should have been able to find them here, even if GTE was unable to trace them.

Now I had my three questions. As he set up his computers Murph said it was going to take a while to do the database search, so I told him I would ring him back in a while and hung up. Shortly afterwards I realized we'd both completely forgotten that Levord had been listening on the line.

Because the PBX installers were still working at Netcom and phones kept being taken off-line, I moved to the opposite side of the building from Robert's office where I settled in a vacant carrel with a still-functioning telephone. I called Murph back after about a half an hour to check on the results of his searches.

We started with the local calls to Netcom's Raleigh POP.

"I think I've seen that first number," he replied.

"Good! Can you give me all the calls to the Raleigh POP?"

"I can't tell you the actual calling numbers because you don't have a warrant," he replied. "I can't give you the actual MIN-ESN pairs." The MIN and ESN—electronic send number—are the two separate numbers that define a particular cellular telephone. The MIN is the assigned cellular phone number and the ESN is the permanent serial number embedded in the phone.

"I don't want the number," I explained, and told him that I was trying to match calls to the sessions we had seen from the Netcom Raleigh dial-up. I was more interested in the pattern of calls than in the actual data. I wasn't looking for the actual number, I was curious to see if there was a pattern to the calls that Mitnick might be making to Netcom through Sprint. If we were lucky we might discover that all the calls came from a small number of MINs or from the same physical location.

We began playing a game that was a lot like the classic children's game Battleship. He couldn't tell me what the number was, but he could tell me if it was the same as some other number under certain conditions.

What I could say was, "Do you see this call at this time?" I took two lists, the Netcom list of dial-in numbers from around the country and the summary of gkremen's log-in sessions.

"On Friday at 15:29 do you see a call to 404-555-7332 duration approximately 44 minutes?"

"Yes, I have that."

"Do you have a call of duration 49 minutes at about 20:22 your time on Friday to 612-555-6400?"

"I have it."

"Do they both come from the same MIN?" I asked.

"Yes," he replied.

"Do you have a phone call on February 11 at 02:21 to 919-555-8900?"

"Yes, I have that one, too."

I asked the same question with five more log-ins taken at random. In each case the answer was the same: they'd been placed from the same cellular telephone number. Occam was right.

"So where is it?" I asked.

Murph walked across the room to a map of Sprint's Raleigh cell sites.

All of the calls were coming from cell number 19, located on the northeastern outskirts of the city, near the airport. We now had another important piece of information: Mitnick was at a fixed location. I thought it was unlikely that the calls would be made while he was driving, but I had been worried that he might be changing locations with each call.

"Do you have sector information?" I asked. Some cellular systems can determine which direction the calling phone is actually located in relation to the cell site —that is, the particular transmitter-receiver tower in a certain area.

"No we don't have that information, but to the east of the cell site is Umstead State Park and to the northwest is the airport. My guess is he is transmitting from somewhere south or west of the cell, based on the locations of our other cells."

It was almost one in the morning. By the time we were through we had his location narrowed down to a radius of less than a kilometer.

"I'll fly out first thing in the morning," I told him. "I'll see you tomorrow."

He gave me his numbers and told me he would meet me at the airport.

Even though it was late, I called Kent back and told him it was more important than ever to get trace orders for both the cellular phone companies. After I got off the phone I remembered it had been hours since I'd heard from special agent Burns. It was four in the morning on the East Coast when I called him back to tell him we'd pinned Kevin down.

"You hung up on me," he said when I woke him up.

I suspected that he'd actually fallen asleep on us and hadn't noticed, but I apologized for forgetting him.

"We have it down to within a kilometer," I told him. "I'm flying to Raleigh tomorrow morning, and we're going to need to get a radio direction finding team out there."

It was late. All I got was a noncommittal, "Unnnh."

I'd seen Markoff leaving a half an hour before and I called him on his car phone. Since I didn't know who in the Valley was listening, I was circumspect.

"We're within tactical nuclear range."

CHAPTER 15

I got very little sleep that night. Andrew and I returned to the Residence Inn, but I stayed up making phone calls and trying to get things organized in Raleigh. I was trying to persuade the FBI to send agents and a radio direction-finding team there quickly. I wanted to go to Raleigh so I'd be in a better position to get information and to make decisions in case our target's behavior changed.

At 4:30 A.M. I paged Kathleen Cunningham in an effort to get a Triggerfish radio surveillance team sent to Raleigh. She said she would do her best, but after I hung up I had a moment of panic wondering whether she was going to contact the Los Angeles FBI, and whether they were going to try to get in the way. From what I could see, Kevin Mitnick was a creature of habit in the network world. It was becoming apparent that he wasn't that clever and he was prone to mistakes. At the same time it looked as if he thought he was invulnerable. All this should have made him relatively easy to take down. But for the FBI, who had mastered traditional investigative techniques, yet was ignorant of computers and computer networks, he might as well have been Casper the Ghost. If the L.A. FBI did decide to take a role, however, there wasn't much I could do about it. Kent Walker was helping me, and I'd just have to see what kind of support I could marshal when I arrived in Raleigh.

I called American Airlines and made a 9:20 A.M. reservation

through Chicago for Raleigh, scheduled to arrive there at 7 P.M. that evening. I arranged for a first-class seat because Kent had asked me to have easy access to an AirFone, and I wanted to be able to stretch out and sleep.

Feeling ill from fatigue, I got up the next morning and staggered through the hotel's continental breakfast. Andrew drove me to the airport shortly after 8 A.M., and as we pulled up to the departure gate I asked Andrew if he would contact Julia and tell her where I'd gone. But something else was bothering me, for I was worried that if Mitnick had an accomplice, we were likely to lose the stolen software and find it spread throughout the Internet by members of the computer underground.

"Would you put together a list of all the sites where Mitnick has stashed software and come up with a plan for collecting evidence and cleaning up when he's arrested?" I asked him. "Don't do anything yet—let me clear the legality with Kent Walker first."

As I settled into my seat on the plane I thought to myself, *This is weird, it feels like a movie.* I'd been chasing an electronic chimera for more than a week, and now in the last few hours it had been transformed from some tenuous image on the Internet to a real person in the real world. It's not the kind of situation an academic researcher usually finds himself in. We track this guy down, and then five hours later I'm on the first flight out to try to locate him.

I dozed only a little on the flight across the country. After I'd been airborne for a couple of hours I discovered that Andrew had managed to secretly slip some apples and bananas into my gray daypack. It was a nice thought and it explained why my baggage had suddenly become so heavy.

I had a short time between planes in Chicago, during which I called Levord again. I asked him if he'd had any luck getting in touch with Cellular One, the other cellular carrier in Raleigh. We would still need their help as well. He told me he still hadn't been able to find a phone number.

"Have you tried 1-800 CELL-ONE?" I asked him pointedly.

"No, I haven't tried that yet," he said, clearly annoyed with the suggestion. Things between Levord and I had begun poorly and were rapidly deteriorating. I could tell he didn't like taking orders from a civilian, but he was in an awkward position, since the

Justice Department had told him to cooperate with me. My sense was that he was in over his head technically, and I could see that he resented my having taken charge of the search.

Next I called Kent and asked him about the legality of cleaning up after an arrest. He said that as far as he was concerned, it was legitimate because we were protecting the victims' property.

On our plane's final approach into Raleigh I called Murph, who promised to meet me with one of his partners at the terminal. Even though it was the middle of winter in the East, I was still wearing California clothing: hiking shorts, a purple Gore-Tex jacket, Birkenstock sandals, and no socks.

Julia had told me about growing up in Durham surrounded by the smell of tobacco, and as I walked through the terminal I was immediately struck by its sweet smell everywhere.

We're not in Kansas anymore, Toto, I thought to myself.

While I was waiting for Murph I went to a bank of telephones and called Levord again. I still hadn't been able to extract a commitment of support from him, but he was beginning to say that he was considering showing up. I was anxious to be ready in case Mitnick jumped from one cellular system to the other in Raleigh, but Levord said he was still having trouble contacting Cellular One. I kept remembering what Kent had said about not taking orders from law enforcement officials, and that in our case law enforcement would provide legal and administrative backup for us. I didn't actually share that with Levord, as I didn't see any reason to rub his face in it. By the end of the conversation he agreed to contact a local agent in Raleigh.

For all my persistence, I still wasn't certain Mitnick was actually in Raleigh. What if he had set up some kind of ingenious repeater? I could imagine FBI agents going to an apartment and finding nothing but an elaborate communications system and an alarm to let Mitnick know that his cutout had been discovered. It wouldn't send us all the way back to the beginning, but it would be one more door that we would have to break down.

I was still standing at the bank of phones in the airport when Murph came in to meet me along with another engineer, Joe Orsak. Murph was a large, stocky man who looked as if he had played football earlier in life. He had a direct, no-nonsense manner and just a touch of a Southern accent. His companion was even larger, a burly guy with a friendly face and a moustache. They both seemed excited about the prospect of an adventure that would take them away from the normal day-to-day engineering and maintenance of cellular telephone switches. Recently, they had been involved in a successful bust of an illegal cellular ring in the Raleigh area that had been using cloned phones and selling stolen cellular phone time for international calls from a farmhouse outside of town, and that incident seemed to have whet their appetites for chasing down more phone fraud. As we went out to the Sprint Cellular truck at the curb I thought to myself, *If Mitnick believed he could hide away here in some backwater, he clearly chose the wrong place.*

I needed to pick up a rental car, and wound up with a Green Geo Metro in which I followed the Sprint van. Freeways are much the same all over America, but the one thing I noticed immediately about Raleigh was that there was a lot of road construction. Everywhere I went I saw roadwork. Freeways were being widened, or entirely new ones were being built.

The Sprint MTSO, which Murph pronounced "mitso", using the cellular telephone industry jargon that stands for Mobile Telephone Switching Office, was located on the opposite side of town, in a wooded lot on the edge of a newly developed office park. It was dark when we arrived but I could see a concrete two-story building behind a high chain-link security fence. Behind the building was a tall antenna with a flashing red light on top.

Inside we met Lathell Thomas, an FBI agent from the local Raleigh office, who was known to everyone as L.B. He was on the telephone when I walked in trying to get more information about the situation into which he had been thrust. He was a black man in his late fifties or early sixties, and he had come equipped with the same confidential AirTel memorandum describing Kevin Mitnick as had the FBI agents at the Well meeting. He seemed pleasant and professional, but I could tell immediately that telecom fraud and computer crime were not his areas of expertise.

I called Andrew and set up two pager codes to use in the event of an arrest. One was a "get ready" signal. I asked the FBI agent for the date of Mitnick's birthday, but he was busy so I went over and grabbed his AirTel and read the date off the wanted wire: 080663. Next I came up with 122594, the date of the first break-in to my computers in San Diego, which would serve as the "go" signal for Andrew to start cleaning up the stolen software.

Andrew told me Mitnick had been on again, and they had seen a couple of intriguing keyboard chat sessions. The first one took place about noon with a friend who was a member of Mitnick's old gang in Los Angeles. The friend's home and office had been searched by the FBI at the same time Mitnick disappeared. He had sued the Justice Department over the search and he was publicly taunting the FBI agents who were hunting for Mitnick. Much of their conversation was cryptic, Andrew said. His friend referred to Mitnick as "Kremlin," and Mitnick called him "banana." They were talking about a pre-arranged signal that would come later and permit a direct telephone conversation.

It was an odd conversation and Andrew and I puzzled over what appeared to be other codewords in their conversation. The friend complained about a "mosquito," and then a while later Mitnick typed, "hahahaha. yup I didn't understand your message re: news, mosquito. I guess." What did mosquito refer to? Did it mean that they were worried about being bugged? At the end Mitnick typed, "I heard jl assistant was at hottub's." We both recognized "hottub." In messages that the same friend had posted on Usenet conferences in the past he would include a line at the bottom of each message referring to one of the FBI agents searching for Mitnick as Kathleen "Hottub" Carson.

After our conversation Andrew faxed me some of the material from the monitoring sessions. That morning, Mitnick had connected to escape.com with a new log-in—yoda, the Star Wars character—and found a letter from jsz. He was warning Mitnick his father had had a serious heart attack and that he would be away from the net for the next three to four days.

"One more thing," Andrew had told me before we hung up. "I might have screwed up and sent Julia to Denver instead of Raleigh."

"Oops," I responded. "What happened?"

When Julia had left on Friday night we were still thinking the most likely upstream location would be Denver. On Sunday morning after I departed for the airport Andrew called her to relay the message to come ahead and join me if she wanted to. Since the resort where she was staying was very rustic, none of the rooms had telephones, and the public pay phone wasn't working, so he'd left an urgent message at the office for Julia to page him. Andrew was worried about the stories he had heard about Mitnick's prowess as a wiretapper and when he and Julia finally connected they had an especially cryptic conversation so there would be no danger of giving anything away.

Andrew said, "Tsutomu went to the place he was planning to go next."

Some time after he hung up he realized that he had no idea if she thought they were talking about Denver or Raleigh, but by then it was too late to reach her again. There wasn't anything I could do about it, either, for I had no idea how to get in touch with her. I'd just have to wait and see if Julia checked in with us.

Before long, she did page me. I called her back and she told me that she had booked her flight to Denver and was calling me to make contact.

"Good," I said, "but I'm not in Denver, I'm in Raleigh." I told her briefly what had happened in her absence and she said she would make a reservation and be on the next flight out. A few minutes later she called to tell me she would be on a red-eye flight and would be arriving in the morning.

Inside the Sprint switching center we once again began playing a waiting game. Mitnick had disappeared from the Sprint system. Andrew was seeing activity at Netcom, but today Mitnick wasn't showing up on Murph's consoles. The Sprint Motorola mini-computer that controlled the switch was agonizingly slow at sorting the call detail records we needed to match the profile we had from the previous day's activities. After a while one thing was clear: There was no Mitnick. The calling number from the day before had disappeared. I suggested broadening the search net to see if he'd simply changed his behavior or was using another phone number. We'd wait and wait with each query. I could tell this computer wasn't designed to do this kind of searching—it was designed for customer billing.

"Can you dump some of the calling data onto a floppy disk?"

I finally asked him. "If you can get it out of your system we can put it on my RDI and do more sophisticated searches."

Murph said it was possible and we started to unload his data. But then he stopped and after thinking for a second decided to try something else first. He called an engineer he knew at Cellular One and asked him to look through his records for any suspicious activity. We gave him a profile of things to look for, but the technician said he didn't have any matches either.

I'd flown all the way back to the East Coast, and now Mitnick was starting to look a little like Houdini. If he was on Netcom, but not going through either Sprint or Cellular One, where *was* he? I was exasperated—he had to be on one system or the other.

"Try some more," I said. "He has to be there."

I found several other Netcom dial-in numbers elsewhere in the country and read them to him. The Cellular One engineer took another pass through his data, and a short while later he came back to the phone and said he had caller activity matching our description. Mitnick was on the air, but where was he?

"I can't give you guys any more help unless I've got a warrant," the engineer said.

We were blocked again by the same problem Murph and I had on Saturday night, for we didn't have a subpoena for the Cellular One records. Although on Sunday morning Sprint had received a subpoena for trap-and-trace and call-record information, and a court order permitting real time monitoring, Mitnick must in the meantime have "tumbled" his cell phone. He'd obviously swapped the fraudulent Sprint MIN-ESN pair for one that must have belonged to a Cellular One subscriber. I called Kent and with Murph's help he wrote a second subpoena, which was faxed to Cellular One.

However, at this point things seem to come to a halt. It had been my plan to assemble a team of law enforcement agents, to go to the cell site, and when Mitnick went on the air, to use homing gear to track him down. Again the FBI had put on the brakes. Special agent Thomas had been called out on a case he knew nothing about on a Sunday night and he made it clear that he wasn't ready to make any decisions about the next step to take without the involvement of some higher authority.

I couldn't believe it. We had Mitnick, and could track him down immediately. But the longer we took to pull things together, the more likely something was to go wrong. "This is why Kevin Mitnick is still out there after disappearing to avoid an FBI search in 1992," I grumbled.

I went into the back room of the switching office and called Kent back to express my frustration. "It's really messed up here," I told him. "I'm getting really tired of this."

He was becoming familiar with my annoyance and promised he'd make some calls to see if he could speed things up. But the situation only became worse. After I got off the phone we began discussing the operational details of conducting surveillance and an arrest. Special agent Thomas assured me that law enforcement agents would have no problem staying in contact with each other, for they all carried scrambled radios.

"You can't use scrambled radios," I had to explain to him. "This guy isn't a normal criminal. He works with his scanner on."

"He won't stick around for one moment if he hears encrypted traffic nearby," Murph chimed in, and we eventually got our point across.

By now it was almost 10:30 P.M. Despite the FBI agents' hesitation, we decided we could still go to the cell site and use Sprint's diagnostic equipment to get a better fix on Mitnick's location. Murph suggested we follow the same approach they'd taken in their recent phone fraud investigation. Every time a cellular phone call is set up it is allocated to its own frequency. That frequency was visible to the engineers monitoring at the cellular telephone company switch, and so they had used a system in which each time the frequency changed, the engineers would send it to a pager the technician in the field was carrying. The technician would then tune the direction-finding equipment accordingly. It seemed like a good idea. It was unlikely Mitnick would be monitoring both cellular and paging frequencies. Even if he was, it was unlikely he would attach any significance to an occasional three-digit page.

We called the Cellular One technician back to help alert us when new calls were made. He was monitoring his switch from home and was able to see both caller data and also sector information. Since there was a Cellular One cell site located immediately next to cell 19 in the Sprint system, we were now able to determine that Mitnick's calls on the Cellular One system were being placed from a phone in the same general location as the previous evening's calls. We were in luck!

The phone calls were coming from the area immediately south of the cell transmitter, confirming Murph's earlier suspicion about Mitnick's location. Murph, Joe, and I walked over to a large map of the Raleigh area. The transmitter was located off Route 70, also known as Glenwood Ave. Directly to the south was Raleigh Memorial Cemetery; to the east and southeast was William B. Umstead State Park.

Immediately our eyes were drawn to Duraleigh Road, which ran almost directly south from where it intersected Glenwood. On the east side of Duraleigh for about a kilometer stretched a neighborhood named Duraleigh Woods. It looked like it would be a good place to start hunting. Murph wasn't sure about Mitnick's distance from the cell, but he drew an arc around the antenna site and said he would probably be within that range.

On the floor of the backseat of Joe Orsak's van was a device about the size of a desktop PC called a Cellscope 2000, which was actually an amateur radio transceiver connected to a note-book personal computer. Used by cellular phone companies to test signal quality, it could function as a radio direction finder as well. Orsak also had a hand-held Yagi antenna connected to the Cellscope, that he could hold inside the cab of his van. The Yagi wasn't designed for radio direction finding, but it would work in an approximate fashion.

Mark Lottor's software was running in my HP 100 palm-top PC in combination with a hand-held Oki 1150 cellular tele-phone, a setup that performed some of the same functions, but in a smaller and cheaper package. It wasn't directional, but for my application it didn't matter. In the cellular telephone world the base station to cellular telephone link is called the forward channel and the link going back from the cell phone to the base station is called the reverse channel. The Cellscope could mon-itor either channel, but not both simultaneously. Using it in tandem with my hand-held system, however, we were able to track both sides of a call.

Mark and I had designed a custom cable to connect the com-puter to the Oki phone. Inside it was a microprocessor chip that did the data conversion between the Oki and the HP computer so that the two devices would be able to talk to each other. The little chip has as much processing power as the first personal computers. It's emblematic of a story Danny Hillis likes to tell. During the 1970s at a computer conference at the New York Hilton a speaker made a wild estimate about the number of computers that would be in the world a decade later. Somebody in the audience stood up and said, "That's crazy! For that to be true there would have to be a computer in every door!"

A decade later Hillis returned to the Hilton for another conference, and sure enough, there was a computer in every door— in the Hilton's newly installed electronic door locks!

As we drove to the cell site I began to assemble my gear and to tinker with the Cellscope while Joe gave me instructions about how to use it. Intercepting cellular phone calls with a device like this is outlawed for private individuals by the 1988 Electronic Communications Privacy Act, but cellular phone companies have an exemption to monitor in order to detect and prevent fraud.

Anticipating the possibility of a long stake-out, we pulled into a 7-11 and I grabbed some food and something to drink while Joe got a cup of coffee. The Cellular One engineer reported that Mitnick wasn't active, so we drove to the cell site and waited. Special agent Thomas had followed us in a conspicuous FBI Crown Victoria sedan. We parked in front of a windowless room-sized concrete block house hidden behind another chain-link fence. Inside were banks of cellular radio transceivers to handle the phone calls through the cell.

Joe and I took the van out for a short drive to test the monitoring gear and get the lay of the land. We asked special agent Thomas to wait until we returned, but when we came back about twenty minutes later the Crown Victoria was gone.

Around 11:30 P.M. Markoff paged me. I'd called him from the airport in San Jose before I left and he'd flown to Raleigh several hours after me and checked in at the Sheraton Imperial hotel near the airport. I put Joe on the phone and he gave Markoff directions to the cell site. While we waited for him to show up we went back outside and we both turned on our scanning gear. On a Sunday around midnight in the suburbs of Raleigh things are really pretty quiet on all of the cellular telephone frequencies.

It was a cold still winter night. Joe was standing outside his truck listening to the Cellscope with the Yagi antenna under his arm and he was having trouble finding any traffic at all. Suddenly he picked up a voice call on a Cellular One channel. He listened for a second and immediately heard someone with a distinct Long Island accent talking about "Phiber Optik."

"Hey, that's it!" I said, "Let's go."

Phiber Optik was the cracker who had served a year in prison, and who was now working for Echo, a New York City on-line service as a system administrator.

We both jumped into the van and raced out the driveway to the cell site and turned onto the street. A car was coming slowly down the street toward us.

"I'll bet that's John Markoff," I said.

Joe flashed the high beams of his van, and as the car pulled up next to us, I recognized Markoff behind the wheel.

"Park your car and get in, we got him on right now!" I yelled out the window. He pulled into a parking lot and jumped into the back seat. The voice with the Long Island accent was coming out of the speaker of the Cellscope unit. We could only hear one side of the conversation, the side that was coming from the cellular base station; the cell phone itself was too far away and too faint to hear.

"I recognize that voice!" Markoff said immediately. "That's Eric Corley!"

I'd heard of him. As the editor of *2600* he had frequently defended Kevin Mitnick in public, arguing that Mitnick was simply a misunderstood and mistreated computer hacker who broke into systems out of curiosity. There were no victims when a hacker stole software, he claimed. We could hear Corley chatting with someone about how to improve his public image.

Several years earlier, *2600* had published Mitnick's own rebuttal to *Cyberpunk*, the book Markoff had coauthored. Mitnick claimed he'd been framed by his partner Lenny DiCicco. Now as we listened to the side of the conversation being broadcast by the Cellular One transmitter, it sounded as if Corley was counseling the person on the other side of the phone on how to deal with being persecuted by law enforcement agencies. I wondered if Corley knew that Mitnick was still lying to people, reading their e-mail, and stealing software.

Joe steered the van out onto Glenwood Ave. and then turned right and headed south on Duraleigh Road. As he drove the Cellscope locked onto the reverse channel going from the cell phone back to the cell-site antenna and we briefly heard the voice on the other side of the conversation. Although Markoff had spoken with Mitnick years ealier on the phone and once heard him speak as a computer security "consultant," he couldn't identify the second voice definitively as Mitnick's.

I watched the signal strength display, until it suddenly dipped. "You've passed it," I said.

We continued picking up snatches of the voice until at one point we heard him saying "bye" to Corley and asking if he'd still be up at 5 A.M. The call then disappeared into static.

I thought to myself, *Let's be patient.* I was confident now that Mitnick was actually nearby. He might have been able to set up an elaborate cutout scheme with a pair of data modems, but it would have been much harder to build a relay that would handle voice and data. Joe looked for a place to turn around, and we cruised slowly back up Duraleigh waiting to see if we could pick up another call.

As we neared the intersection, we could see a succession of reasonably new low-slung apartment complexes. On our right was a shopping center and gas station. We looked over Joe's engineering maps as we drove. It seemed likely that the signal was coming from somewhere inside one of the apartments. We picked the farthest one down the road and drove into its parking lot while we monitored. It was easy because there were no other conversations in the cell. It was almost 1 A.M.

Our monitors now captured another call while it was being set up. This time we could hear the whistle of a modem, which meant it was a data call. On my display I saw the MIN, the cellular telephone number, 919-555-6523. I quickly programmed the monitor to track it in the future.

The signal was strong. Somewhere within a few hundred meters of where we were driving, Kevin Mitnick was sitting, probably huddled over a portable computer, preparing to sniff passwords, install back doors, and read other people's mail. Every few minutes the signal would drop, and then after a pause of thirty seconds or so a new call would start.

"The poor bastard," I said. "He's getting really lousy cellular reception."

Joe drove back onto Duraleigh turning north and immediately turned into the driveway of a larger apartment complex called the Player's Club.

As we circled we all began to feel uncomfortable. The parking lot was full of cars, but there were no people visible, and almost all of the apartments on the outside of the complex had darkened windows. What would someone looking out a window think if he saw three men in a truck circling in the parking lot at this hour?

We drove slowly, in a counterclockwise direction. At the rear of the complex we could see the apartments backed up against open fields. "If I was Mitnick I'd have my escape route planned right through those fields," Markoff said. "I'd also set my computer up to have a good field of view out the window."

I swung the Yagi antenna back and forth as we drove. When we'd entered the driveway of the Player's Club, I'd seen the signal strength on the Cellscope display get stronger. I could tell he was somewhere to our left. Now at the back of the complex, it fell off. The antenna didn't have much precision, because I was inside the truck, and I was trying to remain inconspicuous. I was also trying to keep a mental model in my mind of where the signals would be coming from in real space rather than car space—ignoring the orientation of the car. At the same time all three of us were looking for windows in which the lights were on.

The Player's Court was circled by rows of parking spaces. The complex itself appeared to be a square with arms jutting out, separated by other parking lots. As we approached the southwest corner of the complex the signal strength jumped again. It was clear that the call was coming either from along one of the arms or from the interior of the complex on the inside corner.

We decided that circling the complex again would be too risky, so Joe drove across the street and parked in the shopping center lot. I was certain we'd pinned down Mitnick's location and now all we needed was the FBI.

"Why don't we drive back to the cell site and see if we can persuade the FBI to come out again?" I suggested.

Back inside the concrete block house I called Murph at the

Sprint central office switch, and he called the FBI and beat on them for a while, pleading with them to take some action. After he was told they had no agents available, I called the local office of the Bureau myself.

"This guy is on right now," I told the FBI watch officer. "It's like having a search light that you follow right to his door."

"I'm sorry," he responded. "There are no agents here now. All I can do is take a message."

I hung up and called special agent Thomas, and got somebody who was very unhappy to hear from me at 2:30 A.M. "I'm afraid I can't help you tonight," he explained. "He's wanted on a U.S. marshal's warrant, not an FBI warrant—it's not an FBI problem."

I paced back and forth in the tiny room. I called Kent again who promised me that reinforcements would be on the way soon, but it was becoming increasingly clear that nothing was going to happen that night. We waited for another forty-five minutes while Mitnick's data calls came and went. Finally we decided to give up and drive back to the Sprint switch.

On the way back to the switch I thought about making another phone call to Levord, but I decided a cellular phone call was too risky. We were probably out of scanner range, but if Mitnick was using software stolen from Mark Lottor he would have access to the forward control channel, and he might see my telephone number show up in the system in Raleigh. It was extremely unlikely, but those are the kinds of things that can trip you up.

Joe dropped me off, and I got in my car and followed Markoff back to the Sheraton. We walked into the empty lobby at 4 A.M. I had hoped we would arrest Mitnick tonight but now I was worried that each new delay might allow him to slip away.

CHAPTER 16

Julia found me.

She had arrived at the Sheraton at 8:30 A.M., where I had intructed the front desk to give her a key when she showed up. I was asleep when she slipped into my fourth-floor room, but quite happy to be gently awakened. I was exhausted but delighted to see her and we held each other.

"Did you find anything last night?" she asked.

I told her that we had almost certainly found Kevin, but as I related the details of our surveillance, my frustration with the FBI quickly returned. "I can't believe it," I said. "These guys are going to let him slip through their fingers again."

But I could see that Julia, too, was exhausted. "How was your weekend?" I asked.

"Surprisingly smooth," she murmured. "We communicated more clearly than we have for a long, long time." She paused. "It was really hard," she finally continued, "but we both agreed that splitting up is the right thing to do."

She slipped into bed and we were soon both sound asleep.

When I awoke two hours later, though, my mind immediately returned to the case, and I began making phone calls.

The first was to Levord Burns in Washington, who told me he was planning to make the drive down to Raleigh later that day. *Finally*, I thought, *the FBI is moving into action*. I asked if he was planning to have a team of people who could stake out the apartment complex.

"No, Tsutomu, it's just me," he replied, with the air of some-one who moves at a deliberate pace regardless of what's going on around him. "I'm leaving in two or three hours."

His apparent lack of concern just wasn't acceptable to me. I didn't really regard Levord himself as a problem, so much as a symptom of the FBI's plodding approach, so as soon as he hung up, I decided to take my nagging to a higher level.

Kent Walker in San Francisco once again assured me he was still on the case and help was on the way. I could tell that he, too, was impatient with the creeping pace of this hunt, now that we were so close to our target. He said he would call John Bowler, an assistant United States attorney in Raleigh, to see if he could look into the case, and also promised to lean on the FBI, although we both realized there was only so much he could do from the other side of the country.

Next I phoned Marty Stansell-Gamm, the Justice Department prosecutor who had been so supportive at the CMAD conference in Sonoma, and brought her up to date. "This is exactly why I never bothered to go to the FBI in the first place!" I concluded.

"Who have you been dealing with?" she asked.

"Levord Burns."

"Oh, I know what you mean," she said. "Whenever you talk to him, he sounds half-asleep."

"Maybe that's because we're always waking him up in the mid-dle of the night," I answered. I told Marty that our most pressing need was to get a Triggerfish surveillance team on the scene so we could figure out Mitnick's precise location. She gave me her assurances that she would do what she could.

Julia was up by now, only partly recovered from her night of travel, but like me, was hungry. Around 2 P.M. we went down-stairs and met Markoff in the Sheraton restaurant. It didn't look like the most promising of dining spots, but because we were staying within five kilometers of Kevin Mitnick's apartment, and with my picture having run in newspapers and magazines all over the country, I couldn't risk going somewhere he might see me. And since Markoff's picture had been on the dust jacket of *Cyberpunk*, there was reason to think that Mitnick might recog-nize him, too. From the uninspiring lunch menu, Julia selected a white-bread club sandwich, I took my chances with grilled cheese and what appeared to be vegetable soup straight from the can, and Markoff made do with a chicken breast sandwich. He was far more intent on getting his daily news fix than lunch, poring through the *Times* and *The Wall Street Journal.* Julia and I were picking at our food and chatting idly, when I got a page from Mark Seiden at Internex.

"What's happening?" Seiden asked, when I called him back from a payphone in the lobby. "The clean-up's all done on this end, but it looks like Mitnick is still loose."

"Huh?" was all I could say.

Seiden explained that he had been called the night before by Andrew, who told him that, since Mitnick was about to be hauled in, he should begin cleaning up and securing the Internex computers.

"This is really bad!" I exploded. "The FBI isn't close to catching Kevin yet. What if we spook him?"

It sounded as if we already had. Seiden related that after he had done a fairly thorough shutdown of Mitnick's back doors, Kevin had returned through one that Mark had missed and started making mischief, including trying to close Seiden out of his own account. Then, in what seemed a deliberate act of provocation, Mitnick had deposited a 140-megabyte file called japboy that was a copy of my file that Bruce Koball had stumbled upon several weeks earlier at the Well.

"I have no idea why Andrew told you to start cleaning up," I said, incredulous.

Seiden, who is a computer security pro, was angry at having been misled into such an error. "Last time I take orders from Andrew," he muttered. His task now, we agreed, would be to resume monitoring Mitnick's activities on Internex for indication of how deep his suspicions now ran. Seiden was still fuming with indignation as we ended our call.

I punched in Andrew's number. "What the hell's going on?"

"I'm sorry, I screwed up," Andrew said, knowing immediately what I was talking about. He realized that he had misunderstood my message from when I had called him the night before, and that he jumped the gun with Seiden. It was just a case of being overtired and overly optimistic.

"Look," I said. "We're really close to catching Mitnick, but we haven't caught him, and we may have blown the whole thing now." I told Andrew to start monitoring Netcom for signs that Mitnick had detected our operations there, and give me an update later.

Walking back to the restaurant table still shaking my head, I told Julia and Markoff what had happened. "We don't need screwups like this when we're so close," I said.

Locating Mitnick, it seemed, might turn out to have been far easier than actually catching him.

With Levord not due to arrive for several more hours, we returned to our rooms, where Julia went back to sleep, while I started working the phone with a new sense of urgency.

Before long, my efforts were rewarded with a piece of good news: Marty Stansell-Gamm told me that the FBI's Technical Services Division in Quantico was dispatching a two-man surveillance team with a Triggerfish radio direction-finding unit, and they would be arriving in Raleigh that evening. She gave me the SkyPager number of one of the agents, and soon I was on the phone to him and his partner.

As law-enforcement technical specialists tend to do, the two agents were more interested in asking questions than answering them. They were trying to determine what gear to bring along, and one thing they wanted to know was whether the Sprint or Cellular One cell sites supported NAMPS, an analog cellular phone technology that can double the capacity of a cell site by narrowing the frequency band that each phone uses. Cellular companies that employ NAMPS will often compensate the customer with lower rates for helping conserve frequency spectrum, but using the system requires a special phone, and monitoring it takes special surveillance gear that they didn't have. I told the agent that Joe Orsak had switched off NAMPS on cell 19 the previous night and that I thought that Cellular One's site didn't have the technology. Before I hung up I put them in touch with the Sprint guys, who could give them other, more detailed information about the cell sites they'd be dealing with.

Sometime after 5 P.M., I reached Levord, who had recently arrived at the Bureau's Raleigh office. He was trying to find a place to stay for himself and the Quantico team, whom he had just heard were coming, and he sounded irritated to be playing travel agent. "Why are you having to mess with this, Levord?" I asked, sympathizing.

He didn't answer.

Without revealing to Levord that a foulup on our side of the investigation was now making me more anxious than ever, I observed that it looked as if we were going to need a much bigger team of agents if a stakeout and arrest were to take place.

"We're not going to get any more agents tonight," he said matter of factly.

"Look, we've *got* to be ready to move tonight," I argued, but he seemed unwilling to do anything unless he was in control of the situation. Nevertheless, we agreed to meet at 8 P.M. at the Sprint switching office, where we could hook up with Murph and Orsak, and then have dinner nearby while we waited for the two Quantico agents.

At 7:30, just as Julia and I were preparing to leave the hotel, Seiden called, sounding worried. Mitnick had returned to Internex less than an hour before, and it was evident that he knew something was up. "Looks like he's added an account called Nancy, deleted Bob, and changed a lot of passwords—including mine and root's," Seiden said. "This looks vindictive. He's getting destructive now." And, in a show of spite, Mitnick had made Markoff's account accessible to anyone on the Internet.

When I called to check in with Andrew, he said that he, too, had watched Mitnick's session on Internex, and that Mitnick was clearly acting paranoid. After leaving Internex, Mitnick had next gone to check his back door on Netcomsv that John Hoffman had closed on Friday. It was only one of several of Mitnick's ways into Netcom, but finding this particular entry barred he now seemed truly suspicious.

His next action, according to Andrew, was to head directly to another Internet site we hadn't seen Mitnick use before, operated by the Community News Service in Colorado Springs, where he had a spare copy of test1 salted away. This was the program which allowed him to use Netcom as a base of operations without leaving a record. It appeared that Mitnick brought back this fresh copy of test1 to compare to the one he already had squirreled away on

Netcom, presumably to see if we had doctored the Netcom version so that it might no longer hide his tracks. Comparing the two copies, he found the Netcom version intact. He was using an account named Wendy on Netcom with a password "fuckjkt."

"Who's jkt?" Andrew asked.

"I have no idea," I said impatiently.

Andrew then described a series of activities that were fairly routine, by Mitnick's standards, which indicated to us that once he had verified that his copy of test1 had not been tampered with, he had begun to calm down, perhaps concluding that the one barred back door was a fluke having nothing to do with his problems at Internex. Or so we hoped—at this stage in the game it was becoming hard to tell what was calculated and what was coincidental. After a few minutes, Mitnick had headed back to Internex, and Andrew stopped watching him. We could tell Mitnick was trying to see if he had been detected and if so, where.

"He's still on, so that's good," I said to Andrew. "But he's suspicious. That's exactly what we don't need. After all the prodding I've been doing to get the Triggerfish team here, it would be really embarrassing for him to go radio silent for a week."

Markoff was hesitant about accompanying Julia and me to the Sprint office. He was certain that when the FBI discovered a *New York Times* reporter on the scene they would go nonlinear.

"Don't worry about it," I said. "Just tell them you're on our team."

"There's no way I'm going to lie to them," he replied. "That kind of stuff always blows up in your face." But he was not about to miss the story, so he decided to come along, bringing his own car in case he had to bail out at some point.

As Julia and I drove in my rented Geo Metro, I received a page from a local number I didn't recognize. When I called it, I discovered it was the home phone of John Bowler, the assistant U.S. attorney whom Kent Walker had promised to call.

"Kent said you needed help," Bowler said. "What can I do for you?"

"I'm on a cell phone," I warned him.

"Oh, okay."

"There's someone coming down from Washington," I said.

"Tell him to call me," Bowler replied, and we quickly ended the call.

Joe Orsak and Murph were waiting for us at the Sprint office, joined by a third technician who was even larger than they were—Fred Backhaus, a burly man with an unkempt beard, a ponytail, and a motorcycle jacket. Despite looking like a Hell's Angel, he turned out to be as friendly and hospitable as the others, and all three were eager to get on with the chase. We talked cell phones for a while, until Levord Burns arrived.

Special agent Burns was an athletically trim black man with his hair cut military short, whom I guessed to be in his late thirties. His well-tailored gray suit, starched white shirt, Rolex-style watch, and black wingtips would have put him in good standing on Wall Street. But his big Ford Crown Victoria, with its ominous whip antenna, looked like nothing but a cop car—a cop car with Virginia plates. *Look out, Kevin*, I thought, *the Feds are in town.*

The three engineers and I introduced ourselves, and I gave Levord the message to call John Bowler at the local U.S. attorney's office. He nodded noncommittally, not thrilled to have yet another person to be accountable to.

Burns told us that his bosses in Washington had ordered him to bring along a set of Clipper phones—the government's new standard-issue devices for encrypted digital conversations over regular phone lines. They were in the trunk of his car. "In fact, they're useless unless you're talking to someone who has one on the other end," he said, rolling his eyes.

"The trunk's a fine place to leave them," I agreed. Levord might turn out to be okay, after all.

Before we left the Sprint parking lot I introduced him to Julia and Markoff, using only their first names. Levord asked no questions, and I offered no explanations.

We drove in three cars to Ragazzi's, an Italian restaurant about two kilometers from the Sprint switch. As we all sat down at a single long table, I noticed that Markoff had picked the seat farthest away from special agent Burns.

The restaurant was all done up with Chianti bottles and braided garlic, but the breadbaskets were plastic. And while the breadsticks were freshly baked, the salad turned out to be strictly ice-berg. During dinner Levord talked a little about how the FBI now routinely tracked cellular phone calls during investigations. He acknowledged that they usually monitored people who didn't know anything about the technology they were using—not peo-ple who were cell-phone savvy like Kevin Mitnick. As he dis-cussed his work, it was clear that Levord Burns was a guy stretched pretty thin by a heavy caseload. "This kind of travel puts a lot of stress on your family life," he added. "My wife is pregnant, and I'm not around a lot."

The Sprint guys followed suit and told us about their jobs, and gave more details about the fraudulent cell phone ring they had taken down. The raid had taken place at a farmhouse whose liv-ing room had no furniture, just lots of cell phones on the floor. The conversation turned to telephone fraud generally, and Markoff recounted some of Kevin's history of manipulating the phone system and how he had last been seen running from a copy shop in Los Angeles.

At one point Levord went off to a pay phone to return some pages. While he was gone we moved to the topic of Mitnick's social engineering, and I recalled how he had tried to social-engineer me at Los Alamos.

"We've had a problem like that just in the last couple of weeks," Murph said, surprised. "Somebody called one of our marketing guys pretending to be a Sprint engineering employee, and he managed to talk the guy out of several MIN-ESN pairs."

"You don't happen to remember what name the caller used?" I asked.

Murph turned to Joe. "Do you remember?" Neither did.

"Was it Brian Reid?" I offered.

"Yeah, that was it," Joe said.

"Kevin!" Markoff and I said in unison.

What an amazing creature of habit to stick to the very name he had used on me several years earlier. The real Brian Reid was now an executive running DEC's Internet networking business.

The Sprint technicians were clearly chagrined to learn that Kevin had weaseled information from their company. It wasn't their fault, but it was a point of honor with them that they ran a secure shop, and they were newly irritated by their colleague's lapse.

The more our conversation focused on Mitnick, however, the more nervous I became. If we'd had good operational security, we wouldn't have been having such a discussion in a public restaurant. I looked behind me and noticed a middle-American-looking couple sitting in a nearby booth, obviously interested in us. This made me even edgier. I began asking the Sprint guys technical questions to steer the talk in another direction.

We had been back from dinner less than twenty minutes when the two-man team from Quantico finally showed up at the switching office, driving an old station wagon loaded with gear.

They looked more like Simon and Garfunkel than G-men. One was tall with a rather sallow complexion, and the other was short with a fleshy nose and ears. Both appeared to be in their forties, and had a slightly rumpled look about them—tweedy academic with a touch of the racetrack—and the short one was wearing the type of cap favored by men who drive British sports cars.

After introductions were made we decided that the best plan would be to use Fred Backhaus's white family van to transport the team and their direction-finding gear. As they began to unload the station wagon, Levord went off to the restroom to change from his business suit, emerging in work clothes and a baseball cap, an outfit that made him look like a house painter, though a painter a bit thick around the middle, thanks to the soft body armor he wore under his clothes.

I volunteered to go along, because none of them had any idea of what the terrain was really like. Levord studied me, and in his slow, deadpan style said: "Tsutomu, there's no way you can come with us. Your picture's been everywhere. If he sees you and recognizes you, he'll disappear."

I persisted, though I knew I wasn't endearing myself to any of them. "Look, I should be along," I argued. "We made promises to all these computer sites that we'd be looking out for them. Nobody knows how Kevin might react. If he does something bad before you grab him, I need to see what's on his computer, so I can tell my people how to counter it. Until then, I can stay out of sight."

Levord was unmoved. "Nothing's going to happen tonight."

I got the clear message that he wasn't going to want me around even when he did think something was going to happen. I suspected that he felt intimidated by all this technology that he didn't understand, as well as not wanting to get blamed if I wound up in a chase or a shootout.

The Quantico team did talk to me a little about the technology they had toted along in the station wagon, especially something called a cell site simulator, which was packed in a large travel case. The simulator was a technician's device normally used for testing cell phones, but it could also be used to page Mitnick's cell phone without ringing it, as long as he had the phone turned on but not actually in use. The phone would then act as a transmitter that they could home in on with the Triggerfish directional antenna.

Clever as the technique sounded, I pointed out that it might be risky to use on Mitnick. "You're dealing with someone who has source code for all sorts of cell phones," I said. "He might be able to detect it."

They conceded that it might not be worth the risk, while adding an unstated *Go away kid, you're bothering us.* I don't think they liked the idea of dealing with a civilian, particularly one who was in a position to learn all about their techniques.

Backhaus had by now backed his van up to the front door of the Sprint building, and the agents began moving back and forth between their station wagon and the van, installing their gear. The Triggerfish direction finder, a rectangular box of electronics about a half a meter high, controlled by a Macintosh Powerbook portable computer, was placed in the center of the van's back seat. From one of the agents, who was sitting in the van calibrating the unit, I was able to extract that the Triggerfish was a five-channel receiver, able to monitor both sides of a conversation simultaneously. Next they strung a black coaxial cable out the van's window and ran it up to the radio direction-finding antenna they had placed on the roof. The roof unit had a black base, about 30 centimeters square and several centimeters thick, which held four long silver antenna prongs, each nearly 30 centimeters high, reaching skyward.

This apparatus seemed none too subtle, and I pointed out again that they weren't dealing with some technically illiterate cocaine dealer. "This guy's paranoid, and he's been known to use scanners to monitor the police before," I said. "He's wiretapped the FBI in the past."

They didn't want to talk to me at all now, but I wasn't going to give up. "No, this is ridiculous," I said. "You guys are going to park out there, and he's not stupid. I'm sure he knows what a direction-finding antenna looks like."

They didn't buy it. "It's not that visible," the short agent replied.

I looked at it ruefully. "Can't you put it inside?"

"No, that would degrade the performance," the taller one said.

"Why don't we put a box on top of it?" Murph suggested.

"No, that would be too obvious," he said.

I looked again at the top of the van, which had two parallel rails running across it from side to side, as a carrying rack. What we needed was a box that looked as if it was meant to be carried there.

"Wait a minute," I told them. "Murph, you have fluorescent lights. Do you have any of the boxes they come in?"

We were in luck, they were in a storage locker in an equipment room off the switching center's main room. We came back out with a two and a half meter long box that could be lashed on top of the van. I cut a hole in it so that it could be placed over the antenna, completely hiding it in case Mitnick was in an upper-floor apartment and might see the van from above.

After we were done lashing and taping the box, the vehicle looked like a respectable electrician's van. I could tell that the agents had agreed to the camouflage mainly to humor me, but they had to concede that the disguise worked pretty well.

It was nearly midnight when the three FBI agents were ready to roll.

"So what happens if we actually see him outside his apartment?" one of the Quantico team asked. It seemed probable that Mitnick would frequent the shops in the strip-mall shopping center across the road from his apartment complex. "Do we grab him?"

"He's a probation violator, so we can take him in," Levord said, "but would any of you recognize him on sight?" The photos that all of us had seen were old, and the FBI documents indicated that his weight had fluctuated.

We decided that it seemed unlikely they would get further

tonight than simply identifying which apartment was his, so the Quantico team left with Orsak and Backhaus, while Joe and Levord followed in my green rented Geo, which they decided was the least suspicious vehicle in our fleet. Levord said they would do a quick surveillance and be right back.

While we waited Murph gave us a tour of the switch, a windowless building filled with equipment that looked a lot like mainframe computers, racks of dumpster-sized batteries, and standby generating equipment. Then we settled in to wait—for minutes, and then, to our growing anxiety, for hours.

A little coffee room off the main operations center gave us a place to sit, and we passed the time eating crackers and drinking soft drinks from a small refrigerator. A handmade sign listed prices for different items, including Gatorade, of which there was none left, unfortunately. Payment was on the honor system, and the large jar that had been provided for that purpose was slowly filling with our dollar bills. To keep occupied, I studied the bulletin board with all of the relevant OSHA notices, and read a newspaper clipping about the farmhouse cell phone bust that Murph and Joe had been involved in.

Markoff and Julia began to play with the HP 100 that was part of my RadioMail terminal. At one point Markoff started a program that was supposed to edit icons for the device's user interface, which somehow caused the computer to abruptly crash, corrupting all my wireless communications software.

Grrrrr.

Markoff apologized profusely, but the computer's communications system was quite dead. I remembered that all the backup files were safely in San Diego, where they would do me little good now, which brought to mind a quote I'd once read, from someone I couldn't recall: "Fate is infatuated with the efficient."

Mitnick was not using the Sprint system. And while we could find out that he was active on Cellular One by calling in periodically to check with Gary Whitman, a Cellular One engineer who was monitoring the cell site from home, we could not follow Mitnick's calls as closely as would have been possible if they were being switched through the building in which we now sat.

At around 3 A.M. I paged Joe Orsak. He quickly called back, but he couldn't tell me much, other than to say he was calling from one of the pay phones at the strip mall across Duraleigh Road from the apartment complex.

I asked him to please call one of the FBI agents to the phone. A couple of minutes later, one of the Quantico agents came on the line, and without waiting to hear what I wanted, asked furiously, "Who's this guy named John who's with you?"

"He's a writer," I replied.

"What does he write?"

"He's a writer. He writes books."

"Does he write anything else?"

"Lots of stuff." I thought I understood his problem—he'd be in deep trouble with his superiors if he had knowingly let a newspaper reporter observe the team's activities. I was trying to give him the option of plausible deniability, but he pressed on.

"He wouldn't be John Markoff, the *New York Times* reporter, would he?

"Yes, that's him," I was forced to concede.

"And did he write that book about computer hackers?"

"Yes. *Cyberpunk*. The book on Kevin Mitnick. He's our Mitnick expert."

Now he was really enraged. "Why is he here? Why is he along?" he asked. "You're endangering the operation! Reporters are not allowed to take part in FBI activities! You lied to me!"

"No," I answered. "I never lied to you. You never asked who he was."

My explanation didn't satisfy him, and he hung up.

Markoff had heard my end of the conversation and decided it was time to make a quick and graceful exit. He had made his identity perfectly clear to Joe and Murph the night before, even exchanging business cards with them, and one of them had apparently mentioned it to the FBI men.

"I don't want be caught in the middle of this and have to explain my presence to an FBI agent," Markoff said before he drove back to the Sheraton.

Forty-five minutes later, at nearly 5 A.M., Levord Burns returned with Joe Orsak.

Levord, forgoing his customary slow-motion approach, stormed into the room and tore into me as soon as he saw me. "Look, you've been jerking me around, and now I find out you have this *New York Times* reporter shadowing us. What's going on here!?"

"Let's talk," I said. I saw that I needed to peel Levord off the ceiling, and I didn't think it was going to do any good for him to lay into me while Joe, Murph, and Julia looked on. I motioned toward the storage room.

We closed the door behind us, and Levord started pacing back and forth. "What are you trying to do?" he said. "What's your agenda here?"

I told him I wasn't trying to grandstand by bringing along a reporter, but merely relying on a friend I trusted, someone who had been writing about Mitnick for many years and had some expertise on his habits and motives.

It was clear that I had run afoul of Levord's FBI obsession with operational security, and he let me know that the Quantico agents were terrified that the secrets of their surveillance procedures were going to show up in a *New York Times* article. The agents were going to have to report the encounter to their superiors, and they were very unhappy about it. Although Burns looked exhausted, he lectured me for a full twenty minutes about the Bureau's specific protocols for dealing with the press, and said that many had been violated by us.

"Is he going to tip Mitnick off so he can escape and make it a better story?" Levord asked.

"No way," I assured him. Obviously, as a reporter, Markoff was here because it was going to make for a good story, but the best story would be if Mitnick got caught. So Markoff's interests and Levord's were completely in synch, I explained to him.

"Why didn't you introduce him as a reporter? Why didn't you come clean with me?"

"You never asked me," I replied.

"Where is he now?"

"He went back to his hotel."

Finally, as Levord's rage seemed to peter out, I asked him if they'd nailed down Mitnick's location.

"We're close," he said gruffly, "but we still haven't pinpointed the exact apartment." The Quantico agents were still trying.

Although I was fairly certain that he still would have liked to throw me out, Levord probably knew that right now was when he needed me most. He was going to have to put together an affi-davit for an arrest warrant. And that would require much of the data we had collected so far, which he had no way of interpreting without my walking him through it.

With that in mind, I offered to help.

"Okay," he said, "but no more surprises—right?"

I nodded, then suggested the types of data I could correlate for him: Netcom log-in records, the cellular company records, and Mitnick's actual sessions that we had monitored. Cross-referenc-ing these would demonstrate irrefutably that Mitnick was our man. I called Andrew and asked him to fax me some more of the relevant material.

As Levord and I headed for the coffee room to get started, Julia came up, saw that we had apparently reached a cease-fire, and then slipped into the storage room behind us to take a nap.

"Sorry," she said. "I've got to get some sleep."

Andrew's backup material started rolling off the fax machine a short while later. For the next hour and a half, I sifted through Andrew's data and mine, while Levord spent most of the time on the phone, briefing various Bureau officials and making arrange-ments for backup and reinforcements.

I wound up with a listing of thirty separate sessions, which took place between the afternoon of February 9 and the early morning of February 13, for which we could match the Netcom log-in times with Cellular One or Sprint call-detail records. From these I selected a handful for Levord, and began explaining how the phone records and Netcom sessions corresponded, and what Kevin's actual keystrokes for each session told us about his activ-ities. For anyone without a good grounding in phone networks, and Internet and Unix commands, it was a daunting amount of information to digest; given Levord's and my relationship at this point, the process was particularly painful. But soon Julia awoke and took over, proving to be a much more patient instructor.

When Julia and Levord wrapped up, she and I stepped outside for some fresh air, having been holed up all night in a fluorescent-lit, windowless building. I was surprised: daylight, a leaden, over-cast sky, but morning all the same. It was nearly 8 A.M.

Back inside, I called Andrew and Robert Hood, who were still waiting at Netcom in case something happened, and sounding grumpy about it. I told them that Levord was now saying that the FBI would probably go out and pick up Kevin before noon Eastern time, as soon as his affidavit and the arrest and search warrants were complete. The "get set" and "go" signals might be coming to them in the next few hours, I assured them.

A little later, the two Quantico agents returned, with the haggard appearance of two middle-aged men who had been up all night. They gave me a baleful look, but neither they nor I had the energy for a confrontation about Markoff. Agents from the Raleigh office had just relieved them, and now they intended to check into their hotel and catch some sleep while Levord chased the paperwork. He was heading downtown to the Bureau office, and because the monitoring had still not produced a precise apartment number, he wanted to have someone go by the Players Club complex for some old-fashioned, discreet legwork. I got Levord to promise he would contact me before going out to make the arrest. I didn't believe he'd keep to it, but I kept stressing the vulnerability of the Well and Netcom and other sites and the need for me to alert the people there.

The cellular telephone switching center was starting to come back to life, as the small crew of workers arrived for their day shift. Julia and I headed back to the Sheraton in the Geo, and she pointed out that it was February 14—Valentine's Day.

I woke with a start. The curtains were drawn, and I had to roll over and look at the clock to see the time: nearly 2 P.M. I grabbed my pager from the nightstand and pressed the backlight: no new pages. *Shit.* They must have gone to arrest Kevin without notifying me. The bust had happened, and Andrew and Robert were probably sound asleep.

I fumbled through my belt pouch, found the note with the scribbled number of the local FBI office, and dialed.

"I'm trying to reach Levord Burns," I said as soon as someone picked up.

A sleepy voice on the other end of the line said, "Uh-huh." It could only be Levord.

"What's going on with the warrant for Mitnick? Have you raided yet?"

Instead of getting an answer, I listened as it sounded as if my call was being transferred. Then the line went dead.

Whom had I just been talking to? Had I been conned?

Now it was my turn to be paranoid. What if Kevin Mitnick had been able to tamper with the FBI's phones and had forwarded their calls to himself? If it was Mitnick, I had just given away everything. I immediately called back the same number, and a different male voice answered: "FBI."

I asked for Levord Burns.

"Who?" the voice said.

"Levord Burns," I said. "He's down from Washington."

"I don't think he's here, but there must be thirty-five people rushing around. It's pretty busy." I thanked him and hung up.

Maybe the raid was going down now? By now Julia had awakened, and I told her, "I think we should go back over and see if anything is happening at the apartment complex."

The Player's Club apartments were on the other side of the airport from the Sheraton, and Julia drove us there through what seemed an endless maze of road construction and detours. When we finally reached the complex we drove past it once, but I saw nothing that looked remotely like a surveillance operation, a stakeout, or the flurry of activity one might expect if a Federal arrest had taken place during the last few hours.

Not wanting to hang around the area any longer and risk being seen, we drove a short way down Glenwood Avenue toward Raleigh and found a pay phone at a gas station.

I called Kent Walker, who said he had not heard from Raleigh that day. It appeared that nothing at all had happened yet, which surprised him and totally baffled me. At Kent's suggestion, I called John Bowler, whose message I'd passed on to Levord the night before.

"I've had no news," Bowler said. "I just had this dropped in my lap. But I haven't seen any paperwork and I haven't heard from special agent Burns." Despite being in the dark, Bowler sounded willing to be helpful.

"I think we need to talk as soon as possible," I said.

Bowler gave us directions downtown to the Federal Building. The afternoon traffic slowdown had already begun, so it took us a while to wend our way down to the courthouse. We parked on the street in front of the boxy, glass-front modern building and walked in, passing the guard stand in the lobby.

Shortly past four o'clock Julia and I finally reached the U.S. attorney's suite up on the top floor, where we signed in and received visitor badges. We had to wait for a while for Bowler to finish a meeting, before he came out to the reception area, introduced himself and invited us into his office.

The prosecutor, a balding man in his early forties, had a toothy smile and a rosy-cheeked, almost mischievous demeanor. He carried himself like an athlete and it was obvious he was something of a bicycling fanatic, for biking magazines were scattered around the office and there was a framed cartoon about the funny clothes cyclists wear. There were also several family pictures of his wife and his two preteen sons.

We sat down in two chairs in front of his desk and began to explain our reason for turning up at his office late on a dreary Tuesday afternoon.

"How much of this do you already know about?" I asked.

"Very little," Bowler said, but he seemed intrigued that two California computer hackers had wandered into his office with a tale to tell.

I told him that we were pursuing Kevin Mitnick, who was wanted by the FBI and the U.S. Marshal Service, and I gave him as precise a rundown as possible of the events of the past weeks, up through tracing Mitnick to the Player's Club apartment complex on Sunday night.

"The FBI has been in town since last night," I said, "and since we all now know where Mitnick is, I don't understand why things aren't moving more quickly. He's managed to elude the Bureau for more than two years, and it looks as if they're giving him every opportunity to get away again."

"Is he armed, or is he dangerous in any way?" Bowler asked.

I said I doubted that he was armed, but that he was dangerous in unpredictable ways. Whether or not he would actually wield that power, at the moment he was in a position to damage computer systems used by tens of thousands of people and containing property worth hundreds of millions of dollars. Several Internet companies were operating at considerable risk in an effort to help us catch this criminal, and were not likely to keep exposing themselves much longer.

"Mitnick isn't your ordinary criminal," I emphasized. "This is a game to him, and he understands telephone and computer technology a lot better than the law enforcement agents who are pursuing him."

I told Bowler the special agent on the case, Levord Burns, had expected to have an affidavit for search and arrest warrants by noon, but I hadn't heard from him since early morning. I was concerned that this not carry over to yet another day, because we now had reason to believe that Mitnick might be on to us.

"Sounds like I need to talk to Levord Burns," Bowler said. He called the Raleigh FBI office, which referred him to Levord's hotel.

When he reached Levord in his room, Bowler said, politely but firmly, "I understand you're working on the affidavit." He paused and listened for a moment. "Can you get over here as soon as possible?"

Bowler looked at his watch—it was nearly the close of the business day in the Federal Building—and said, "I'd better line up a judge for these warrants." He placed a call to the office of Magistrate Judge Wallace Dixon, whom he subsequently tracked down at the building's fitness center. Bowler and the judge arranged for us to bring the paperwork by his house later.

Bowler's next calls were to a friend, who agreed to sub for him that evening as coach of his son's soccer team, and to his wife, saying he'd be missing the game and would probably be a little late getting home.

Soon he was busy pulling together documents and delegating tasks to two assistants. The younger of the two women, who looked to be in her thirties, was plump, with curly blond hair, well-polished nails and a Betty Boop scarf. The older woman, who also seemed to be more authoritative, was plainer, with the husky voice of an inveterate smoker. As they were working, I received a page from Pei at the Well.

"Something new has happened," she reported when I reached her. Kevin had destroyed some accounting data, she said, and while they had been able to recover it, the Well officials were concerned that he might have suddenly turned vindictive and would now aim to do permanent damage. "Tsutomu," she said, "our management is worried about leaving ourselves vulnerable like this."

"Management" sounded to me like "Claudia," so I gave Pei a status report, concluding, "We know where he is and we're going through the paperwork for the arrest right now." I told her I would call Bruce Katz as soon as I got a chance.

Hearing this exchange seemed to further galvanize Bowler, who once again called Levord, telling him more firmly and a bit less politely this time, "We really need that affidavit!"

I was grateful to Kent Walker for having hooked me up with Bowler, so I called to give him an update. He, too, was pleased to hear that someone in Raleigh finally recognized the urgency of the case, and was dumbfounded that Levord still hadn't produced the necessary documents. "What's going on with this guy?" Kent said. "We don't need to write a book on the subject. The affidavit doesn't need to be that involved."

Because Julia and I had not eaten since dinner the previous night, and the Federal building was about to close, she went downstairs and found a Subway sandwich shop and brought back some sandwiches. We sat on the floor of Bowler's office and ate, sharing our food with Bowler and his assistants, who were now working through dinner.

I phoned Katz, who recounted what Pei had told me about the deleted accounting file. "Tsutomu, I want your advice," Katz said. "How vulnerable are we?"

Katz raised a series of questions. Had Mitnick actually figured out that the Well's staff were watching him, and had decided to take them with him if he himself was about to be taken down? What were they risking by not shutting their systems down or locking him out immediately? "What's going on here, Tsutomu? Is he trying to get revenge?" Katz asked.

"We haven't done anything to turn Mitnick against the Well," I answered honestly. "We're this close to getting him," I said. "Give us a little more time."

While I didn't think Mitnick had any reason to believe the Well was on to him, I couldn't say the same for Netcom. I phoned Andrew, who reported further signs of paranoia from Mitnick. He was continuing to move his data stashes and change passwords, and as a gesture of contempt for all who cared to review the log files, he had attempted to log into Netcomsv with the password .fukhood, no doubt for Robert's special attention. And unfortunately, there was also an indication that Mitnick was suddenly approaching the Well with new wariness: the dono account, which he had been using for weeks with the same password, fucknmc, now suddenly had a new one. There may have been some hidden meaning in the choice of dono's new password—no,panix—but what mattered far more to us was that Mitnick had apparently felt a need to take a counter-security measure at the Well, even though it turned out to be an ineffectual measure, given the level of our surveillance. Had something, or perhaps someone, tipped him off? Had he discovered Pei's use of his log-in?

Levord finally arrived, glaring at me briefly as he walked in, and seeming to move even more glacially than his usual deliberate pace. He placed the affidavit on Bowler's desk and said that he might have been there sooner but he thought it might be a good idea to organize his team if there was to be a proper stakeout and arrest.

"I've also taken some extra time to make sure that the affidavit is correct. It might be your intent to catch him," he said, eyeing me, "but it's necessary to do everything by the book in order to keep him."

The continuing obstacle, Levord told Bowler, was trying to determine the correct address from among the several possibilities to which the Quantico team had narrowed it down the previous night. The layout of the buildings was making it difficult to get a precise fix on the cellular radio signals.

That morning, the local FBI agent, L.B. Thomas, had gone to the Player's Club and talked to the manager in hopes of winnowing their list by determining whether any men in their early thirties had recently moved into one of the suspected apartments. Two new tenants had arrived during the last two weeks, it turned out, but one of them was the manager's girlfriend, and the other lived on the wrong side of the complex. So Levord was still left with a list of three possible addresses, any of which might be the right one. There was also a chance that none of them was the apartment from which the radio waves were actually emanating.

The difficulty, Bowler explained to Julia and me, was not in obtaining an arrest warrant, which could be issued for the entire

Player's Club complex as long as Mitnick was somewhere on the premises. The sticking point would be the search warrant. To look for and seize evidence, it was necessary to have a judge's permission to search a particular residence, which in this case would have to be specified by building number and apartment unit.

Levord went out to the reception area to put out more calls to see if his team had come up with any new leads. Meanwhile, Bowler and his assistants, now that they had the affadavit to work from, set about preparing warrants for each of the addresses on Levord's list. For good measure, Bowler had them draw up a fourth set, with the address blank. He hoped he could persuade the judge to sign the three that were completely filled out, and leave the blank one to be authorized later, if necessary, with a phone call to the judge, if the agents on the scene should determine that Mitnick lived in some other apartment.

I helped Bowler compile a list of items to include in the search warrant, such as computers, hardware and software documentation, floppy disks, modems, cell phones, and cell phone parts. It was rather eerie trying to picture Mitnick's lair and what it might contain. Word of his latest machinations at Netcom and the Well had once again underscored his potential for maliciousness. And when one of Bowler's assistants went to print the warrants, only to discover that her computer was suddenly unable to talk to the printer over the office's local area network, Julia suggested that it might somehow have been Mitnick's handiwork. But we quickly discovered that the problem was a bug, not a saboteur.

Finally, shortly after 7 P.M., we had the warrants assembled. Since Levord had gotten no further on narrowing the address list, Bowler bundled up all four packets and we headed off for Judge Dixon's home.

As we walked through the anteroom outside Bowler's office Julia noticed a jar full of small candy Valentine hearts. She poked through it and found one that had YES DEAR written on it and handed it to me. She meant it as a joke because I sometimes teased her by saying that, but I was so distracted that I only looked at it absentmindedly before popping it into my mouth. The four of us headed out of the suite for the elevators, cheered on by the two assistants.

"Go get 'em!" called the one with the husky smoker's voice.

We decided to ride to the judge's house in Bowler's customized van, so we could proceed directly to the Player's Club afterward. I was still hoping to get to the apartment complex before 8 P.M., to catch Mitnick on the air before he signed off for his dinner break, which usually lasted until 11 P.M. or so. The van, outfitted with louvered windows and curtains, would make it easier for me to stay out of sight during the stakeout. It would also be more comfortable than the Geo, since it was a mobile family room, complete with wood paneling, fuzzy upholstery, and food wrappers and plastic action-figure toys on the floor.

As Levord followed in his Crown Victoria, we drove to an affluent north Raleigh suburb which turned out to be quite near Mitnick's place. Julia and I waited in the van while Bowler and Levord went into the judge's house, a modest-sized brick home with a small, roofed porch. It was dark enough outside that we could easily watch through the judge's uncurtained living room picture window and see people moving about inside.

While we waited I decided to send Andrew the ready code we'd agreed upon, which turned out to take some doing. I wanted to bracket the number 080663 with dashes, to make clear at a glance that this was not a regular phone number. On many numeric pagers the dash is created by punching the * key, but when I entered the combination *080663* followed by the # key to send it, I got a fast busy signal, indicating some sort of error. After I tried it again, with the same result, I entered the code number without the dashes, and after it was successfully transmitted, hoped Andrew would interpret it correctly.

Procedures were not going smoothly inside the judge's house. Judge Dixon, as we learned later, was requesting various changes in the warrants, including a proviso that an arrest could be made after 10 P.M., a necessary legal stipulation, since arrests are generally supposed to be made during normal waking hours. It was clear that additional documents were going to be needed, so Bowler made arrangements for someone from his legal staff to prepare them and meet up with him at the stakeout. Just before 8:30, Bowler and Levord emerged.

We drove several kilometers to the shopping center parking lot across Duraleigh Road from the apartment complex, and Levord peeled off down a side street to the far side of the Player's Club, where the action would be. We had no idea at this point how many or what sort of reinforcements Levord had assembled, but I assumed that since this part of the show was totally in the FBI's hands, they would know what they were doing.

Bowler circled the small shopping center parking lot while we considered how best to position the van. He finally parked so that we could view the Player's Club complex, though not Mitnick's side of it, through the windshield. I sat far in the back to be inconspicuous. After setting up my monitor, I switched on a tiny flashlight I had borrowed from Julia to watch the display as I began searching both the Cellular One and Sprint frequencies. There was no sign of Mitnick.

"Looks like he's having dinner," I said. Maybe he'd gone out; maybe he was even here in the strip mall. We peered around outside the van, but there was no foot traffic along Duraleigh Road. Bowler and Julia decided to take a walking tour of the area to see if they could see anyone who might be Mitnick, though neither of them knew exactly what he looked like.

For the chilly February night air Bowler was wearing a fedora and a trench coat, and as he got out of the van he turned to me and said slyly, "Do you think I look too much like an undercover agent?" He was obviously enjoying this unexpected adventure.

With the side curtains now closed so that I wouldn't be seen, I couldn't tell what Bowler and Julia were up to, but they were back within fifteen minutes with a reconnaisance report. As I listened, Bowler let me wear his fedora so that I wouldn't feel left out of the caper. He and Julia had passed a Chinese take-out restaurant, a pizza delivery shop, and a bar, glancing through their windows, then entered the convenience store to buy some Gatorade, popcorn, and AAA batteries for Julia's flashlight.

"I didn't see anyone who looked like Mitnick," Julia said drolly, "but there were sure some suspicious-looking characters across the parking lot." On the way to the shops, they had walked past two men somberly sitting in the front seat of what looked distinctly like a government car, facing the Player's Club.

Julia had decided to go into the Chinese place to get us some more food, and while waiting for the order to be filled she noted that one of the counter people looked out at the same car and said to a coworker, "Something must be going on; those guys haven't moved for the longest time." One of the pizza parlor employees had also ducked his head out the door several times to see what might be taking place in the parking lot.

For the next two hours I encountered nothing but silence on the scanner, and I couldn't banish the thought that Kevin might have fled, a scenario that seemed increasingly plausible, given the lack of subtlety of what little we could see of the stakeout.

"We saw him talking about seeing *Sneakers* the other night, maybe he's gone to a movie," Julia said at one point, trying to lighten my mood.

A cluster of outdoor pay phones stood near the gas station in the corner of the parking lot, which we could see by peering through the side curtains. A remarkably large number of calls were being placed from them for a weeknight in midwinter. Several times we were paged by Markoff back at the Sheraton, wondering if there was any news, and Julia would get out of the car and walk to the pay phone to return them. Then, close to 11 P.M., there was a page from Andrew, at Netcom.

"You're not going to like this," Julia warned, when she returned from talking to Andrew. He had realized that he'd screwed up again. Three hours earlier, when it had taken me several attempts to transmit the "get ready" message, Andrew had interpreted the flurry of signals to mean that Kevin had already been arrested. For evidence, he had started to make backup copies of the files that Mitnick had stashed around the Internet, and then begun deleting the intruder's own versions.

There was also one piece of good news—Andrew had analyzed Mitnick's deletion of the Well's accounting file earlier in the day and had determined that it was the result of a simple typo, not an act of sabotage. But the bad news was devastating: our surveillance had now been irredeemably compromised.

And it had happened several hours ago. Again, Andrew had not called sooner, fearing my anger. This was unbelievable. Here I'd been riding the FBI as hard as I could, and now if everything fell apart and Mitnick escaped they were going to be able to come to me and say, "Your guys blew it."

But there was no time to fret about the error now: my monitor indicated that Kevin Mitnick had just signed on for the night shift. And if he hadn't noticed before dinner that his stashes had been destroyed—and his presence now indicated he might not yet know—he was about to find out.

I wasn't the only one who'd heard Kevin come back to life. Suddenly Levord's car and several other vehicles sped through the parking lot and disappeared behind a bowling alley at the end of the shopping center. It was a quick, final coordinating meeting of the federal and local law-enforcement agencies, and Bowler drove the van around to join the half-dozen plainclothesmen who had assembled. He handed Levord the amended warrants, and I warned the group that Mitnick might have been inadvertently tipped off, so haste was more crucial than ever. Someone mentioned the Quantico agents now had a "beacon" to home in on and could now use a hand-held signal-strength monitor for close-up work, so it shouldn't take long to find him. The meeting lasted less than a minute, and the others were off to take up their assigned positions around and on the far side of the Player's Club.

Bowler eased the van back to our parking spot, and I resumed monitoring, picking up Mitnick as he came and went for the next hour or so. Usually, upon concluding, or dropping, a data call, he would redial immediately. But at one point, I didn't hear him come back on, so I began checking the adjacent arcs of the Cellular One cell site, to see if his signal had been bounced to another sector. And then I noticed something strange.

Although Kevin was south of the cell site, I was now picking up a data carrier from the north. It was the first time I'd seen another data call being placed within this cell from anywhere but Mitnick's vicinity since I'd come to Raleigh. Because of the spotty reliability of cellular connections, and the fairly high cost of the service if a person is not stealing it, it is not common to use cellular radio for transmitting data.

I reported my discovery to Bowler and Julia, and we began conversing in hushed voices. Had Mitnick moved? Did he have a partner? Or had he gone mobile after being alerted by Andrew's premature cleanup?

After I picked up the MIN of this new data caller, I told Bowler, "Drive over to the phones." It was 12:40 A.M. He positioned the van as close to the pay phones as he could get it, with the vehicle between me and the apartment complex, and I slid out and called the Cellular One technician.

"Gary," I said, when Gary Whitman picked up his phone. "Are you watching?"

He was indeed monitoring the Cellular One site, so I read him the new MIN and asked him to let me know each time our mysterious caller placed a new call and moved to a different frequency. He could do so by paging me with the new channel numbers.

Once again Bowler returned to our parking spot, and almost immediately I got the first of a series of pages, which allowed me to quickly flip back and forth between Mitnick's sector and the mystery man's, confirming that we indeed had two separate data callers using the cell site. For forty-five minutes, I continued watching the two.

Then, at almost precisely 1:30, Kevin's carrier went dead. We immediately saw the Quantico station wagon zip past, first down Duraleigh Road, and then a short time later speeding past in the other direction. The car now had the directional antenna that had been on Fred Backhaus's van the previous night. The second data carrier was still on the air, and it was obvious that the Quantico agents had spotted it, too.

Other vehicles were now moving in on the Player's Club as well—including our neighbors from the parking lot. "Something's happened," Bowler said. "Let's go have a look."

He slowly pulled the van out of the parking lot and onto a side street nearer the apartment complex, stopping behind some bushes just to the east of it, where we could see directly into the parking lot. We stepped out of the van. We could now see that the area was well staked out. There were at least four government cars, and at least a dozen plainclothesmen standing or walking around. The Quantico station wagon returned.

I wanted to go tell the agents what I knew about the new signals from the north, but Bowler came over. "No, no, no," he said, standing close to me. "There's nothing you can do at this point. Besides, we don't know if they have Mitnick yet. He might see you."

"But I've got the MIN," I objected. "Cellular One is sending me the channel numbers."

"Why don't you send Julia over with a slip of paper?" he suggested.

She walked over. They were annoyed at first, but when they realized she had valuable information, they took the MIN and my pager from her, and the Quantico teams' wagon roared off once more, now heading north. Julia returned, and we sat in the van, listening to the soft hiss of the mysterious data caller's modem.

Ten minutes later, Levord strode over.

"We're inside," he said. "We've got Mitnick. But we're going to need to call the judge to authorize the warrant to search a new address."

I handed Bowler my cell phone so we could wake Judge Dixon for authority to search Kevin Mitnick's home. Then I sent Andrew the "go" code on my pager. Finally, it really was time for him to start alerting the Well and the other sites on our warning list. I hoped he was still awake.

As Bowler talked with the judge, Levord described for Julia and me how he and several other agents had knocked on the door of his apartment and waited a full five minutes for it to open. When it finally did, the man inside refused to admit that he was Kevin Mitnick.

They went in anyway, and Mitnick rushed to lock up some papers in a briefcase—a futile act, under the circumstances. He said he was on the phone, talking to his lawyer, but when Levord took the receiver, the line was dead. America's most-wanted computer criminal began vomiting on the floor of his living room.

"We haven't Mirandized him yet," Levord said. "We're actually worried about his health. We found prescription drug bottles. He's on some sort of medication."

Now it was safe to leave the van. The Quantico team had returned, and I walked over to where they were standing next to their station wagon. The clammy night air had finally given way to a light rain. The agents had the air of weary veteran athletes after a big victory—content, but far too tired to celebrate. The radio echoes had continued to bedevil their directional antenna, so they had finally tracked down Kevin by walking through the complex with the signal-strength meter, watching the cellular signal grow stronger and stronger until it led them to Mitnick's front door.

I asked about the other data signal. They said they'd chased it for a while but had been unable to pin it down. It, like many other threads in the investigation, would remain a mystery.

I never saw Mitnick that night. It would be at least another hour before he was finally hauled off to a holding cell downtown in the Wake County Jail. Long before then, Levord Burns obtained a valid search warrant from the judge, via Bowler, and had his agents start gathering up the evidence.

Levord came over to the van again to report this progress. I asked if I could have a look at the apartment, to see how my opponent had spent his days and long nights, but he declined to let me do so.

"We've taken lots of pictures of the inside of his apartment, but they're evidence for the trial, and no one else will see them until after it's over." But he did point out Mitnick's car, an old, light blue Plymouth Horizon.

Levord's mood was noticeably improved, despite the steady cold drizzle that was now soaking us all, and he came around to the side of the van and shook my hand.

"Congratulations," I said. "We managed to do this without killing each other."

He didn't reply, but for the first time since I'd met him, special agent Burns smiled at me.

CHAPTER 17

I was awakened the next morning by a call from Markoff.

"Kevin's court appearance is at ten o'clock," he said.

I looked at my watch and saw that it was already a few minutes past nine. "We'll meet you in the lobby as soon as we can get dressed," I told him, gently shaking Julia awake, then pulling the hotel room curtains back on a gray wet Raleigh morning.

Markoff drove us downtown through a light rain, and because I was feeling a bit out of touch since the crashing of my RadioMail terminal, I decided to use my cell phone to check my voice mail in San Diego. I couldn't believe it. There was a new message in that phony Asian accent, and it had been delivered just before 7 A.M. West Coast time, a full eight hours after Mitnick's arrest but well before any news of his capture had been reported by the media.

The message was long and rambling with none of the cockiness or bravado we'd heard before but, instead, in a delivery so nervous and rapid that the accent occasionally fell away altogether. After listening to it, I played back the message twice more, first holding the phone to Julia's ear, then to Markoff's:

"Hi, it is I again, Tsutomu, my son. I just want to tell you—very important, very important. All these phone calls you received with, ah, making reference to Kung Fu movies—nothing to do with any computer thing whatsoever. Just a little, ah, interesting call.

"I see now that this is getting too big, way too big. I want to tell you, my son, that these have nothing to do with any computer activities whatsoever. Just making fun of Kung Fu movies. That's it. That's it.

"And making reference to, ah, you know, trying to make a reference to putting Kung Fu movies into the . . . into a computer reference. That's it. Nothing to do with any Mitnick, hacking, anything, nothing. I tell you it was just a interesting call that's . . . it. All coincidence. This is getting too big, and nothing wrong has been done by anybody who left any messages on your voice mail. Just to let you know. Okay? It's getting way too big."

We were amazed. "So the tables have turned," I said. I wondered aloud where Mitnick's friend had gone to ground. I was curious if he was hiding right here in Raleigh. Whom had Mitnick called in the minutes before he opened the door for the FBI the night before? Was this the owner of the second cellular phone that had been making the data calls that the Quantico team had been chasing?

We were still talking about this new mystery, as we entered the Federal building. It was just a brief prearraignment hearing, and word hadn't yet gotten out that Kevin Mitnick had been arrested. We walked into a small empty courtroom and sat down in the last of the three short rows that had been reserved for spectators. It was like U.S. courtrooms all over the country, an austere, windowless space with a high ceiling.

After a short time Mitnick was led in from a door at the front of the room to the right of the judge's dais by a dour U.S. marshal. Kevin didn't look ill, but he also didn't look anything like the overweight, bespectacled "dark side hacker" who had once terrorized Los Angeles. We saw a tall young man, neither thin nor stocky, who had metal-rim glasses and shoulder-length flowing brown hair. He was wearing a gray charcoal sweatsuit, and he was handcuffed and his legs were chained.

Halfway into the room he recognized us and paused for a moment. He appeared stunned, and his eyes went wide.

"You're Tsutomu!" he said, with surprise in his voice, and then he looked at the reporter sitting next to me. "And you're Markoff."

Both of us nodded.

It had become clear to both Mitnick and me that this was no longer a game. I had thought of the chase and capture as sport, but it was now apparent that it was quite real and had real consequences.

Having spent several weeks on this man's trail, seeing the damage he had caused, coming to learn that he was not only single-minded in his invasion of other people's privacy and his pursuit of their intellectual property, but also petty and vindictive, I knew one thing for certain about Kevin Mitnick: he was in no way the hero of a movie about some mistreated computer hacker whose only crime was curiosity. There was nothing heroic about reading other people's mail and stealing their software.

He was led to the defendant's table and Judge Dixon came in. The hearing was over in under ten minutes. A public defender had not yet been appointed and so Mitnick sat at the defense table alone with the U.S. marshal close behind him. I was curious to see if he'd continue his masquerade, but when asked his name he identified himself as Kevin David Mitnick. The fight had gone out of him, and he was clearly tired.

As the judge read the charges—telecommunications fraud and computer fraud, each carrying a maximum potential sentence of fifteen years or more—it was clear that Kevin was beginning to understand what was in store for him. This game had real penalties. In a soft voice he said he wanted the court's permission to contact his attorney in California. The judge noted that whatever happened in his legal entanglements, the U.S. Court of the Eastern District of North Carolina would "have its way" with him first. The detention hearing was set for two days later on Friday morning.

The whole thing lasted less than ten minutes. After the judge adjourned the court, Markoff made his way up to the railing that separated the spectator gallery from the rest of the courtroom. Julia and I followed him. Kevin rose and turned to face us.

He straightened and addressed me. "Tsutomu, I respect your skills," he said.

I returned his gaze and just nodded. There didn't seem to be much to say. In our contest he had clearly lost.

Strangely, I felt neither good or bad about seeing him on his way to jail, just vaguely unsatisfied. It wasn't an elegant solution—

not because I bought some people's claims that Mitnick was someone innocently exploring cyberspace, without even the white-collar criminal's profit motive, but because he seemed to be a special case in so many ways. This was the sixth time he'd been arrested. He certainly knew what the stakes were, and I hadn't seen any evidence of a higher moral purpose to his activities or even just innocent curiosity.

The marshal started to lead him away and Markoff said, "Kevin, I hope things go okay for you."

Mitnick appeared not to have heard him at first, but then he stopped for a second and turned back toward us. After giving a slight nod of his head, he turned away and was led out of the courtroom.

The three of us walked back to the elevator. Kevin was in deeper trouble this time than ever before. He was a second-time offender on at least two federal crime statutes, and he was a probation violator. More than half a dozen federal districts and several states were waiting to file charges against him.

None of us could figure out the psychology of his obsession. Did he imagine himself the innocent voyeur that his friend Eric Corley believed him to be? Or was he wrapped up in his own legend, living out some Robert Redford–inspired vision of being a last American hero on the run? Was he some new kind of cyber-addict, as a federal judge decided back in 1988? I'd read somewhere that gamblers and check forgers exhibit similiar behavior: even though they realize they will lose or be caught sooner or later, they're trapped by an irresistible urge to keep going until they fail. Maybe somewhere deep inside, Mitnick had been so seduced by the game that he accepted the same fatal certainty that sooner or later he would be caught. There was no way of knowing.

Afterwards we drove back to the Sheraton. Markoff went off to file his story for Thursday's *New York Times*, and Julia and I spent the rest of the day in the hotel room— much of it on the phone with Andrew, officials at the Well and Netcom, and other systems administrators around the Internet whose networks Mitnick might have compromised. That evening, around 9 P.M., Markoff, Julia, and I drove back to the Sprint switch and waited until Murph and Joe could go out to dinner. By the time they got off their shift it was late, and we drove around for a long time before finding a place to eat.

The next day I woke up to find that the real chaos had begun. Kevin Mitnick's arrest was big news, and the media deluge was happening in earnest. That morning I also discovered one last message from the mysterious caller. It had been left on my office voice mail at 7:23 P.M., San Diego time, the night before, in an urgent voice:

"Tsutomu, my friend. I just want to say . . . want to reiterate it is big joke. It is big, make fun of Kung Fu movies, has nothing to do with computer hacking, Mitnick, nothing! You tell them, do not send them to come and get me. No, do not fly out to come and get me. I'm not worth it . . . just make fun of Kung Fu movies. That is it. Thank you."

The game really was over.

EPILOGUE

In July of 1995, Kevin Mitnick agreed to plead guilty to one charge of cellular telephone fraud and, without a trial, was sentenced to eight months in jail. As a result of his arrest in Raleigh, Federal prosecutors had originally charged him with twenty-three counts of telephone and computer fraud, but all but one of the charges were dropped as part of his plea bargain.

However, Mitnick's legal problems aren't over. He is now in jail in Los Angeles awaiting new charges including federal probation violations, tampering with the State of California Department of Motor Vehicles computers, and computer and telephone fraud charges that may be filed by more than a half dozen federal districts. Unless he agrees to a new plea bargain, a trial is now scheduled for late November, and it is likely that he will spend more time in prison.

Today, as I look back on the events of the past year, I'm still troubled. In the wake of his arrest in February, Mitnick's legend continued to grow. For many months after his arrest, heated discussions about his actions took place on the Internet. Some people continued to argue that because Kevin Mitnick never physically harmed anyone, what he was doing was innocuous.

The fact is that this is also the case of a man who has had fifteen years and six arrests to figure out what is right and wrong. In the late 1980s, a federal judge made a special effort to give him a second chance.

For me, Kevin Mitnick's real crime is that he violated the original spirit of the hacker ethic. It's not okay to read other people's mail, and to believe that software and other computer technologies should be freely shared is not the same as believing that it's okay to steal them.

The network of computers known as the Internet began as a unique experiment in building a community of people who shared a set of values about technology and the role computers could play in shaping the world. That community was based largely on a shared sense of trust. Today, the electronic walls going up everywhere on the Net are the clearest proof of the loss of that trust and community. It's a loss for all of us.

October 25, 1995

INDEX